# WORSHIP IN THE WORLD'S RELIGIONS

*By the same Author*

West African Religion
Bible and Polygamy
West African Psychology
Religion in an African City
African Traditional Religion
Story of Ketu
Introduction to Asian Religions
Witchcraft
African Ideas of God
Comparative Religion
Upanishads, Gita and Bible
What World Religions Teach
The Christian Debate
The World's Living Religions
Jesus in the Qur'an
African Mythology
Religion in Africa
Avatar and Incarnation
Dictionary of Non-Christian Religions
Man and his Gods
The Indestructible Soul
The Bhagavad Gita: a Verse Translation

# WORSHIP
# IN THE WORLD'S RELIGIONS

by

### GEOFFREY PARRINDER

1976

### LITTLEFIELD, ADAMS & CO.
Totowa, New Jersey

First published in the United States 1976 by

LITTLEFIELD, ADAMS & CO.

by special arrangement with Sheldon Press

First published in 1961
by Faber and Faber Limited

Second edition published in 1974
by Sheldon Press

**Library of Congress Cataloging in Publication Data**

Parrinder, Edward Geoffrey
  Worship in the World's Religions

  (A Littlefield, Adams Quality Paperback No. 316)
  Reprint of the 1974 ed. published by Sheldon
Press, London.
  Bibliography: p.
  1. Cultus. 2. Worship—Comparative studies.
I. Title.
[BL550.P3  1975]        291.3        75-34031
ISBN 0-8226-0316-0

Geoffrey Parrinder is Professor of the Comparative Study of Religions in the University of London. After ordination he spent twenty years teaching in West Africa and studying African religions, before becoming the founder member of the Department of Religious Studies in the University College of Ibadan, Nigeria. He has travelled widely in Africa, and in India, Pakistan, Ceylon, Burma, Israel, Jordan and Turkey and held lecturing appointments in Australia, America and India and at Oxford. He is the author of many books on world religions.

My brother kneels (so saith Kabir)
  To stone and brass in heathen-wise,
But in my brother's voice I hear
  My own unanswered agonies.
His God is as his Fates assign—
His prayer is all the world's—and mine.

KIPLING

All God's names are hallowed.

M. BUBER

# CONTENTS

# INTRODUCTION

The study of the religions of the world is of great interest and importance. Three reasons for this may be mentioned in particular. Far more is known about the great religions of the world today than ever before, outside the regions in which each prevails; a great deal of impartial and accurate study during the last hundred years makes it possible to know the faith of others as never previously. It is no longer permissible to speak, as did medieval miracle plays, of Muslims worshipping an idol called Baphomet! And it should be no longer asserted that the Chinese adore Confucius, or that Christians regard the Virgin Mary as the second of three gods.

Secondly, far more people from the West have visited the East than in any earlier age, and many Easterners have come to see the West. The ease of travel, imperialism, and the movement of troops during the wars, have brought the world together. Many Europeans and Americans have been confronted with Hindu temples and Korean monasteries, Asians have visited Christian cathedrals, and African soldiers have seen Burmese pagodas.

A third reason for the importance of this subject is the revival of life in many of the world's religions. With the rise of nationalism and the recovery of self-government, many eastern lands have turned again to the religion on which their culture has been based. With the example of Christian missions before them Buddhism and Islam, themselves historically missionary religions, have begun to send literature and envoys to other peoples. Even in Hinduism and Sikhism a similar awakening and outward looking is apparent. The modern world has not yet done with religion. Our scientific age, with its pride and its uncertainties, is only just beginning to realize the strength of the faiths that men have held dear for thousands of years and that are reviving today.

Most universities until recently ignored the subject that has the greatest amount of historical literature of any, and the study of man's most cherished convictions has small place. Nevertheless detailed studies and translations of scriptures continue to appear and have a wide sale. Because of this it is important to have works available that cover the whole field of modern religion in a general way. For while it is true that no one man can hope to have full knowledge of all the religions of the world, and perhaps only of one, his own, yet if the needs of ordinary readers and general students are to be met it is imperative to have books that summarize what experts in special fields have written.

There is a number of general up-to-date introductions to man's religions, and of recent works one may mention the books of Noss, Smith and Finegan, all Americans. Here are invaluable introductions to the origins and history of the great religions and philosophies. There is no attempt in the present book to duplicate what they have done so well.

But too often introductory works give most of their space to the history of the religion, its founder, sects, and leading ideas and philosophy. They are informative, but the effect is often dead or merely historical. What I have attempted in this book is to show these religions as living organisms, to answer the questions, What is the nature of their worship? What is their faith and prayer? How do they appear to their worshippers?

The history of the religions has hardly been touched, and readers must look to other books for that. The philosophical systems have barely been mentioned. But the state of the religion today is depicted, inadequately no doubt, but the attempt is worth making in the cause of international understanding. And since the number of the world's religions has been so large, only living religions are discussed. Thus the modern Parsis are considered, but ancient Zoroastrianism is mentioned only as far as it provides the necessary background.

Worship is taken in the broad sense of what is seen and shared by the laity. This is not a study of rituals performed by priests alone, which is a subject that would demand many volumes and achieve other aims. Only so far as the layman witnesses and joins in the rituals are they described. In general this common participation is more frequent in the 'western' religions, Judaism, Islam and Christianity, than in the Eastern, except for some of the Mahāyāna Buddhist and Shintō sects.

Concepts of God and other spirits have been thought important for this study, because the God in which a man believes, and his nature as revealed in doctrine and myth, inevitably affects his worship. So efforts have been made to show how the deity appears to faith and devotion.

Temples to which the public may go, the relics they enshrine, and the pilgrimages made to them, are all significant to the layman. His part in temple worship may be small or private, and the inner sanctuary hidden from him, nevertheless it is his support that maintains the temples and the very hands of his fathers that built and adorned them.

Laymen's worship in public, and devotions made in private, are of great significance. These play a greater part, even among illiterate peoples, than is commonly recognized. And from there we go on to those mystics, of all ages and lands, with their many lay followers, who link up with seekers after God everywhere and who find their inspiration in the same source. As the Ṣūfī Rūmī said, 'The lamps are different, but the Light is the same.'

There is no attempt here, however, to suggest that all religions are of equal value or can make a vague synthesis. It is hoped that the day of that facile solution is passing, for no man can lightly contemplate abandoning his own cherished beliefs for the dubious gain of a vague hotch-potch. The need today is for a fair and sympathetic understanding of the facts of other religious beliefs and ways of worship. Only by impartiality and charity can we recognize different viewpoints and work towards a greater harmony than in the past which was clouded over by so much misunderstanding.

To do this it is valuable to have religious faith oneself. An atheist, who looks upon all religion as superstition, cannot hope to enter into the spirit of other faiths as can a man of religion.

# INTRODUCTION

Religion is such a personal matter that it makes a great deal of difference if the student has a faith of his own. As a leading anthropologist has said, 'Even in a descriptive study judgement can in no way be avoided. Those who give assent to the religious beliefs of their own people feel and think, and therefore also write, differently about the beliefs of other people from those who do not give assent to them.'[1]

After half a lifetime of the comparative study of religions, and years in Africa, I have made numerous visits to India, Pakistan, Ceylon and Burma, as well as Iran, Turkey and Egypt entering temple and mosque, pagoda and monastery. To those many friends who, in Tagore's words, have 'given me seats in homes not my own', I wish to express deep gratitude. To the kindness of many leading Hindus and Muslims, Buddhists and Parsis, Sikhs and Jews, and to innumerable Africans and Christians, I owe immeasurable thanks.

## GENERAL BIBLIOGRAPHY

Brandon, S. G. F., ed. *A Dictionary of Comparative Religion*, Weidenfeld, 1970.
Eliade, M. *From Primitives to Zen*, Collins, 1967.
Eliade, M. *Patterns in Comparative Religion*, E. T. Sheed & Ward, 1971.
Finegan, J. *The Archaeology of World Religions*, Princeton, 1966.
Hinnells, J. R., ed. *Comparative Religion in Education*, Oriel, 1970.
James, E. O. *From Cave to Cathedral*, Thames & Hudson, 1965.
James, E. O. *Sacrifice and Sacrament*, Thames & Hudson, 1962.
Noss, J. B. *Man's Religions*, Macmillan, 1969.
Parrinder, E. G. *A Book of World Religions*, Hulton, 1965.
Parrinder, E. G. *A Dictionary of Non-Christian Religions*, Hulton, 1971.
Parrinder, E. G., ed. *Man and his Gods*, Hamlyn, 1971.
Smart, N. *The Religious Experience of Mankind*, Collins, 1971.
Spencer, S. *Mysticism in World Religion*, Penguin, 1967.

[1] E. E. Evans-Pritchard, *Nuer Religion*, p. vii.

# PART I

---

*Religions Without Scriptures*

## Chapter 1

# PRE-LITERARY RELIGIONS TODAY

There are millions of people in the modern world who hold to religions that are pre-literary, that is to say they have no written history and no scriptures. Such peoples are found in most continents, in America and Asia, in Australia and Africa. They are most numerous in Africa, where there are about a thousand times as many pagans as in Australia.

There are a hundred million or so inhabitants of Africa south of the Sahara. Millions of these, however, have adopted Christianity or Islam. They have taken the Bible and Qur'ān (Koran) as their scriptures, and learn and treasure their teaching with great earnestness. For this reason most Africans who visit Europe are Christians, or have undergone some Christian influence, because the missions have taken western education to African and other illiterate peoples.

Nevertheless there are still great multitudes who cling to the old faiths, certainly more than half the population of Africa. They will not be met with in the West, but many travellers to Africa and Asia have been confronted with strange manifestations of religion which do not belong to the great historical religions.

These pre-literary religions are often neglected in comparative works of this kind, or they may be dismissed as 'primitive'. But this word is ambiguous. It suggests that the religious manifestations are crude or materialistic, and even more that we can see in them the forms that religion first took when it appeared among men. This assumption is quite arbitrary, for there is little evidence that backward people today hold the same beliefs as did the first prehistoric men to show signs of religious ideas. All modern peoples have a history, even where that history is unwritten and largely unknown. They are modern men, not primordial beings.[1]

Professor Elkin, writing of the Australian aborigines, says, 'the Aborigines, being food-gatherers, living perforce in semi-nomadic fashion, are lower than most horticultural and village peoples. But even so, we must remember that their lowliness is not to be equated to a primeval state or one just above the animals.' He goes on to maintain that 'their philosophy and ceremonial life are, in some respects, no lower or less complicated than our own'.[2]

The comparative study of religions has suffered a great deal from the theories of investigators which have warped their interpretation of religion. In a modern work of outstanding importance Professor Evans-Pritchard, an eminent anthropologist, has protested against what he calls 'rationalist influence on anthropology'. This, he says, has led writers to discuss religious beliefs and practices together with a medley of other rites, 'all having in common only that the writer regards them as irrational'.[3] Pre-literary religions have been explained as 'primitive', and their supposed origin has been sought in magic, mana, fetish, totem, animism, and the like. 'All this was for the most part conjecture.'

Then the psychologists came on the scene and tried to explain religion away in terms of the personification of nature, fear, awe, anxiety, projection, taboo, and such terms. 'Most of these theories have long ago been discredited as naïve introspective guesses.'[4]

A good deal of tinkering has been done at the theory of religion, without coming to grips with the facts of religious experience. It is significant that the attack has been at the lower levels, among so-called primitive peoples, rather than directly at the great religions about which we know much more through

[1]For a study of really primitive religion see E. O. James's *Prehistoric Religion*, and note his careful qualifications in problems of the origins of religion.

[2]*The Australian Aborigines*, p. 20.

[3]*Nuer Religion*, p. viii.    [4]*ibid.*, p. 311 f.

their history and scriptures. Yet even here the rationalist approach is erroneous, for it tends to equate lowly culture with primitive religion.

That many of the illiterate people of the modern world are living at a low level of material culture is true. So are many followers of highly sophisticated religions, like Hinduism and Buddhism. That men live in poverty, with a very elementary standard of existence, does not necessarily imply that their religious beliefs are primitive. Evans-Pritchard, who writes of the religion of the Nuer cattle herders living in the swamps and savannah of the eastern Sudan says, 'The Nuer are undoubtedly a primitive people by the usual standards of reckoning, but their religious thought is remarkably sensitive, refined, and intelligent. It is also highly complex.'[1]

And similar words come from Elkin in Australia: 'We are very apt to underrate the philosophical powers of primitive peoples, but the absence of clothes and complicated economic systems does not imply an absence of thought. Primitive peoples have more time than we for contemplation, and we err in thinking that when an Aborigine is sitting, apparently idle, looking into vacancy, his mind is necessarily blank. . . The Aborigine has, in fact, developed the art of contemplation to a much greater degree than most of us.'[2]

In discussing a religion that has no scriptures to explain and defend it, it is too easy to adopt a superior attitude and regard it all as superstition. The external ritual can be observed, but the inner meaning may be hidden in the absence of written explanations of it. But religion is not just outer ritual; it depends on an inward conviction. 'Nuer religion is ultimately an interior state. This state is externalized in rites which we can observe but their meaning depends finally on an awareness of God and that men are dependent on him and must be resigned to his will. At this point the theologian takes over from the anthropologist.'[3]

[1] *ibid.*, p. 311.
[2] *The Australian Aborigines*, p. 188.
[3] *Nuer Religion*, p. 322.

# PRE-LITERARY RELIGIONS TODAY

## BELIEF IN GOD

'How can the untutored African conceive God?' asked an eminent traveller. The simple fact is that most, perhaps all, African peoples have had some idea of God, although they have taken up differing attitudes towards him. Many other illiterate peoples have had comparable beliefs.

When Charles Darwin visited Tierra del Fuego in 1833 he brought away the idea that the Fuegians had no religion. Darwin stayed about two months in the country, he was interested chiefly in the flora and fauna, and spoke none of the native languages. Yet his remarks received wide currency, and the Fuegians were long quoted as an example of a pre-religious stage of mankind. A modern scholar, who has spent years in Tierra del Fuego, and speaks the Yamana language, declares that the idea of a supreme God has long been well known there. His name is Watauináiwa, meaning the Eternal or Unchangeable, and another name is Father.[1]

The theory that there was a primitive monotheism, from which all peoples fell away, is a simple hypothesis. It concerns prehistory and need not detain us here. Suffice it that belief in God is a widespread phenomenon. In what follows we shall have to speak generally, since the illiterate peoples of the world are too numerous and scattered to take separately.

But is the supreme God a person or a vague power? Some say that what is called God is really an abstract power, never regarded as akin to man, and that to speak of him as a Supreme Being is misleading.

Against this it must be said that in Africa notably, although God is regarded as the source of power he has his own personality. He is distinct from other beings and from the sky and the wind. 'The Nuer do not regard the sky or any celestial phenomenon as God and this is clearly shown in the distinction made between God and the sky in the expressions "Spirit of the sky" and "Spirit who is in the sky". Moreover, it would even be a mistake to interpret "of the sky" and "in the sky" too literally . . . God is

[1] W. Koppers, *Primitive Man and his World Picture*, p. 137 ff.

Spirit, which, like wind and air, is invisible and ubiquitous. But . . . God is not these things.'[1]

God has a personal name, he has life and consciousness, and he responds to the appeal of man. Sometimes he is said to have a wife and children. But he is not normally spoken of as if he were human, or had ever been a man, or were a deified ancestor. He is usually regarded as male but sometimes female or of dual nature. Dr Aggrey said that he always thought of God as Father-Mother.

What men believe about God, and the attitude they adopt towards him, may partly be deduced from the names they give to him. His personal name may indicate his nature clearly, or it may be an ancient name whose meaning is almost forgotten. It may contain veiled references to his nature. Or the name may be taboo, and never spoken or revealed to strangers.

The titles men give to God are of great number and variety in different places. They help to show his attributes. Roughly, they may be taken under several headings. Some titles refer to God as Creator: he is the moulder of children, maker of souls, founder of the universe. Then he is controller of nature, giver of rain, sunshine and the seasons; the thunderer and the firelighter. He is almighty, ancient of days, irresistible; he roars so that all peoples are smitten with terror, yet is also the one you meet everywhere. His providence is important: God is father of little children, greatest of friends, full of pity, the one on whom men lean and do not fall. Then there are the mysterious names: God is the great pool contemporary with everything, the immense ocean whose circular headdress is the horizon, beyond all thanks, the high up one, the inexplicable.

All these names are given to God in different places.[2] Since they express men's feelings about God they affect the attitude adopted towards him in worship and decide whether it is worth praying to him or not. In praise names and in proverbs, in riddles and myths, as well as in worship, the names and titles of God throw light upon what men think of his character.

[1] *Nuer Religion,* p. 1 f.
[2] Lists are given in *African Ideas of God,* ed. E. W. Smith, p. 305 f.

Is God worshipped? To the monotheist the question will be strange, but in a polytheistic system the lesser gods may receive more attention than the supreme God. Is he then supreme? Yes, as father of gods and men, though in some myths he has removed to a distant heaven because of human presumption. Moreover, in many places God is believed to uphold the moral law; he is the judge of men both now and after death, and so men are responsible to him for their deeds.

If worship is defined as requiring temples, priests, and sacrifice, then many illiterate peoples give God little worship. Rarely are temples built for him in Africa. 'Will God in very deed dwell on the earth?' Solomon is said to have asked, and many illiterate people are sufficiently thoughtful to reject the notion that any temple, however grandiose, could be adequate for the great God whose headdress is the horizon. The Ashanti of Ghana have a few, very few, temples where God is worshipped with his own priests, and they are almost alone in this provision of temples.

Images of God are almost non-existent among illiterate peoples. There is one of Mawu in Dahomey, and none known elsewhere in Africa. There are countless representations of other gods, in wood, clay, brass and stone, but not of the Supreme One of all. Medieval Christian paintings depicted God as an old man with beard and crown. William Blake painted God speaking out of a cloud to Job and appearing to Adam. In India, Brahmā, Śiva and Vishṇu, all called supreme, appear in innumerable images and paintings. But Africans will laugh if one speaks of the possibility of representing God in art. In this they are most akin to the Muslims.

Sacrifices are rarely made to God. The Kikuyu of Kenya were unusual in worshipping him in sacred groves where communal sacrifices were offered of rams without blemish. On special occasions, in drought or disease, and in thanksgivings for bumper harvests, God was worshipped and offerings were made to him. In other places, an occasional libation of water or spirits poured on to the ground, a few nuts held up to the sky, an obeisance made to the rising sun, are all that may be offered.

Yet prayer is worship, and in many places prayers are offered to God. They may not be uttered as frequently as to more troublesome spirits. But when all else fails, when the thunder god or smallpox spirit do not hear, and the ancestors slumber or have turned aside, then the great God can be appealed to. He is the final court of appeal, the judge of all, and to him men turn in despair. They may approach him without priest or intermediary, with empty hands and in any place; since he is almighty and omnipresent he can hear the slightest voice and humblest cry.

Such beliefs are held by millions of illiterate people. They are not without nobility or subtle discrimination.

## OTHER SPIRITS

The universe is regarded as the abode of many spiritual beings, some of them vaguely spirits of fable, and others in whose honour rituals are performed, like the corn spirits to whom boys and girls dance in spring-time. In polytheistic belief many spirits are honoured, and they are not neglected in favour of one only in case they are offended and bring harm.

The spirits may roughly be divided, and some peoples do clearly distribute them thus, between the sky, the earth, the waters and the forest or the wild. The Nuer believe that the spirits of the air are the most powerful, they are responsible for storms, lightning and winds. In some places, notably in West Africa, there are temples and priests for many of the gods; here the sky gods are some of the most powerful, their wrath in casting thunderbolts and lightning flashes is dreaded, and their favour sought in sending rain. Rain, of course, is particularly sought after in the drier semi-desert lands. The sun and moon are often not worshipped in tropical regions, where they are ever-present, as they were in the olden days in the colder regions of the north, in Europe and Mesopotamia.

After the sky spirits the gods of the earth are very potent. The chief earth spirit is often female, like the Greek Demeter and Roman Ceres, and is venerated because of her production of the crops. Also the dead are buried in the earth, and she keeps both men and plants in her pocket or womb. Hence many rites designed to encourage the fertility of the earth are also ceremonies of human fertility, whereby the dead are reborn, and are at times performed with considerable licence. The earth has many temples, those of the Ibo of Nigeria are famous. But even if it has no temple a libation of wine may be made on the ground at birth ceremonies, the blood of a cock is shed before the spring hoeing, and again when digging a grave the earth is warned by knocking three times—a practice still preserved by Jamaican Christians. An old Nigerian Yoruba chant, preceded by a prayer and offering of split kola nuts, goes:

> *O Earth I call thee,*
> *Thou who shavest thy head with hoes;*
> *Please call me not back quickly to thee;*
> *Consume me not speedily.*
>
> *O God of heaven, O God of earth,*
> *I pray thee uphold my hand.*
> *My ancestors and ancestresses,*
> *Lean upon earth and succour me*
> *That I may not quickly come to you.*

Spirits of the water include the naiads who sport in every stream, the local denizens of wells and springs, gods of lakes and rushing rivers, and the mermen and mermaids who dwell in the sea together with all kind of sea serpents and monsters. Women dare not draw water at night from the streams because of the spirits there, and to bridge a river permission must first be sought from the guardian spirit that lives in its depths.

There is in Ashanti a strange lake called Bosomtwe, cradled between hills and having no outlet. It is round, five miles across each way, and the water evaporates in the heat. It is said that a female spirit lives in the lake, who every so often 'explodes her gunpowder' and comes out of the water to sit on the banks with her children. The explosion is caused by gases which accumulate from decaying vegetable matter at the bottom of the water. The lakeside fishermen, who are the children of this spirit, so revere her that they will not use paddles for canoes, but push themselves along on logs with their hands, and use no metal hooks to catch fish but simply cane basket traps. They offer sacrifices of white cocks to the lake goddess.

Spirits of the wild, the desert or forest wastes, include beings of many kinds. There are one-legged spirits that speak a kind of whistling language intelligible only to the initiated, fairies who impart herbal secrets to hunters on payment of a sacrifice or oath of loyalty, many strange creatures in fantastic forms, and the ghosts of those who have died violently ór before their time. Often these spirits receive no worship, unless it be an occasional gift in a pot at the foot of a tree or on a rock, but they are much feared and woe betide the wanderer who gets into their clutches unawares.

## ANCESTORS

Quite a different category of spirits is that of the souls of men who have died, the ancestors who still live in the world beyond the grave. They may be thought of as inhabiting a 'heaven of cool breezes', or living underground and appearing at their own tombs, or even being reborn as babies in their own families. But wherever they are the departed are given great attention. It is often said that people do not fear their gods half as much as they do their ancestors. A man will perjure himself in the names of many gods but he will speak the truth when swearing on the bones of his fathers. The ancestors are near at hand, they know their children, and punish them if they do wrong. Perhaps for this reason many of the totems that some peoples use to represent their ancestors are aggressive animals.

Totem is an American Indian word indicating the emblem of a family or clan, generally an animal, and to which they believe themselves related. In North America and Australia particularly totemic cults have become famous, though these peoples are small in numbers today. In totemistic ceremonies men dress up as animals, birds, or human beings, to represent the past heroes of the clan and enact rites and dances illustrating incidents in the lives of the heroes.

The ancestral spirits of all peoples are concerned with any matters which affect the life and property of the family; they may fertilize the ground, promote the growth of crops and receive the first-fruits of the harvest. They are naturally interested in the increase of their family and childless women pray to them for offspring. Since many peoples believe in rebirth, it is natural for them to think that the ancestors keep the channels of birth open in order to facilitate their own return to their families. Sickness or disease may be attributed to the ancestors, but this is often put down rather to the troublesome activity of an unsettled ghost and rites are performed to pacify it. An ancestor may be angry at neglect, or unhappy because of an unfinished funeral ceremony, and haste is made to placate him when he plagues his family with bad dreams or sickness.

Some of the most prominent figures in many parts of the world are the mediums who profess to be in touch with the spirit world. Some of these work under the direction of priests, others operate on their own. They may claim to be controlled by many kinds of spirits, giving prophetic messages and warnings. They are particularly concerned with the spirits of the dead, like the medium of En-dor who raised up Samuel for Saul. They go into a trance and often act violently as if 'possessed' by a strange power. Men consult them as oracles, to discover hidden things of the past or to probe into the future. The ancestors are believed to have special knowledge, which they have acquired by entering the spirit world and obtaining powers beyond the reach of mortals, but their secrets can be tapped through the mediums whom they control.

The ancestors receive great attention, but is it worship? Some writers maintain that to speak of ancestor-worship is misleading. There is a continuous community between the living and the departed, and there is no radical distinction between men and their ancestors, except that the latter are now more powerful. When men go to their graves with gifts, it is like going to a chief with a present. So, it is asserted, this is not prayer but a projection of social behaviour.

The answer to the problem depends largely upon the definition of religion. If religion may be defined as dependence upon supersensible powers, then the cult of the ancestors is religious. If one studies the type of gifts offered to them, and the language used in sacrifice, it is found that frequently these differ little from those used for the gods also: 'We beg you for life, life to the hunters, life to the rulers, may the women bear children, let no misfortune come to us.'

It has been suggested that the religious complex of many illiterate peoples may be represented as a sort of triangle.[1] At the apex is God, the supreme and creator spirit. The two sides of the triangle are the gods and the ancestors, both important, and one made more of than another in varying places. The base of the triangle is composed of those superstitious beliefs and practices, often called magical but all depending upon belief in their spiritual efficacy.

Magical practices occupy a large part of the thought and time of many people all over the world. Amulets for wearing on the neck, wrists, waist and ankles; charms for hanging in the house or farm, philtres to obtain love or induce rain, are innumerable. Every market has stalls with magical medicines: red parrot feathers, porcupine quills, gourds, horns, skulls, dried snakes, bats, rats. All these are used for their magical virtues. Sir James Frazer called magic a primitive science and said that it came at the early stages, before religion. There is no evidence for the latter assumption. Religious and magical beliefs are intertwined at most stages of culture, and indeed a case can be made out for banning the word magic and including it all, however crude, under the heading of religion; for these strange practices all depend upon spiritual conceptions and largely work by faith.

The beliefs in different kinds of spiritual beings: God, nature spirits, ancestors, and magical powers, may be comprehended under the name polytheism. This is a better word than the old and

[1] E. W. Smith, *African Symbolism*.

27

misleading 'fetishism', 'juju', or animism, for most peoples believe their gods to be persons and to have more than local sway. To call the pre-literary religions polytheism links them up with other great religious systems, such as those of ancient Egypt or Greece, and removes the stigma of primitivism.

## SHRINES AND IMAGES

Building in stone is unknown to most illiterate peoples, either through lack of soft stone in their territory or more commonly because the necessary techniques are absent. Hence there are no great temples, monuments of the past, such as we find everywhere among the literary religions. There is scarcely any abiding architecture at all. Apart from some central African ruins, e.g. the stone Zimbabwe in central Rhodesia, there is hardly a native building in all Africa south of the Sahara that is more than two hundred years old at the most. Mud buildings do not last long, and the oldest constructions are the stone forts of the Portuguese and Danes along the coastline. In the Pacific Islands there are ruins of stone temples in some places, such as Tonga and Tahiti, which may have been influenced by Indonesian or American styles.

There are, however, some fine temples built of clay which bear witness to vigorous artistic instincts. They are often decorated with geometric designs or set with patterns in bright pieces of pottery. These are found especially in West Africa; elsewhere temples are smaller and more temporary. The hill and jungle tribes of India, like the descendants of the American Maya, though not far from stone temples of higher civilizations, are content to build small huts with thatched roofs to contain the images of their gods.

Even the largest temples are usually quite small, buildings of one or two rooms at most. They are only entered by priests and are not intended for communal worship. In tropical countries generally, as we shall see again later, most temples contain a relatively small sanctuary into which priests go alone. A large courtyard, or simply an open clearing, is for the use of the laity.

Every village has at least one shrine, of the local chief deity. Often there are many small huts, or little mounds with a tree or stone at the foot of which offerings are placed. There are wayside shrines, and sacred trees, for guardian and fertility spirits, at which occasional gifts are laid.

Many shrines have an air of neglect, and except for quiet corners of the forest where the romantic imagination of the visitor may fancy an air of dread, they often appear singularly lacking in sanctity. They are, however, normally barred to strangers and on great festivals they are repaired and redecorated if the means are present.

Some shrines contain an altar, of stone or clay. Many enclose an image of wood or stone. Frequently there is a pot of water. Often a tree stump or a rod of iron is thrust into the ground. There may be visible remains of a sacrifice: bones, feathers, shells, nuts, flour, oil.

Images are found in many, but by no means all, shrines. The commonest material is wood, and the lively wooden carvings of Africa, New Zealand, Polynesia and the American Indies are well known. Fine pottery is done in many places, without the use of the wheel, and is highly decorated. Elephant tusks, animal horns, and fish bones may be carved. Bronzes are known, often of masks used in rituals.

Stone images are rare but there are some in Nigeria, and gigantic stone sculptures on Easter Island and the Marquesas, to beguile the imagination in wondering what purpose they served and who carved them. They are rarely used in rituals today.

Exaggerated praise is sometimes given to the art of illiterate peoples, as if there were little comparable inspired art in the world. Perhaps we are jaded with our own traditional art forms, but there is plenty of variety and superb craftsmanship in India and China, in Persia and Japan, that far outshines the illiterate world. One must keep a sense of proportion. The fine brasses of Africa are small beside the splendid bronze works of Cellini, Bellini and others in many Italian towns. The carvings pale before the abundance, skill and vigour of the sculptures of many a south Indian city.

Illiterate peoples have lacked the techniques and the traditions to produce and preserve much art of abiding quality, for most of what they have today is fashioned out of highly perishable material. That is not their fault; it is due to their isolation, geographical and cultural, and the worth of what they have produced demands recognition nevertheless.

There are no scriptures, by definition, among illiterate peoples. This has been said already, but its implications are not always realized. There are no written records of the past, because these peoples never learnt the art of writing. If some of them migrated from areas of higher culture centuries ago, as some writers claim, then they have lost invaluable skills, such as writing, the use of the wheel and the plough. Hence they will long be handicapped by the lack of a great cultural tradition.

As there are no writings, so no religious traditions of the past have been preserved except what could be transmitted orally. There were, no doubt, original thinkers and teachers in the past, but their thoughts have perished with them and have not been enshrined in books to teach later ages. So whatever prophets there may have been, their influence has been restricted both in place and time. There are no historical religious founders, and the few priests or prophets that can be remembered date from recent centuries. Pre-literary religions, then, are not historically founded. Neither are the religions of much of India and China, but at least they have had many teachers and reformers, and their scriptures are innumerable.

## RITUAL AND SACRIFICE

It has often been said that primitive religion is entirely a communal affair, and that personal religion arises at a later stage. This is only a half truth. But most ritual is communal, performed on behalf of the family or the village.

The ritual often has the appearance of being casual. As there are no written texts, words may be uttered that have been handed down orally but these are varied by the priest to suit current needs.

Exact pronunciation of ritual words belongs to the realm of magic spell rather than to divine sacrifices. Prayers are similar to those addressed to ancestors: 'May we have long life, may death not get us, let us not be impotent, give life to the village head, and life to the children.'

Many rites are concerned with agriculture, or whatever is the main occupation of the people. When the fields are ready to be hoed the chief calls his family or village together. A libation is made to the spirit of the earth or of fertility, and a prayer uttered for success in harvest and protection against accidents and snake-bites. When the harvest comes the first-fruits go to the gods and ancestors who have given them and from whose land they come.

At harvest the old food of the previous year is eaten first, if there is any of it left; the lack of old supplies of grain explains why in some parts this ceremonial eating is called 'hunger-hooting'. Then when the new corn is tasted by the people it is a communion meal with the gods who have eaten the first-fruits. In Swaziland there was a harvest ceremony which was believed to strengthen the kingship, and during much feasting and dancing the king himself danced to demonstrate his power.

Rituals are performed either by specially designated priests, or by the chief or elders of the family. One often finds that in worship of the gods it is a priest who presides, while in ancestral cults it is the family head or the oldest living member who performs the sacrifice, since he is nearest to the ancestors.

Great sacrifices of sheep or bulls are made on occasions when drought reduces people to despair. The whole village gathers, watches the slaughter of the sacrificial animal, and shares in its flesh when cooked. Under the leadership of a chief or priest they chant the praises of the spirits and shout out their need of rain. Perhaps a rain-maker, skilled in watching the weather signs, has directed the time of sacrifice and rain may fall soon after.

Sacrifices are made of any object. The simplest are libations of water or alcohol, or gifts of a few shells, beans or grains. Vege-tables are laid at the shrines at harvest festivals, and presents of almost any material may be placed there as votive gifts by grateful worshippers. The gift type of sacrifice is of any object that is thought adequate or necessary to the god.

Blood sacrifices, now abandoned in most higher religions, are commonly made by illiterate peoples. Often the blood is poured out on the altar or left to soak into the earth, that is the god's share, while the worshippers eat the carcase after cooking it. In a propitiatory sacrifice, designed to avert some great evil or obtain a special favour, a costly animal sacrifice is made and perhaps all of it dedicated to the god as a whole burnt offering.

The commonest animal sacrifice is a fowl whose neck is wrung, it is left in the shrine and the village dogs may come to clear up the carcase. A cock often hangs at the entrance to a village to keep away evil influences. A dog or goat is more costly, while a sheep is an even more fitting offering. A bull is the most expensive sacrifice, but it is commonly made on great occasions by cattle-rearing peoples.

Human sacrifice has been made, as the most costly of all and therefore the most potent. This is not peculiar to illiterate peoples; there are examples of it in the Old Testament, India and elsewhere. Human sacrifice might be performed to avert some great danger in war-time, or to provide a powerful charm in front of a village or a chief's house. Men were killed as scapegoats on whom the sins or evils of the people would fall, and as they were paraded through the village streets the crowds would touch them to transfer guilt to them.

On the whole it seems that human sacrifice was unusual, and today it is generally abandoned though one hears of cases sometimes; some of the Burmese hill tribes are said still to practise it. But the great massacres of human beings that took place in the 'cities of blood', the warrior and slaving kingdoms of Kumasi, Abomey and Benin, in the last century, were not strictly religious sacrifices. Men were killed at the death of a monarch to serve as his retinue on the journey to the underworld, and more were slaughtered on the anniversaries of his death to take him news of this world. Many of those who were killed were condemned criminals whose execution had been delayed until the anniversary, or prisoners of war, or slaves. This does not excuse the massacres, but shows their proper setting. Some early travellers grossly exaggerated the numbers of people involved. Today the tendency is to deny or forget that human sacrifices ever existed. Yet they are not so far away. It is better to recognize their existence and try to understand the reasons, now outmoded, that prompted these cruel actions.

## PERSONAL RELIGION

In the communal rites mentioned above, and in many others, the layman may be a passive spectator or at most one in a crowd of dancers. It is beyond our purpose to inquire further into rituals that may be performed by priests privately, since the aim of this book is to describe worship only as it affects the mass of the people, or at most the devout.

In addition to communal festivals, at the beginning of the year, harvest, and other times in the agricultural or pastoral year, there are occasions in the private and family life of every individual when religious rites are performed.

Sacrifices and prayers are made at the birth of a child, and at its naming ceremony. In puberty boys and girls pass through rituals of preparation for adult life. Many of the 'secret societies' are concerned with rites of adolescence; instruction in tribal customs and circumcision may take place then, and the idea of rebirth is linked with the passage from childhood to man's estate. The dances, costumes and masks often worn at the initiation cere-monies are popular subjects for European photographers and journalists on the look-out for exotic rites.

Marriage has its customs, more social than religious, in the provision of dowries and linking families together. But the ancestors are informed of what is taking place in their family. Death has its special rituals, serving to separate the corpse from its family and send the spirit safely away. Often a second funeral ceremony, or even a third as in Burma, is performed before the relatives can be sure that the spirit has actually reached the land of the ancestors. Then the cult of the ancestor is established at the grave or in a little hut near its relative's house.

In addition to family rites there are more personal prayers. In many places when a man rises in the morning he goes to his private or family shrine, bows before it, utters words of petition and dedication, and perhaps places a small offering there. Or he may face the rising sun and lift up his heart in adoration. At night he commends himself to the protecting deities against the dangers of ghosts and witches who may suck his blood and devour his soul. There are no set forms of prayer in widespread use, since there are no scriptures.

As well as villages shrines, most houses have some religious symbol. It may be simply a wisp of straw or a calabash amulet hanging over the door, to ward off evil influences. It is often a true shrine, in the corner of the room or on a shelf, where there are carved images or pots with symbols of the gods. Both men and women have divinities to whose care they commit themselves.

On special occasions, before undertaking any new venture, men present themselves before the gods and the fathers. A hunter dedicates himself and his weapons and implores protection from accidents and wild beasts. A merchant demands success to his enterprises. A traveller seeks safety for a journey and on return offers sacrifices in gratitude. Women pray for children and give thanks for safe delivery. Those spirits are most popular which promise a cure for 'unpregnancy'.

The help of the spirits is sought in every need. Their unwelcome attention is diverted or satiated in time of disease or misfortune by propitiatory sacrifice. A large part of religion is taken up with offering to the gods and ancestors to obtain their help. In conversion to a new religion a man expects the same and greater benefits. If the Christian convert does not prosper more than his pagan neighbour there must be something wrong. It takes a long time to learn the virtues of the patience of Job.

In all these personal and family rites offering and prayer can be made by any individual. A priest need not be called in. But if that expense is incurred, then additional blessings will be expected from his more potent incantations.

Is there solitary religious experience? In a recent work by an anthropological authority it is stated, 'Never does the worshipper face his god in solitude'.[1] This assertion may be questioned, for obviously the observer cannot see a man in solitude. And in view of the way in which certain of the same people, when converted to Christianity or Islam, go into retreat in the loneliness of the hills and at times return with an experience of God and a message from him, it need not be denied that the same happens in pagan religions. There are always thinkers who emerge from seclusion and announce a prophecy.

To ordinary men and women as well, as individuals and not merely as units of society, religion means a good deal more personally than is commonly supposed. There is communion with the spirits who surround all beings and fill the universe with their presence and power.

## BRIEF BIBLIOGRAPHY

Bastide, R. *African Civilisations in the New World*, Hurst, 1967.

Berndt, R. M. *Australian Aboriginal Art*, Collier Macmillan, 1964.

Eliade, M. *Australian Religions*, Cornell, 1973.

Eliade, M. *Shamanism*, E. T. Routledge, 1964.

Evans-Pritchard, E. E. *Nuer Religion*, Oxford, 1971.

Evans-Pritchard, E. E. *Theories of Primitive Religion*, Oxford, 1965.

Fürer-Haimendorf, C. von. *The Naked Nagas*, Thacker, Calcutta, 1962.

James, E. O. *The Ancient Gods*, Weidenfeld, 1960.

Krickeberg, W. *Pre-Columbian American Religions*, E. T. Weidenfeld, 1968.

Lévi-Strauss, C. *Totemism*, E. T. Penguin, 1969.

Maringer, J. *The Gods of Prehistoric Man*, E. T. Weidenfeld, 1968.

Parrinder, E. G. *African Mythology*, Hamlyn, 1967.

Parrinder, E. G. *African Traditional Religion*, Sheldon, 1974.

Poignant, R. *Oceanic Mythology*. Hamlyn, 1967.

Steiner, F. *Taboo*, Penguin, 1967.

[1] S. F. Nadel, *Nupe Religion*, p. 273.

Te Rangi Hiroa, *The Coming of the Maori*, Wellington, 1949.
Turner, V. W. *The Drums of Affliction*, Oxford, 1968.
Vaillant, C. G. *The Aztecs of Mexico*, Penguin, 1961.

# PART II

*India and Southern Asia*

*Chapter 2*

# HINDUISM

## The Divine

Hinduism has such a long history, and indeed is said to be the oldest living faith in the world, that it is puzzling to know where to begin before this vast complexity. This is not a history of religion and only brief reference can be made to historical developments to illuminate present trends.

The Indus city-civilization which preceded the Aryan invasion of India left a few traces in pottery and seals, but it is likely that a great deal of popular Hindu religion goes back to the Indus peoples or beyond, because it is so different from the Aryan religion revealed in the Vedic scriptures. Sir John Marshall said of the Indus civilization, 'Their religion is so characteristically Indian as hardly to be distinguishable from still living Hinduism or at least from that aspect of it which is bound up with animism and the cults of Śiva and the Mother Goddess—still the two most potent forces in popular worship'.[1]

The Aryans who swarmed into India from the middle of the second millennium B.C. composed hymns, prayers and spells to their many gods, which were gradually formulated into the Rig Veda and other scriptures. Only a few of the sacrifices prescribed in the Vedas are performed today, but the Vedic texts and hymns are revered and recited daily by countless people. The Vedas are believed to have been divinely inspired, revealed by the creator Brahmā to the ancient seers. Every devout Hindu recites as many

[1] *Mohenjo-daro and the Indus Civilization*, Vol. I, p. vii.

times as possible every day the Gāyatrī mantra, the sacred text called 'the mother of the Vedas': 'We meditate on the adorable glory of the radiant sun; may he inspire our intelligence'.[1]

In the Rig Veda there are many gods, and this polytheism appears to the outsider one of the perplexing features of Hinduism. But already in the early texts is a suggestion that all the gods are manifestations of one: 'They call him Indra, Mitra, Varuṇa, Agni, and even the fleet-winged celestial bird Garuḍa. The One reality, the learned speak of in many ways.'[2] This tendency is brought into full prominence in the Upanishads. One of the most famous asks, 'How many gods are there?' They are brought down from three thousand and three to one. And again, 'When they say, "Sacrifice to this or sacrifice to that god", each god is but his manifestation, for he is all gods.'[3]

Teaching about the divine as impersonal, the one spiritual reality, brought out the great element of immanence in Indian religion. The Upanishads many times speak of the infinite Brahman, the universal principle of nature, and its unity with the self, the Ātman. 'Verily, this whole self is Brahman. Tranquil, let one worship it as that from which he came forth, as that into which he will be dissolved, as that in which he breathes . . . This is the Self within the heart, this is Brahman.'[4] This leads on to the famous formula, 'That thou art' (*tat tvam asi*), which unites the soul and the all in Brahman-Ātman. This monistic trend has remained strong in Hinduism and colours many modern writings.

But God is also known as personal, in some of the later Upanishads and especially in more popular texts. Through his grace the creator may be seen in his greatness, and those who practise faith and austerity eventually go to him. Theism is still immanental, especially in its incarnational forms.

The Hindu deities must be considered against this background. The creator Brahmā plays but a small part in modern religion.

[1] Rig Veda III,62, 10.
[2] Rig Veda I, 64.
[3] Brihad-āraṇyaka Upanishad III, 9; I, 4.
[4] Chāndogya Upanishad III, 14.

Perhaps his most famous representation is in the caves on Elephanta Island near Bombay. Here is the ancient colossal stone Trimūrti, the three-faced bust, with faces that represent Brahmā the creator, Vishṇu the preserver and Rudra the destroyer. But these are all manifestations of Śiva, in whose honour the sculptures were made. In popular art Brahmā is shown as four-faced and four-armed, carrying a scroll and seated on a swan. His more popular consort, Sarasvatī, goddess of learning and the arts, is worshipped by teachers and students.

## INCARNATIONAL RELIGION

Vishṇu is a leading figure of the Hindu triad: Brahmā, Vishṇu and Śiva.[1] He is a god of grace, protecting and sustaining the world, and is worshipped as the supreme God by his Vaishṇava followers. He is accompanied by his wife Lakshmī and Garuḍa the sun-bird. Lakshmī is much invoked as goddess of good fortune, holding a flower in her hand and sometimes a child in the other arm.

Vishṇu is supremely the god of incarnations or descents (*avatāra*) and is worshipped under various forms. The stories of the avatars are found in the Purāṇa tales. There were many avatars of Vishṇu, but ten are generally accepted. These are: as fish, tortoise, boar, man-lion, dwarf, brahmin, Rāma, Krishṇa, Buddha, and Kalkī or the avatar yet to come. The most important of these are Rāma and Krishṇa.

*The Rāmāyaṇa,* 'the career of Rāma', composed in Sanskrit by Vālmīki about the second century B.C., and later translated into other Indian tongues, notably into Hindi by Tulsīdās in the sixteenth century, is one of the favourite religious writings of India. It is a noble story of the north Indian prince Rāma who married Sītā, was defrauded of his throne and took up the life of an ascetic in the jungle with his wife. Sītā was carried away by Rāvaṇa, the demon king of Lanka (Ceylon). With the help of

[1] Ś represents a palatal sound about midway between s and sh, often pronounced sh by Europeans (i.e. Śiva as Shiva).

Hanumān, the monkey god, and his followers Rāma recovered his wife, crossing the sea in an aerial chariot or by the islands that are still called Rāma's bridge, and bringing her safely home to his regained throne.

Rāma with his bows and arrows, accompanied by his faithful brother Lakshmana, is a popular figure as an incarnation of Vishnu. Sītā is held up to Indian women as the ideal of female purity and constancy. Hanumān is worshipped as Great Hero (Mahāvīra) at many village shrines; pictures of him in an attitude of devotion before the glorified Rāma are very common.

A further work attributed to Vālmīki, the *Greater Book* (Mahā Rāmāyana), is not so popular but is a mystical treatise of great beauty and depth. It describes the inner life of Rāma, how he conquered himself and came to the apprehension of the Supreme Self.

The eighth avatar of Vishnu is Krishna, but some regard him as god himself and not just an avatar. His cult is even more widespread than that of Rāma, and its origins seem to go back to prehistoric times.

Krishna first appears in the Bhagavad Gita, the Song of the Lord, which is the most renowned of all Hindu scriptures, a small part of the great epic Mahābhārata perhaps about the third century B.C. In this account of tribal wars the warrior Arjuna hesitates on the field of Kurukshetra, beset with scruples, unwilling to slay his kinsmen. Krishna, who appears as his charioteer, gives the stern reply that the soul is imperishable, 'that by which all this is pervaded is indestructible . . . he is never born, nor does he die at any time'. One should therefore perform one's duty without thought of result: 'Let not the fruits of action be thy motive; neither let there be in thee any attachment to inaction. Fixed in yoga, do thy work.'[1]

This is the way of Yoga, training the mind in detachment, but it goes on to devotion (*bhakti*). Krishna reveals himself to Arjuna as God, and Arjuna adores confessing his attributes: 'In thy body, O God, I see all the gods and the varied hosts of beings as well,

[1] *Bhagavadgītā*, 2, 17–20.

Brahmā, the lord seated on the lotus throne and all the sages . . .
Thy fiery rays fill this whole universe and scorch it with their
fierce radiance, O Vishṇu . . . O thou Great God-head, have
mercy. I wish to know thee, the Primal One.' So he is told that the
way of salvation is through devotion to Vishṇu: 'Fix thy mind on
Me; be devoted to Me; sacrifice to Me; prostrate thyself before
Me; so shalt thou come to Me. I promise thee truly, for thou art
dear to Me.'[1]

In a supplementary work called Harivaṁśa, and in the Purāṇa
stories, there is much additional matter about Krishṇa. His birthplace is fixed at Mathura (Muttra) in north India, a town that is
still a great centre for pilgrims who perform the 'pilgrimage of
the groves' connected with his birth. Stories of his birth and
childhood, pranks and adventures, conflicts with demons and
gods, are very popular. Later ages dwelt much on Krishṇa's love
affairs which are the subject of many erotic and mystical poems.
Probably Krishṇa here embodies old fertility cults, and these are
sublimated into examples of human and divine love, rather in the
manner in which the love poems of the Song of Songs were
sanctified for the devotions of Jews and Christians. The sexual
instinct is glorified and its ecstasies translated into the soul's long-
ing for God. This is the fullest expression of *Bhakti*.

Krishṇa's adventures with the cowgirls (*gopīs*) are all dwelt
upon. In particular one girl, Rādhā, appears as the chief object of
his passions, and their meetings and separations are described in
many ways. In the *Gītā Govinda*, a poem written by Jayadeva in
the twelfth century, these themes find expression in sensuous
terms:

> *He has gone into the trysting-place, full of all desired bliss,*
> *O you with the lovely hips delay no more*
> *O go forth now and seek him out, him the master of your heart,*
> *him endowed with passion's lovely form.*[2]

Other poets took up the theme, and from the fifteenth century

[1] ibid., ch. 11.
[2] W. G. Archer, *The Loves of Krishna*, p. 79.

many were writing of Krishna's life and loves, in lyrics that are still popular. Princess Mirabai sang thus of the divine lover:

*How shall I ever live without thee, Beloved?*
*Thou art the root of my life-herb.*
*How can the bond between thee and me sever?*
*As sap pervades the stem of a lotus, so is thy love immanent in me.*[1]

Artists depicted the scenes of Krishna's amours, and especially in Kangra State there were produced lovely pictures of Rādhā and Krishna. All over modern India, in countless houses and shops, there are coloured prints of the blue-skinned Krishna in a yellow vest playing to the *gopīs* on his flute. The scenes of his exploits are depicted on temple walls, and he appears in images, crowned, with the Vishnu mark on his forehead. The praises of Krishna, often under the name Hari, are chanted endlessly in daily repetitions of the Bhagavad Gītā, and beggars sing for alms in his name.

## Śiva and Śakti

Śiva has been referred to as the great god manifested in the Trimūrti as Brahmā, Vishnu and Rudra. By his Śaiva followers he is called God himself, and all the other gods are looked upon as his subordinates. One of his favourite titles is Mahādeva, 'great God'.

The very ancient character of the worship of Śiva is illustrated by his function of destroyer, representing the destructive side of the universe, but he is also a creator and sustainer. Similarly his constant symbol of the *linga* or phallus, often set in a female *yoni*, is no doubt derived from an ancient fertility cult. Yet both of these symbols are conventional in form and are not necessarily suggestive to the worshippers who deck them with flowers as other images. Śiva is also the god of dance, and one of his best known representations is as Naṭarāja, the dancing lord, where the four-armed god performs the world-shaking dance.

[1] A. J. Appasamy, *Temple Bells*, p. 69.

Further, Śiva is always accompanied by animals. He has his attendant snake, and is often clothed in a leopard skin. Nandi, the white humped bull is always found in Śaiva temples facing the shrine, and is worshipped by women. Gaṇeśa, the elephant-headed god, is Śiva's son, and as patron of learning and fortune is invoked at the opening of books and undertakings. Another son, Kārttikeya, is associated with the stars.

Yet Śiva is also lord of ascetics (Mahāyogī), and his ash-smeared followers, with his characteristic horizontal marks on their brows, and trident stuck in the ground beside them, are one of the commonest sights in India. A favourite subject with artists is Śiva and his consort Pārvatī in the Himalayas with their children. Śiva sits as an ascetic, his body smeared with ash but recognizable by his third eye and crescent moon in his forehead.

Many Śaivites follow the monistic philosopher Śaṅkara, who is said to have put down some of the grosser manifestations of the cult in south India. The Śaṅkara school maintained that the way of knowledge (*jñāna mārga*) was better than that of devotion. The popularity of the way of devotion (*bhakti*) however led to its introduction into Śaivism. Especially in south India Tamil poets, like Manikka Vachakar, had a great influence in bringing *bhakti* into Śaivism. His songs are widely used:

> *I am unreal! My heart is unreal! My devotion is unreal!*
> *Sinner as I am. I can attain thee if I but cry for thee!*
> *O Sweet Lord! O Honey! O Clear Juice of the Sugar Cane!*
> *Be gracious, that I may reach thee!*[1]

There are many sects of Śaivism and ascetics with peculiar practices. The Sitta Śaivas of south India are monotheists whose sacred books express a passionate belief in the unity of God and a hatred of idolatry. The Tridandrins bear about the trident as a symbol of Śiva the great ascetic. The Lingāyats wear a small liṅga and are very important in the political scene, especially in Mysore. Others perform many kinds of asceticism and are visible at the great festivals.

[1]ibid, p. 60.

Śakti, another name for the consort of Śiva, is the third most popular deity today. She is often called Mahādevī, Great Goddess. As mother she is referred to in the Mahābhārata and the Purāṇas. Women pray to her for children and she has strong fertility associations.

Under the forms of Durgā and Kālī the goddess appears in terrifying manifestations, fighting demons and gods, and triumphing even over her own consort. Fearful representations of Kālī are to be seen today in countless pictures in shops and houses. In her most famous temple, the Kālīghat from which Calcutta takes its name, blood sacrifices are still offered daily. This is very different from the non-sacrificial worship of most of Hinduism, and Hindus like Radhakrishnan regret that Śaṅkara could not have purged the Kālīghat. 'He put down the grosser manifestations of Śākta worship in South India, and it is a pity that his influence is not perceptible in the great temple of Kālī in Calcutta.'[1]

Yet Kālī is cherished as the Great Mother. Women go to her shrine and kiss the walls in the hope of becoming pregnant, while others pray for the blessing of their families. A tree in the courtyard of the Kālīghat is hung with votive gifts to the Mother. The great nineteenth-century saint, Ramakrishna, was priest in one of her Calcutta temples and had a deep devotion to her. So had his disciple Vivekananda. The poet Ram Praśad of Bengal in the last century constantly sang of the motherhood of God:

> *Tho' the mother beat him,*
> *The child cries 'Mother, O Mother',*
> *And clings still tighter to her garment.*[2]

The name Śakti is given to the goddess in her aspect of female 'energy'. The worshippers, Śāktas, have been traditionally divided into 'right-hand' and 'left-hand' worshippers. Most Śāktas belong to the former cult and perform their devotions openly. The 'left-hand worshippers' adore in secret, and follow after salvation by means of the five M's: liquor, fish, flesh, corn, and sexual union

[1]*Indian Philosophy*, ii, p. 450.
[2]Sister Nivedita, *Kali the Mother*, p. 53.

(under their Sanskrit names). These are followed sacramentally, and despite sensual rites sometimes alleged of them, the Vāmā-chārīs (left-hand) have a reputation for high morality outside their cult, and they have worked for social reform and removal of abuses such as *sati* (suttee, widow-burning).

The scriptures of the Vāmāchārīs are special tantras (thread, fundamental doctrine), sacred books that give details of the kinds of sacrifices required. The tantric worship of certain Buddhist sects is closely akin to this. The wives of other Hindu gods are also called their Śaktis, being regarded as manifestations of the Great Goddess.

In the villages the most popular gods are often the gods of the place, as in African villages. These are the tutelary village gods, in addition to which there are personal and family gods. They may be purely local spirits, or chosen from among the greater deities of the Hindu pantheon. Most of the village gods are female, their names ending in *amma*, a feminine termination. The goddess may be simply represented by a piece of stone painted red, with other stones for her children; or there may be a carved image or a tree also painted red. Snakes have a cult of their own, especially in Bengal and the south where the worship of Nāga, the serpent, is ancient and deeply enrooted. Under many village trees are small stones on which snakes are carved in different postures and which receive regular offerings. These are cults of village Hindus, and are distinct from the gods of the aboriginal hill tribes.

## Personal and Family Worship

Worship is largely an individual matter for the Hindu. In the temple it is not congregational, and even at great festivals the devotee observes his own regulations. We may distinguish worship in the home and worship on special occasions.

The twice-born Hindus, that is those who belong to the three higher castes, perform their ritual three times a day. The devout Hindu rises before dawn, utters the mantra Om (or Aum, the mystic invocatory syllable), repeats the name of his God, remembers his teacher, and says a prayer of identification with the Lord which begins, 'I am the Lord, in no wise different from him, the Brahman'.[1]

He then binds up the tuft of hair on his head, which is the distinctive mark of a Hindu, and repeats the Gāyatrī mantra. He proceeds to worship (pūjā) bare to the waist and bare-footed, with the sacred white thread diagonally across his trunk from shoulder to waist, and perhaps with *tilaka* marks of ash or sandalwood paste on his forehead; either horizontal for Śiva or vertical for Vishnu. He sits on a rug on the ground, legs crossed, eyes fixed on the tip of his nose, controlling the breath, facing east. Water is sipped, while the name of God is repeated, and water sprinkled round the seat. He then touches six parts of the body symbolically, to place the deity in his body. He repeats prayers, meditates on the sun, and says the Gāyatrī many times. Water is offered to the image of the god, Vedic verses repeated, and a final water offering and obeisance made.

Evening devotions are similar but shorter, with recitation of verses and offering of lights and flowers to God. Midday worship follows a visit to a spiritual teacher and consists of worship towards and meditation on the deity. The five daily obligations which an orthodox Hindu observes are offerings to gods, to forefathers, to the seers through reading the Vedas, to animals and to the poor.

Worship is performed in a special room or corner where there is an image or symbol, such as the *śālagrāma* stone of Vishnu or *liṅga* of Śiva. Pictures or books may be used as symbols. A symbol called a *yantra* may be used; it is a square with four openings, enclosing a circle with eight spokes and a smaller circle in the middle. This may be of wood or metal, and geometrical designs are engraved on it or put on with paste or ashes. Then there is the *maṇḍala*, a design made with powder of five colours. These

[1]For a detailed account see M. Stevenson, *Rites of the Twice-born*, or more recently K. W. Morgan, ed., *The Religion of the Hindus*, p. 176 f.

*Om* is the most sacred syllable that can be uttered, and is on the lips of pious Hindus all life long.

*maṇḍalas* and *yantras* are of great interest to those who study mystic diagrams; psychologists like Jung have seen great significance in them. They are regarded by the worshipper as the body of the deity and vessels are consecrated for their use in ritual.

If there is an image of the deity its care is taken very seriously. It is clad in beautiful clothes, cooled with water in the hot season, and offered fresh fruit. It is anointed while texts are repeated. Gifts have to be placed carefully according to traditional rules, uncooked food and lamps on the image's left and cooked food on its right.

Household priests come to perform special ceremonies on payment of fees. On important occasions the five great deities, Vishṇu, Śiva, Gaṇeśa, Śakti, and Sūrya the sun, may be worshipped under image or symbolical form. The preliminary rites comprise sipping water while the name of the principal god is repeated, ringing of a bell and sounding a conch shell. The ceremony proper is in sixteen stages: invocation, offering the gods a seat, water to wash their feet, offering rice, water for them to sip, milk and honey to bathe in, clothes represented by *tulasī* leaves, ornaments in the form of leaves, perfumes and sandal paste, flowers, incense, lights, food, walking round the images, giving flowers while texts are recited, and final adoration.

Such elaborate rites are occasional. Even the regular devotions of the caste Hindu sketched above are observed by the devout rather than by everyone. In modern times many Hindus find it impossible to give the time to traditional religious requirements. Full worship may be held once a day, or by one member of the family on behalf of all. Those families that can afford the services of a priest have the care of the image done for them. Others recite sacred texts wherever they may happen to be, in the train or the office. Nevertheless in devotions, meditation, and yogic practices, it is probable that Hindus in general give much more time to religion than do most Europeans.

Women do not observe the Vedic worship and they are not allowed to use the sacred mantras. But they attend upon their husbands, clean the vessels of worship and prepare the food. They often have an image of their own, perhaps of Krishṇa, which they tend with the care given to a child. If they can read they may study the Rāmāyaṇa and the Bhagavad Gītā; in any case they will know much of them by heart. If initiated they may observe Śāktic forms of worship, using Tāntric texts and mantras from the Purāṇas. Children are taught to repeat the names of Rāma, Hari and Śiva, while older people utter these names, telling them over on prayer beads. Rosaries of 108 beads are used.

Tāntric worship is open both to women and to members of the fourth caste, the Śūdras. The Tantras are scriptures which aim at showing practical ways in which the theories of the Vedas may be set out. In an elementary form of Tāntric initiation the teacher delivers a mantra to his disciple, which he is charged to repeat daily and use in time of need. A simple form of worship is enjoined, and fuller observances are left to priests who are called in.

The Śūdra, like women, may not read the early Vedic mantras (*saṁhitās*) but some Upanishads, the Mahābhārata and the Purāṇas are open to him. Despite handicaps many Śūdras have played a leading part in Indian life and religion; many temples have been built by them and they have played privileged roles in the service of the temple gods. Many of the restrictions formerly placed upon them and even more upon the outcasts are breaking down today.

TEMPLE WORSHIP

While the large temples contain pavilions where religious entertainments are held, and instruction on religion is given, yet temple worship is not congregational. The ceremonies are performed by priests, and many of the temples, especially in north India and the villages, are too small to admit large crowds.

The sacraments of family life, birthdays, initiation, marriage and funerals, are performed at home and not in the temple.

India is world famous for the number, beauty and lavish decoration of its temples; but these are mostly in the centre and south. Multitudes of great buildings were destroyed by the iconoclastic Mughal Muslims in the seventeenth and eighteenth centuries. The ruthless Aurangzeb (died 1707) in one year destroyed 252 Hindu temples in Rajasthan alone; how many more were sacked in the course of his forty years' reign no one can tell. As a result many Hindu temples in the north are small and undistinguished; often they are little shrines in the middle of busy streets, at which people bow and prostrate before a tiny image, oblivious of the bullock carts, trishaws, tongas, taxis and buses that whirl by. Even at the great religious centre of Benares the temples are crowded in the bazar or hanging along the River Ganges.

There are famous ancient groups of temple buildings at Ellora, Khajuraho, Bhuvaneśvar and Puri, but the south Indian temples are the most numerous. In the great temple at Madura, for example, there is a Hall of a Thousand Pillars, with wonderful and elaborate stone sculpture. The only European parallels that come to mind are some of the Gothic cathedrals, and even their wonder and variety are far outnumbered by the innumerable temples of south India.

All temples of any size are built on a definite plan. The central part is the sanctuary (*vimāna*) in which an image or symbol of the god is enshrined in its 'womb'. This is covered by a tower or pyramid. There is a pavilion in front of the shrine for worshippers and a veranda or processional passage around it for ritual circumambulation. It is an essential part of worship to make the circuit of the shrine, one or many times. There is always a large tank for ritual washings. The south Indian temples are characterized by the *gopurams*, high wedge-shaped pyramidal porches in the stone walls, decorated with lavish profusion by scenes from the mythologies. These tower above thousands of villages and towns and mark the landscape, like pagodas in other lands.

There are many modern temples, but of lower architectural standard, though they swarm with worshippers. There is the much publicized Birla temple in New Delhi, a pretentious structure in pink and yellow, with sugary statues of many deities, and even a shrine of the Buddha; que fait-il dans cette galère? The skill and vigour of building that lasted a thousand years, till the seventeenth century, has not yet been regained.

Temple worship is performed by the priests, and it is not intended here to make a study of priestly rituals, but only to refer to what may be shared in by the layman. The temple symbols, *linga* or *śālagrāma*, or images are cared for like those at home, bathed and anointed. The laity may come especially in the evening to see the royal clothes of the image in a lamp ceremony before retiring. They bring offerings of flowers, garlands, scent and cooked food. Animal sacrifices are never made to Vishṇu and are generally repugnant to Brahmins, except in the worship of Kālī. But the village gods of south India receive many animal offerings.

The visitors provide lighted lamps for the shrine, pay for the reading of scriptures, walk round the shrine with the right side always towards the image, or prostrate all round the temple in fulfilment of some vow or to obtain a special favour. Merit is also gained by paying for the performance of sacred music and drama.

Gatherings to hear musicians play and sing are very popular in the home, the village square, or the temple. Many of the ancient hymns of devotion are sung thus, with stories of human love applied to God. Paṇḍits (religious teachers) expert in the epics and Purāṇas are invited to give public expositions, which are illustrated by adornments and gestures and lead the audience to applause, tears or ecstasy.

## FESTIVALS

Every temple has at least one annual festival in honour of its principal deity, and this usually lasts a week during which time people flock in from neighbouring villages. There are elaborate ceremonies for the god every day, of which the evening robing is attended by great crowds. The chief item of the festival is the public procession of the temple image, which may be carried on an elephant or in a huge and highly-painted and carved wooden carriage. The image is borne round the temple and through the main streets, down to a river where it is bathed, and returned to the shrine. The temple of Jagannātha (Juggernaut, a title of

Krishṇa) at Puri has long been famous for its festival. In the past devotees dragged the chariot by hooks fastened through their backs and excited pilgrims threw themselves to the ground in front of the cart wheels.

There are many religious festivals at all times of the year in different parts of India. Most of these are associated with some event in the stories of the gods. Some are universally observed.

The Holi festival at the beginning of spring, in February–March, comes clearly from an ancient fertility ritual. The crowds sing songs and carry phallic symbols, and generally behave as in the saturnalia of the ancient world. People delight in squirting coloured water and powder on each other and on any passers by, to the laughter and pranks of children. Coloured water and powder are offered to Krishṇa and Rādhā, and traditional stories connect the feast with the loves of Krishṇa and the demons that he killed. Effigies of demons are made and burnt in bonfires.

Dasera (*Daśarā*), in September–October, is a ten-day feast in honour of the goddess Durgā, and is becoming increasingly popular. It used to be celebrated with particular pomp by the rajas and warrior caste, with elephant processions symbolizing war against other states. The origins of the festival are said to go back to Rāma's battle against the demon Rāvaṇa, when the former invoked the help of Durgā. The first seven days are comparatively quiet, and are each dedicated to one of the manifestations in which Durgā or Kālī fought with demons. There is merry-making on the eighth day, and sacrifices to Kālī on the ninth. On the tenth day huge pasteboard effigies of Rāvaṇa and his associates parade the streets; they are packed with crackers and explosives. There are vivid portrayals of battles between Rāma and Rāvaṇa by masked dancers who go in a carnival procession in decorated cars. The culmination comes when Rāma shoots fiery arrows into the effigies and they explode, thus demonstrating the triumph of good over evil.

Divali, in October–November, comes from a word meaning a 'cluster of lights'. It lasts for four days and is a new year festival. Various stories associate the feast with Rama, or departed souls, and more especially with Vishṇu and his wife Lakshmī. Homes are lit with clay oil lamps to welcome into the house Lakshmī, goddess of wealth and prosperity. Houses are spring-cleaned, flour designs are made on doorsteps, and fireworks scare away evil spirits. Presents and greetings are sent to friends, and children receive supplies of crackers. Business people, in particular, celebrate the festival and open new account books with prayers to Lakshmī for success in the New Year.

Other popular festivals celebrate Gaṇeśa, the god of prosperity, and Sarasvatī, patron of learning and music. The Śaivites observe with great devotion the day of the 'Sight of Śiva' when he manifested himself to his devotees as Naṭarāja, in the cosmic dance of creation and dissolution of the universe.

## PILGRIMAGES

Pilgrimages to holy places play a great part in Hindu religious life, and are a means whereby men gain merit and advance in spiritual progress. They are as significant in Hinduism as pilgrimages were to medieval Europe.

There are seven especially holy places of the Hindus: Benares, Mathura, Ayodhya, Hardwar, Dwaraka, Ujjain and Conjeeveram. Mathura was Krishna's birthplace and Dwaraka his capital. Ayodhya was Rāma's kingdom. Hardwar, where the Ganges comes down to the plains from the mountains, has a footprint of Vishṇu in stone and is also a centre for the worship of Śiva a lord of the mountains. Ujjain is a great centre of Śaiva *liṅga* worship. Conjeeveram (Kanchipuram) is one of the great centres of Durgā worship in the south, as well as of Vishṇu and Śiva.

Benares (Varanasi or Kāśī) is the most sacred of all, a centre of Śaivism and always a place of learning from ancient times down to the establishment of its modern Hindu university. The whole city is sacred to the Hindu, and especially the River Ganges, Mother Gangā, which flows through it. Pilgrims visit holy spots in the town, make the circuit of the city, a distance of about ten miles within which all is sacred, and bathe in the Ganges. All pious

Hindus wish to die within the precincts of Benares, which ensures a direct passage to heaven, hence the place is a favourite one for cremations.

The *ghats*, steps leading down to the river, line the northern bank. Many of them are now being repaired and new concrete steps are in building. Some of the small temples behind them are tilted towards the river. The *ghats* are lined with holy beggars. Large straw umbrellas are dotted about under which men sit in meditation or repeat the scriptures. Men and women go down to bathe in the river, the women separately and half clothed, the men in loincloths.

Most cremations take place at the Burning Ghat, the Jalsain Ghat. Piles of sandalwood are on sale. When a body is brought bearers chant the name of God, 'Rām, Rām', as they carry it, wrapped in a simple white cloth. It is laid in the river and Ganges water splashed into the uncovered mouth. A priest of Yama, the god of death, takes dues and performs the ritual. The relatives ask for the sacred fire and apply it five times to the pyre on which the corpse has been placed. When the burning is over the remains are scattered on the surface of the river, with marigold petals.

Some eighty miles up river from Benares is Allahabad, or Prayag, where the two rivers, Ganges and Jumna unite, and where thousands of pilgrims bathe at the sacred confluence. Pilgrims who wish to gain great merit go on foot the 1,200 miles to the extreme south of India to Rameśvaram, where is a famous Śaiva shrine said to have been founded by Rāma. Other favourite places are Gaya, lower down the Ganges than Benares where there is an imprint of Vishṇu's foot in stone, and Sagar Island where the Ganges-Hoogly enters the Bay of Bengal. The most sacred lake in India is at Pushkar, near Ajmer in Rajasthan. Many other old places are associated with the stories of the gods.

Every twelve years great pilgrimage festivals, known as Kumbha Mela, are held at four places in succession. According to the myth the gods and demons fought for the possession of a pitcher (*kumbha*) of nectar, which the gods finally carried off to heaven. They stopped at four places on the way and sanctified them with the touch of the Kumbha. The sacred spots were Prayag, Hardwar, Nasik and Ujjain.

The Mela is a great religious fair of timeless antiquity; it was mentioned by a Chinese traveller in the seventh century who saw half a million people there. It is even more popular today with modern means of transport. At the last Kumbha Mela, at Prayag in 1954, it is estimated that 6 million people were assembled, and so immense were the crowds that hundreds were killed and injured in a rush towards the water at the confluence.

To these Melas come bands of sādhus (ascetics), some emaciated with fastings and austerities, such as arms withered by disuse or eyes blinded by constant gazing at the sun; others lie on beds of spikes, or swing in the air with their heads down, and many are smeared with ash and chant holy mantras. Some sādhus emerge from their silent seclusion in the forest or mountains only at this festival and pilgrims come especially to see them. Other teachers employ modern methods of instruction, and use microphones to lecture large crowds.

## TEACHERS AND MYSTICS

In the revival and reformation of Hinduism which have taken place during the last century or so, there have been considerable efforts at purification of worship. Ram Mohun Roy (1772–1833), founder of the Brāhmo Samāj, denounced idol worship and caste distinctions and built a rational theistic system based on the Upanishads. In its later developments the Brāhmo Samāj tended to become a synthesis of Hinduism and Christianity; its followers reject images and religious pictures, but adorn their houses with texts from all the world's religious. The Ārya Samāj, a more militant movement now, like the Hindu Mahāsabhā, seeks to reclaim those who have left the ancestral religion; it denounces idol worship and caste and takes its stand on the Vedas alone, curiously neglecting the Upanishads.

Rabindranath Tagore (1861–1941) was a great mystical poet who began with the Brāhmo Samāj but outgrew their limitations.

His devotional poems are sung throughout India and are known all over the world in translations. Here is *bhakti* religion at its purest, as he sings of the divine flautist:

*Thou has made me endless, such is thy pleasure . . .*
*This little flute of a reed thou hast carried over hills and dales, and hast breathed through it melodies eternally new. . . .*
*Drunk with the joy of singing I forget myself and call thee friend who art my lord.*

But his mysticism passes beyond local ties and has a strong universal note:

*Days come and ages pass, and it is ever he who moves my heart in many a name, in many a guise, in many a rapture of joy and sorrow.*[1]

Of great importance religiously today is the Ramakrishna Mission. Śri Ramakrishna (1836–86) was a poor Brahmin of Bengal who in 1855 became a priest in the Kāli temple at Dakshine-śvar in north Calcutta. In 1859 he took as wife Sarada Devi who was later to become known as the Holy Mother. Ramakrishna gave himself up to meditation and for twelve years was as dead to the outer world. He had a vision of Kāli as the Divine Mother, but he was also torn with doubts as to the place of the other faiths of the world. Finally he emerged with his syncretistic gospel: 'He who is called Krishna is also called Śiva and bears the name of Primitive Energy, Jesus and Allah as well—the same Rāma with a thousand names.'

Ramakrishna inspired followers with ideals of renunciation, service of humanity and preaching the unity of religions. His favourite disciple, Swami Vivekananda (1863–1902), toured Europe and America and founded the Ramakrishna Mission which has many centres, in all the main Indian cities and many other parts of the world. Not only does Hinduism now become missionary, by seeking a synthesis of religions, but religious devotees engage in social and educational work and in relief programmes. The headquarters of the mission at Belur in Calcutta has a main

[1]*Gitanjali*, pp. 1–2, 67–68.

temple which is a mixture of Hindu, Muslim and Buddhist styles, and at the far end of the hall is a marble image of Ramakrishna, who is called the 'presiding Deity', to which money, flowers and incense are offered. There are other shrines to the Holy Mother (Sarada Devi), Vivekananda, and Brahmananda the first president of the movement. There are relics of the founders, and schools and colleges.

The importance of the spiritual teacher (*guru*) has always been great in Hinduism. The spiritual life is not to be learned from books, but from the living voice of a *guru* who bestows initiation into worship. The sacred teachings of the Vedānta were not written down for many centuries, but were passed on by word of mouth and so the importance of teaching and of knowledge, rather than mere book-learning, was always stressed. There are innumerable modern teachers to whom serious Hindus go for shorter or longer periods. Many of these have founded ashrams (*āśrama*, hermitage) as did the seers of old, for the purpose of teaching a new way to their followers. Tagore, Aurobindo Ghose, Ramana Maharshi and many others have had their ashrams.

Śri Aurobindo Ghose (1872–1950), the 'prophet of the Life Divine', taught what he called 'integral yoga', by which the higher consciousness of the divine life might be realized and fill both mind and body, so producing Supermen or Divine Men. He believed that all modern social troubles could be solved by producing divine men, and in his ashram at Pondicherry he practised his form of yoga and taught it to the many people who came for instruction.

Yoga (union; related to our word yoke) is the name for systems of mental and physical culture which are widely practised in India and have been for many centuries. There are methods of sense-control, exercise, breathing practices, and posture which aim at increasing bodily powers and developing physical and mental capacities. But spiritual powers are no less included, and the Yoga Sūtras of Patañjali (third century B.C.) are taken as guides on the spiritual path. The aim is 'liberation' (*moksha*) or 'liberty', by which peace of mind is achieved through control of the emotions, health of the body, and the enhancing of psychic faculties. Many schools and teachers set forth methods of training body and mind, and are followed by large numbers of both young and older men.

Sri Ramana Maharshi (1879–1950) is one of the best known of modern Indian saints whose influence is still great, and whose ashram exercises an unfading attraction. As a young boy he became devoted to Śiva, in ways that he himself described: 'I would stand before Iśwara, the Controller of the universe and of the destinies of all, the Omniscient and Omnipresent, and sometimes pray for the descent of his grace upon me so that my devotion might increase and become perpetual.'[1] Soon he ran away from home to the sacred hill of Arunachala in south India, and there after fasting and extreme asceticism comparable with those of Ramakrishna, he attained the peace that so marked him when he became known and followers were drawn to him. By rigorous self-examination, 'Who am I?', he came to see the unity of all beings in the Supreme Being. By seeking beyond the bonds of appearances man realizes his identity with the Absolute. This is the doctrine of Advaita, non-duality, taught by the sages since the time of the Upanishads. 'All religions postulate the three fundamentals: individual, God and world. It is only so long as the ego endures that one says either, "The One manifests Itself as the three," or "The three are really three." The supreme state is to inhere in the Self, the ego extinguished.'[2]

When devotees came to attend on and learn from Ramana, āshram premises were put up, guest-rooms and a dining-hall, office, kitchen and dispensary. Regulations were made for communal life and the whole was put under the rule of the saint's brother. Their mother came to the holy hill and when she died was buried there, not cremated as she had become a saint and would not be reborn; at her grave a temple was finally erected. 'the Temple of God manifested as the Mother'. Ramana Maharshi himself died of cancer in 1950 and was also buried on the holy hill with the symbol of Śiva, the liṅga of polished black stone, over

[1]A. Osborne, *Ramana Maharshi*, p. 23.
[2]ibid., p. 82.

his grave. The āshram is maintained, his followers performing meditation and speaking of the abiding presence of the saint as the Inner Guru.

Mahatma Gandhi (1869–1948) had perhaps as great an influence on modern Indian religious life as on its political fortunes. His application of the principle of non-violence, which he owed largely to the Jain teaching of 'harmlessness' (ahiṁsā) has been of lasting effect. He sought freedom for the outcastes (Harijans) to enter temples. He shared in the growing appreciation of other religions which was apparent in his day, but sought rather to widen and purify Hinduism from within than change it for another faith. Today Gandhi's bust garlanded with flowers is to be seen in every Indian town and countless villages. His grave at Delhi is a constant place of pilgrimage, at which visitors take off their shoes and place marigold flowers in sign of their veneration.

Gandhi's spiritual heir is Vinoba Bhave, who is famous for his land reform movement (Bhudan) based on appeals to religion and service. Vinoba walks from village to village with a group of disciples, usually spending a year in each state, appealing for gifts of land which are distributed to landless cultivators. His message is one of great simplicity, but is given force by his constant appeal to religious traditions and his own ascetic life. He is undoubtedly one of the greatest religious forces in India today.

## BIBLIOGRAPHY

Archer, W. G. *The Loves of Krishna*, Allen and Unwin, 1957.

Basham, A. L. *The Wonder that was India*, Sidgwick and Jackson, 1954.

Daniélou, A. *Hindu Polytheism*, E. T. Routledge, 1964.

De Bary, W. T., ed. *Sources of Indian Tradition*, Columbia, 1958.

Dhavamony, M. *Love of God according to Śaiva Siddhānta*, Oxford, 1971.

Dowson, J. *A Classical Dictionary of Indian Mythology*, 11th edn., Routledge, 1968.

Eliade, M. *Yoga, Immortality and Freedom*, E. T. Routledge, 1958.

Hinnells, J., ed. *Hinduism*, Oriel, 1972.

Ions, V. *Indian Mythology*, Hamlyn, 1967.

# BIBLIOGRAPHY

Klostermaier, K. *Hindu and Christian in Vrindaban*, S.C.M., 1970.

Kramrisch, S. *The Art of India through the Ages*, 3rd edn., Phaidon, 1965.

Morgan, K. W., ed. *The Religion of the Hindus*, Ronald Press, 1953.

Pandey, R. B. *Hindu Samskāras*, 2nd ed. Benares, 1969.

Parrinder, E. G. *Avatar and Incarnation*, Faber, 1970.

Parrinder, E. G. *The Bhagavad Gita: a Verse Translation*, Sheldon, 1974.

Rawson, P. *The Art of Tantra*, Thames & Hudson, 1973.

Rowland, B. *The Art and Architecture of India*, Penguin, 1970.

Singer, M., ed. *Krishna: Myths, Rites, and Attitudes*, Chicago, 1968.

Thomas, P. *Hindu Religion, Customs and Manners*, Taraporevala, Bombay, 1956.

Vidyarthi, L. P. *The Sacred Complex in Hindu Gaya*, Asia, 1961.

Wood, E. *Yoga*, Penguin, 1970.

Zaehner, R. C. *Hinduism*, Oxford, 1962.

Zaehner, R. C. *Hindu Scriptures*, Everyman, 1966.

Zimmer, H. *Myths and Symbols in Indian Art and Civilization*, Bollingen, 1953.

*Chapter 3*

# THE JAINS

The Jain religion has often been neglected because of the small number of its adherents (about a million and a half) and misjudged on account of its special doctrines. Yet this is a notable religious community of monks and laity, almost the most literate in India and eminent both in science and commerce, the purity of whose worship and the beauty of whose temples are outstanding. 'The Jains express their faith not only in their texts, but more in their buildings, and it is certain that Hindu art owes them a great number of its most remarkable monuments. In the realm of architecture, in particular, they have reached a degree of perfection that leaves them almost without rivals.'[1]

## THE JINAS

The early Jinas ('conquerors') are of great importance to Jain teaching and worship. The Jains believe that their religion is eternal and has been revealed in successive ages of the world by innumerable Tīrthaṅkaras, 'ford-finders' or guides over the ocean of transmigration (*saṁsāra*).

There have been twenty-four Tīrthaṅkaras in the present period. A hymn of praise to them begins: 'We praise the Lord Rishabha, who was the first king, the first ascetic, the first head of a congregation'. It continues down through the other Tīrthaṅkaras, giving the age, height, colour and emblem of each until the last two are reached. 'May the Lord Pārśvanātha . . . be for your

[1]A. Guérinot, *La Religion Djaïna*, p. 279.

emancipation. May there be good fortune from holy Vīra's eyes whose pupils are wide with compassion even for sinful people, moist with a trace of tears.' Thus praise turns to prayer.

The last Tīrthaṅkara but one, Pārśva, seems to have been a historical figure. He was a prince of Benares who, after thirty years as a householder, renounced the world to seek for salvation. After eighty-three days he attained enlightenment and then spent the rest of his life preaching to others. The place of his death, or Nirvāṇa, on the Paraśnath Mountain in Bihar, is now the centre of Jain worship in eastern India and is visited by thousands of pilgrims yearly. There are temples to all the Tīrthaṅkaras here and the principal one contains the sculptured feet of Pārśva.

Two hundred and fifty years after Pārśva came his more famous successor Mahāvīra. Vardhamāna, better known as Mahāvīra ('great man') lived about 500 B.C. Like Gautama the Buddha, of whom he was an elder contemporary, he was of the Kshatriya warrior caste. His parents are said to have been followers of Pārśva and finally they fasted to death as he had done. At this Mahāvīra left his home, wife and family (the Digambara sect says that he was always celibate), tore out his hair in ascetic fashion, and after wearing a scanty robe eventually went about naked begging for alms. After thirteen years he attained enlightenment and became a Jina, becoming omniscient.

For the next thirty years Mahāvīra taught with considerable success. He is said to have gathered a community of 50,000 monks and nuns, and nearly half a million lay men and women. He finally entered Nirvāṇa at Pava-puri, near the ancient Buddhist centre of Rajagriha. Many pilgrims still visit this place at the time of the Hindu festival of Divali, which is identified with the day of Mahāvīra's translation. The central temple here contains his footmarks in stone.

## DOCTRINE

Mahāvīra is regarded as the last Tīrthaṅkara and the source of the Jain scriptures; some of them contain discourses uttered, but not written, by him. Previous Tīrthaṅkaras are believed to have taught the same doctrines, but Mahāvīra's authority lies behind the Angas and other scriptures of Jainism.

Jainism opposes the argument for the existence of God which maintains that this faith is necessary to explain the world, on the analogy that the thing made implies a maker (the cosmological argument). No god is necessary or possible for creation, says Jainism, 'There can be no destruction of things that do exist, nor can there be creation out of nothing. Coming into existence and ceasing to exist, things have, because of their attributes and modes.'[1] The universe consists of mental and material factors which have existed from all eternity, and which undergo endless revolutions produced by the powers inherent in nature without the intervention of any deity.

This is all very well for philosophy, but complete atheism would be death to religion. Modern Jains, however, repudiate the charge of atheism. 'Jainism believes in Godhood and innumerable gods; but certainly Jainism is atheistic in not believing its gods to have created the Universe.'[2]

If there is no divine creator in Jainism, still there are the Jinas, the omniscient lords who have overcome all faults. And every soul when it attains perfection becomes a Paramātman, a supreme soul. The Jinas of the past are regarded as the highest godhead, their images adorn the beautiful Jain temples, and to them prayers and divine service are offered after the manner of those practised in Hindu shrines.

Many gods and goddesses, indeed, have found their way into Jainism. Lakshmī, wife of Vishṇu, is a great favourite. When some followers of Krishṇa became Jains the twenty-second Tīrthaṅkara was said to be Krishṇa's cousin and black like him. The gods are recognized because they are also eternal beings in a state of transmigration. But they are inferior to men, in theory at least if not always in worship, for the gods will have to undergo more rebirths, and to attain Nirvāṇa must eventually be born as men, for

[1] S. Radhakrishnan, *Indian Philosophy*, i, p. 329.
[2] J. Jaini, *Outlines of Jainism*, p. 4 f.

only from the human plane may one reach salvation. Radhak-rishnan says, 'Strictly speaking there is no room for devotion or bhakti in the Jaina system . . . But weak man is obliged to de-velop a sort of devotion towards the great tīrthaṅkaras.' The gods help to fill up the place.

The most famous Jain doctrine is that of reverence for life or harmlessness (ahiṁsā). 'One must meditate upon compassion for all living beings, delight at the sight of beings more advanced than ourselves, pity for the afflicted, and indifference for those who mistreat you . . . Compassion for all living beings, compassion for those who have taken vows, charity, self-control, with attach-ment, etc., contemplation, forgiveness, and contentment.'[1]

Ahiṁsā has been practised scrupulously, with respect for all forms of life. Jains are vegetarian, of course; some strain water for fear of destroying insects, refuse to eat honey and some kinds of vegetables, and go through food to see if it contains eggs, worms or cobwebs. Monks walk about with a white cloth across their mouths to stop inhaling insects, and sweep the ground before their paths with brooms of peacock's feathers. The kindness shown by Jains to cattle and birds, with their animal hospitals, is renowned.

Austerities (tapas) are practised especially by monks. But the layman also is exhorted to abstain from intoxicants, from flesh food, from insect-ridden fruit, from gambling, hunting and adul-tery. Employments that might bring him to injure life are for-bidden, notably military service, agriculture, fishing, and certain crafts and trades. As a result the Jains entered commerce, especially money-lending, and count as members some of the richest Indians.

Differences over scriptures and ascetic practices distinguish the two main sects of Jains. The Śvetāmbaras ('white-clad') hold as canonical eleven Aṅgas, and some later writings. The Digambaras ('sky-clad' or nude) reject the Śvetāmbara canon and have their own scriptures. The latter say that Mahāvīra went about naked and was celibate, and that no monks who own property such as clothes can gain Nirvāṇa. They themselves pull out their hair and

[1] S. Radhakrishnan and C. A. Moore, *A Source Book in Indian Philosophy*, p. 257 f.

the monks walk stark naked, but screened by a cordon of lay Jains lest the sight offend the public.

The Śvetāmbaras say that Pārśva wore clothes and they are not a hindrance to salvation; it is interesting that they live mostly in the colder northern parts of India. There have been other schools, of which the most numerous today is the Sthānaka-vāsī which renounces the use of images. This school has its own services and festivals.

## PRAYER AND WORSHIP

This subject is peculiarly delicate in Jainism. Since there is no supreme creator God, prayer cannot be addressed to him. Some lesser gods are recognized, though they also are souls subject to *karma* and seeking Nirvāṇa. Prayers may be addressed to Hindu gods by laymen: 'O God, give me wealth', 'forgive my sins', etc. This is despite the belief in life conditioned by *karma* so that prayer and intercession would logically be excluded.

But officially the Jain outlook on life should be naturalistic. 'A monk or nun should not say, "The god of the sky! The god of the thunderstorm! The god of lightning! The god who begins to rain! May rain fall, or may it not fall! May the crops grow! May the sun rise!" They should not use such speech. But, knowing the nature of things, he should say, "The air; a cloud has gathered, or come down; the cloud has rained".'[1]

The Jinas, who have reached perfection and passed beyond this world, are objects of devotion and the Jain temples are filled with their images. The use of images in worship is justified from the example and inspiration they inspire: 'Contemplating the form of the passionless Lord in a Jaina temple, the mind becomes filled automatically with a sentiment of renunciation . . . The mind is purified by the contemplation and worship of the Tīrthaṅkaras. Images of the Tīrthaṅkaras make one fit, therefore, to enjoy the pleasures of heaven after death—and can even prepare one's mind to experience Nirvāṇa'.[2]

[1] *The Gaina Sutras*, p. 152.
[2] H. Zimmer, *Philosophies of India*, pp. 216–7.

The images of the Jinas, often made of milk-white alabaster to show their clarified state, suggest by their symmetry and perfect naked physique the immobility of the supermen who dwell at the top of the universe. They are models of perfection but they are now so exalted as to be indifferent to human affairs and they cannot show favouritism to those who call upon them, so that it is said that worship of the Jinas is adoration rather than prayer or petition.

Every day Jains rise before dawn and, with rosary of 108 beads in hand, invoke the Five Great Ones, the five classes of superior beings, embodied and disembodied. With folded hands, bowing to east, north, west and south, this invocation is repeated: 'I bow to the *arhats*, I bow to the *siddhas*, I bow to the *āchāryas*, I bow to the *upādhyāyas*, I bow to all the *sādhus* in the world.' These are respectively: the perfect who are still embodied, the disembodied perfect including the Tīrthankaras, ascetic leaders, teaching saints, and all other ascetics.[1]

Religious exercises for monks, and for devout laymen who may be following the monk's rules for a limited time, include worship for forty-eight minutes three times a day, and fasting. In the monastery there is confession of sin, and acceptance of a penance given by the director to get rid of the *karma* which sin entails. At night time again the Five Great Ones are saluted and beads told. The Jain reminds himself of his responsibility for his fate in the words of a popular verse: 'The soul is the maker and the non-maker, and itself makes happiness and misery, is its own friend and its own foe, decides its own condition, good or evil.'

The devotions of a Śvetāmbara Jain include daily visits to the temple, after seven o'clock in the morning. Having bathed and put on freshly-washed clothes, and a sacred thread round his waist which Jains (unlike Brahmins) only wear during worship, he proceeds to the temple and walks three times round it meditating on the Three Jewels of his faith: Right Knowledge, Faith and Conduct. Shoes, socks (and any leather object worn by non-Jain visitors, such as watch-strap or camera-case) must be left outside

[1]Jaini, *op. cit.*, p. 3.

the temple. At the porch the worshipper puts a saffron mark on his brow with his third finger, and utters the word *Nissahi*, to put aside all sin and care.

In the temple the worshipper crosses to the shrine and bids for the right to wash the principal Tīrthaṅkara images there. The jewels and old flowers are removed from the image and it is washed with water, milk and five nectars. When dry it is rubbed over and marked with liquid saffron in fourteen places of the body, from the toes to the head, while verses are sung in its praise. Incense and lamps are waved at the threshold, and an offering of rice (*aksata pūjā*) is made on a table before the door. The rice is placed in the shape of a crescent, in three heaps to represent the Three Jewels of religion, and in the shape of a swastika.

After the image washing and the offerings, the worshipper performs spiritual worship (*bhāva pūjā*), which is regarded as the most important of all. He prostrates three times before the image, then recalls the virtues of the Tīrthaṅkara and sings his praises. Finally he walks backwards to the door, utters the word *Āvassahi*, with bowed hands towards the image, and again as he leaves the temple.

The acts of worship may be performed in differing order or abbreviated; in which case probably the marking with saffron and sandalwood paste, waving an incense stick, and offering rice, will be done. Additional devotions may be offered in praises to the Twenty-four Tīrthaṅkaras from illustrated books which are censed, as are rosaries for telling beads. If the worshipper had time he might go to the monastery to hear a sermon and receive instruction.

The care of the images and temple ritual is entrusted by the Śvetāmbaras to Brahmins or other caste Hindus. At evening worship only this priest enters the inner shrine, lighting lamps and incense sticks before the chief image. The highest bidders from the worshippers receive lamps to wave, singing as they do so while the rest of those present beat drums and gongs.

In the Digambara temples the officiants are Jains and the worship is more congregational. All the rice and dried fruit offered is taken by the priest on a large tray to a table in front of the main image. Then with intoning and kneeling he transfers the contents of the full tray to an empty one marked with a swastika, thus effecting consecration. Then follows the spiritual worship when the priest repeats mantras to himself, bowing, kneeling, and touching the ground with his head. At night a lamp is lit, protected by glass against insects, hymns are sung, and sacred words recited.

## TEMPLES

Many of the historic sanctuaries of Jainism are of great interest. A peculiarity was the Jain love of building temple-cities, some of them with hundreds of shrines of different periods. The most sacred of these in western India is the hill of Śatrunjaya, 'the first of places of pilgrimage, the bridal hall of those who would marry everlasting rest'. It is a city of temples only, 863 of them; nothing else is there and the silence is impressive. 'Street after street, and square after square, extend these shrines of the Jain faith, with their stately enclosures, half palace, half fortress, raised, in marble magnificence, upon the lonely and majestic mountain.'[1] There are so many temples here that it is said that ninety-nine pilgrimages are required to go round them all. The city is especially sacred to Rishabha, the first Tīrthankara.

There are many other splendid temples and sculptures: at Mount Girnar with its magnificent stairway, Gwalior with great statues cut out of the hillside, Śravana Belgola with its 60-ft. nude figure of Gomateśvara, and so on. The most famous of all are at Mount Abu, 'the Olympus of India', in southern Rajasthan; by the intricacy of detail and delicacy of carving of figures and flowers in marble, these temples with their fretted ceilings and pillars contain perhaps the finest marble sculpture in the world.

There are many modern Jain temples in the great towns of today, most of them small and undistinguished. Often there is an

[1] A. K. Forbes, *Ras Mala*, p. 5 f.

inscription: 'Non-violence is the highest religion'. The general plan of Jain temples is of a portal and colonnades, a nave or open courtyard, and a principal chapel for the images. The principal alabaster image is that of the Jina to whom the temple is dedicated, say Mahāvīra. It is flanked by two servants (Yakshas) and by twenty-four smaller images of the Tīrthaṅkaras. In the Śvetāmbara temples the images have big glass eyes and stone loin-cloths, and are adorned with jewels and flowers. The Digambara images have eyes cast down and no loin-cloths.

Every Jain temple has a saint wheel (*siddha chakra*) which is a popular object in the cult. This seems to have been a late introduction into Jainism, from Tantric rites in Hinduism and Buddhism. Some of the more elaborate resemble the wheel in which Śiva dances, but here replaced by Jinas in meditation. The general shape is that of a brass or silver tray, perhaps like an eight-petalled lotus, and always containing figures representing the Five Great Ones, the *arhat* in the centre and others at the four cardinal points. Mantras are inscribed of the Three Jewels of faith, and the word 'austerity'. In paintings of this diagram each of the Five Great Ones has a special colour. The saint-wheel is saluted daily as the Jain tells his beads. Twice a year, in spring and autumn, it receives an eight-day worship and is washed in a tank.[1]

## FESTIVALS

The most sacred season of the Jains is at the end of their religious year, when monks and laymen of all schools observe the fast of Pajjusana. It is in the wet monsoon season, usually in August, and lasts eight days. Special services are held in the monasteries, situated near the temples, with readings and expositions of the scriptures. The birthday of Mahāvīra is celebrated at this time; temples dedicated to him are decked with flags and processions are made in his honour. On the last day of Pajjusana there is strict fasting, even from water. Monks pluck out their hair, laymen dress only in loin-cloths; but women, in a separate building, wear

[1]U. P. Shah, *Studies in Jaina Art*, p. 97 f.

their brightest clothes and jewels. Instruction is given in Jain ethics, quarrels must be mended, and before the close of the fast at night everyone asks each other's pardon for injuries or slights.

During this period there may be a procession of the scriptures in public, and a rich man who has outbidden others for the privilege takes the copy to his house where it is covered with a rich cloth, marked with a swastika. Hymns are sung before it all night and it is returned to the temple in the morning.

The next most important festival is Divali, the Hindu feast of Lakshmī who as goddess of wealth is important to business communities. The Jains say it originated with Mahāvīra, and on the third day of the festival he attained salvation. On this day services are held for business books. After devotions at the temple, a Brahmin comes at night to Jain homes. After putting an auspicious mark on the forehead, pen and book of the worshipper, he writes the word Śrī (Lakshmī) in pyramid form on the book and places an old rupee on it. A lamp is waved and the book sprinkled with red powder.

Phases of the moon are observed, and four of the full moons are special fast days. Pilgrimages are arranged to famous Jain monuments, like Śatrunjaya and Mount Abu. Temples are decorated with lamps and sermons given. On one of these full-moon days the scriptures are especially worshipped, cleaned, dusted and freed from insects. Before the April–May moon fairs are held at the centres of pilgrimage and vows made.

Jainism has been a religion of the more wealthy classes, hence its small numbers but considerable influence and splendid temples. Jainism is close to Hinduism in its rituals and Hindu gods are found in the temples beside the Tīrthaṅkaras, but there has been a modern movement to replace the Brahmin priests in Śvetāmbara temples by Jains. And in its philosophy and ethics Jainism has influenced modern Hinduism, notably by its doctrine of *ahiṁsā* which had a powerful effect on the passive resistance movement.

Some modern Jains try to interpret the asceticism of their religion to fit in with present conditions, 'Do not destroy life, unless it is absolutely necessary for the maintenance of some higher kind of life.'[1] The monks do not countenance even this concession and follow a harder though doubtless shorter road to Nirvāṇa.

## BIBLIOGRAPHY

De Bary, W. T., ed. *Sources of Indian Tradition*, Columbia, 1958.
Finegan, J. *The Archaeology of World Religions*, Princeton, 1952.
Jaini, P. S. 'Jainism', in *Man and his Gods*, Hamlyn, 1971.
Shah, U. P. *Studies in Jaina Art*, Benares, 1955.
Stevenson, S. *The Heart of Jainism*, Oxford, 1915.
Williams, R. *Jaina Yoga*, Routledge, 1963.
Zimmer, H. *Philosophies of India*, Bollingen, 1953.

[1]Jaini, *op. cit.*, p. 71.

## Chapter 4

# THE SIKHS

The Sikh religion, a militant missionary faith, had its forerunners in both Hinduism and Islam, but it claims to come from a new inspiration. Sikh teachers say that the building of the Golden Temple at Amritsar was predicted by the Buddha; it was probably begun in 1577 by permission of the Mughal emperor Akbar, himself an inquirer into many religions and a fashioner of a new synthetic religion of his own. The Sikh scriptures, the Granth Sāhib, contain words from fifteen Hindu and Muslim saints.

In the fifteenth century not only had Rāmānanda brought the fire of *bhakti* to bear against the formalism of his day, but the mystical poetry of the Persian ṣūfīs began to exercise a strong influence and there were efforts at reconciling these elements of Hinduism and Islam. This became potent in Kabīr, born a Muslim in Benares (1440), who was accepted as a disciple by Rāmānanda. When Kabīr developed further on his own lines, composing and singing poems that denounced temples, priests and scriptures, he was subjected to persecution. Thenceforth he travelled through northern India with his disciples.

The Kabīr-panthis, followers of the path of Kabīr, still number about a million people found mostly in north central India, who have scriptures called Bijak written in Hindi. Many of Kabīr's rhyming couplets are preserved orally, and some of them are incorporated in the Sikh scriptures. His tomb is at Maghar where there are both Hindu and Muslim shrines to him.

Kabīr was a monotheist who saw the one God under the many names, 'whether Allah or Rāma':

> *He is one: there is no second.*
> *Rāma, Khudā, Śakti, Śiva, are one:*
> *Tell me, pray, how will you distinguish them?*
> *By the One name I hold fast.*[1]

Yet he constantly stressed the immanence of God, 'Search in thy heart of hearts; there is his place and abode', and he spoke of being lost in God as a stream in a river. So both monotheism and monism seem to meet in the devotion to God who is within.

## GURU NĀNAK

Although the Sikhs have included verses from Kabīr and Rāmānanda, as well as Hindu poets such as Jaidev and Nāmdev, in the Granth, it is to Guru Nānak that they look for the foundation of their religion as a distinct entity.

Nānak (1469–1538) was born at Talwindi in the Punjab, the state where Sikhs are still most numerous. He was of Hindu parentage, but joined with Muslims and others who were seeking after truth. Nānak's religious crisis came with a vision of God who offered him a cup of nectar and told him, 'I am with thee. Go and repeat my Name, and cause others to do likewise'. Faith in God, the True Name, became the central dogma of Sikhism. Nānak preached it in north India, dressed in a costume of mixed Hindu and Muslim styles. His greatest success was in the Punjab where groups of Sikhs, 'disciples', began to follow him.

Before he died Nānak chose a successor, Angad, to be the second Guru (teacher). This institution of the Guru was of great importance in Sikhism; all are accorded great reverence, with special devotion to the founder. The third Guru started common kitchens to abolish caste-distinctions. The fourth founded the town of Amritsar and began building the Golden Temple.

[1]F. E. Keay, *Kabīr and His Followers*, p. 69 f., and see his criticism of Tagore's popular translation of Kabīr's poems.

Arjun the fifth Guru, introduced special Sikh dress, and his successor added to it by wearing two swords and taking up arms in defence of the faith against Muslim persecution. The tenth and last Guru, Govind Singh (1675–1708), founded the Khālsa, the militant Sikh force. He introduced the baptism of the sword, and added the suffix Singh (lion) to the names of the baptized. He also abolished the succession of Gurus and put the scriptures, the Guru Granth Sāhib, in their place.

The Gurus are taken as models of devotion by their Sikh disciples. It is said that 'the Sikh Gurus were perfect', and that 'the Gurus were sinless', indeed 'sins did come to tempt them, but they never gave way'. Guru Nānak is held to have declared, 'Everybody else is subject to error, only the Guru and God are without error.'[1]

Some of the texts speak of the unity of the Sikh and the Guru. In one of Guru Arjun's stanzas we read:

*Nānak, the Guru, has destroyed all my superstitions and defects,*
*And I have become uniformly one with him.*[2]

This theme is developed in the belief that the Sikh 'incorporates the Guru'. A believer is one, but 'when he takes Guru Govind Singh into his embrace' he is equal to a hundred thousand. So it is also said, 'the Guru lives within his Sikhs', and 'the Guru is the Word and the Word is the Guru'.

Moreover, although the names and deeds of the different Gurus are remembered, and constantly recalled on the anniversaries of their great deeds, yet the Guru was also held to be identical with his predecessors. The Gurus always signed themselves Nānak. In a coronation ode, given in the Granth, rulers regarded themselves as mystically joined with the Gurus: 'Thou Ram Das art Nānak . . . The human race comes and goes, but thou, O Arjun, art ever new and whole.'[3] And the whole Sikh assembly, called the Panth, came to be thought of as an embodiment of the Guru.

[1] T. Singh, *The Sikh Religion*, p. 20.
[2] T. Singh, *The Religion of the Sikh Gurus*, p. 323 f.
[3] ibid., p. 325.

To the Sikh, then, Nānak is not just a reformer, a uniter of Islam and Hinduism, but he is the supreme and perfect Guru, with whom men now seek union. A popular picture of him in Sikh homes and shops shows an old man with a beard and turban, wearing the Hindu saffron robe and carrying prayer beads but a halo glows behind his head.

The Sikh prayer, which is repeated every day, begins with the invocation of God and the Gurus:

> *Having first remembered God the Almighty, think of Guru Nānak; Then of Angad Guru, and Amar Das, and Ram Das; may they help us. . . .*
>
> *May the Tenth King, the holy Guru Govind Singh, the lord of hosts and protector of the faith, assist us everywhere!*
>
> *Turn your thoughts, O Khalsa, to the teachings of Guru Granth Sahib, and call on God!*[1]

This is punctuated by exclamations of 'Wonderful Lord' (*Wāhiguru*) from the congregation.


### THEOLOGY

Sikhism is monotheistic. God is called Nām, the Name, so it is the religion of the name. God is creator, timeless and unborn. Incarnations of God are not taught, as in Hinduism. God is known through the grace of the Guru. So although Hindu scriptures are recognized, Krishna, Śiva and the Hindu gods are regarded as creatures.

There is strong insistence on the personality of God. He is called Father, and also beauty and truth. Yet his immanence, as well as transcendence, is stressed. A verse attributed to Guru Arjun says of God: 'He dwells in everything; he dwells in every heart; yet he is not blended with everything; he is separate.'

Guru Rām Dās sang of God in terms of a mystical marriage: 'I have obtained my spouse who is after my heart . . . God himself arranged this marriage, and the Bride's heart rejoices in his name.'[2]

[1] T. Singh, *Sikhism*, p. 120 f.  [2] ibid., p. 138.

# THEOLOGY

The practice of the Name is enjoined frequently in the Sikh scriptures: 'We should worship the Name, believe in the Name, which is ever the same and true.' In the Jāpji, meditations of Guru Nānak, it is enjoined: 'In the ambrosial hours of the morn, meditate on the grace of the true Name.'

This meditation is an essential part of the worship of every individual. After rising early and bathing the Sikh begins his devotions by reciting the opening lines of the Jāpji:

> *There is but One God, whose name is True, the Creator, devoid of fear and enmity, immortal, unborn, self-existent, great and bountiful;*
> *The True One was in the beginning, the True One was in the primal age.*
> *The True One is, was, O Nānak, and the True One shall also be.*

Sikhism is a scriptural religion, in which similar attention is devoted to the written word as to the Qur'ān in Islam and to the Bible in Christianity. The Guru Granth Sāhib, to give its full title, or Ādi Granth is central to Sikh teaching and practice.

The nucleus of the Granth is attributed to Nānak, but the complication was due to the fifth Guru, Arjun. Himself a poet, he included many hymns of his own composition, in addition to those of Nānak, Kabīr, and some Hindu poets. Other Gurus added their quota until Govind Singh, the tenth and last, said that after him the Granth would be the Guru of the Sikhs. The community itself, as we have seen, is invested with the personality of the Gurus, but guides its action by their teachings as found in the Guru Granth Sāhib.

In the temples the Granth is the focal point, it is opened every morning and closed after the evening prayers. It is given great honour, and some have concluded that the book is worshipped when they have seen Sikhs bowing before it. But this is denied, for Sikhs are told to worship nothing but the Name. Great reverence is shown for the book, however. It is kept in the finest draperies, and a silver-handled fly-switch is always at hand to keep away insects. When the Granth enters the temple all stand and bow their heads.

It is thought superstitious to burn incense, ring bells, or wave lamps before the Granth, in Hindu style. But from the time of Govind Singh, at least, the greatest reverence has been given to the incorporated Word, and the Guru himself always chose a seat lower than the Granth. No other book is read in the temple. Whenever a Sikh enters the presence of the Granth he bows to the ground, then stands before the book with folded hands and bowed head and utters the cry, Wāhiguru.

At Sikh festivals, which are mostly of heroes of the faith in their past struggles, the Granth is read through continuously from end to end for two days and nights. On the festival day it is taken in procession through the streets, with five chief Sikhs marching in front with drawn swords.

## CONGREGATIONAL WORSHIP

Sikhism follows Islam, rather than Hinduism, in insisting on congregational worship in the temples (Gurdwaras). There the Granth is kept. The worshipper goes round the temple, clockwise, and comes to bow before the Granth with folded hands.

The Granth must be kept open where a congregation is assembled, and someone must sit behind it; but it is covered with a scarf when it is not being read. At home every Sikh is expected to set aside a room in his house for a copy of the Granth and to read some portion every day. It may be opened anywhere, and reading begins with the first passage on the top left-hand page. The whole book may be read through without stopping by a family in time of trouble. Anyone may buy copies or portions of the Granth, and Sikhs read and recite it in the train in the same way that Hindus recite the Gītā and other scriptures in public.

Every morning and night the Granth is brought into and taken away from the temple with great pomp. At Amritsar it is kept all night in the treasury, guarded by soldiers, at the end of the causeway from the temple. At five o'clock in the morning it is brought out of the treasury on the head of a bearer and put into a large silver ark, covered with a cloth and flowers. The ark is borne on the shoulders of half a dozen men, and during the course of the short procession they are constantly replaced by others who vie for the favour of carrying the sacred ark. An official walks beside it with a fly-whisk. In front of the procession walks a trumpeter, backwards facing the Granth, and blowing on a curved silver horn. It is for all the world like the Jewish procession of the Torah.

The procession passes through the silver gates and on to the pier that joins the temple to surrounding terraces. In the temple the Granth is taken out and placed on a cushion under a canopy, and covered with a silk veil which is removed when it is read. At night, at about ten o'clock, the ceremony is performed in reverse with the Granth being returned to the treasury.

At services in the temples the usual order is: the opening of the Granth, music, exposition, sermon, the Anand (Guru Amardās's 'Song of Joy to the Name'), a prayer, reading of a passage from the Granth, distribution of communion food (a sweetmeat of butter, sugar and flour), and finally the dispersal.

The communion food (Karah Prasad) is said to have been instituted by Guru Nānak to ensure equality among his followers and remove untouchability. It is brought in to the congregation and consecrated by reading the Anand ('The True Name is my support; it is my food and drink', etc.). Before distribution some is set aside in memory of the five first baptized Sikhs and given to five notable living ones. It must be eaten on the spot. It may be given to visitors, without distinction of class and creed.

The Free Kitchen (Guru ka Langar) also dates back to Guru Nānak traditionally. Every Sikh is expected to share his food with others and call for them when taking his meals. He should also contribute to the running of the free kitchens. Here visitors, Sikh and non-Sikh, are received, lodged and fed freely for three days, without distinction of religion. Many Tibetans are seen at Amritsar in the winter, staying at the free hostels on their way down India. The laws of the canteens enjoin observance of Sikh rules:

no smoking or shaving. No beggars are allowed, or tips given; but contributions can be made towards maintaining the hostels. With this social service and self-help the Sikhs have recovered from the strife and massacres that followed partition in 1947.

The Sikh community, the Khālsa, is entered through Amrita, a form of baptism. It originated with the tenth Guru, Govind Singh, who tested the devotion of five of his followers by demanding their lives and apparently executing each one, then showing them to be alive he gave them a drink stirred with a sword and invested them with a uniform.

The Amrita ceremony is held in the presence of the Granth and five baptized Sikhs. The candidates must have bathed and be wearing the five marks of the Khālsa, the five Ks: Kesh (long hair), Kangha (comb), Kachk (shorts), Kara (steel bracelet), and Kirpān (dagger). They are addressed on the Sikh faith and give assent to it. Then the Amrita (nectar of immortality) is prepared in an iron vessel in which water and sweetmeats are put. The candidates, with right knee on the ground and left knee up, the 'heroic attitude', repeat the Jāpji, the Anand and other verses, while the leader stirs the nectar with a two-edged sword. Then each comes and kneels in turn, cupping his hands and receiving five handfuls of the Amrita, and shouting after the leader, Wāhiguru. The eyes and the hair are also touched with Amrita. Then a vow of discipline is administered, directions given as to prayers, payment of tithes, clothing and taboos. Finally the communion food is distributed and the new Sikhs eat it out of the same dish.

TEMPLES

The chief Sikh temples are in their most sacred town, Amritsar in north India, a name which means 'Pool of Nectar' or 'Water of Life'. Here is a sacred artificial lake in which the main temple is built, on a site given by Akbar.

The Golden Temple, called by the Sikhs the Śrī Darbar Sāhib (Divine Court) or Hari Mandir (Temple of the Lord), was destroyed and rebuilt in 1764. It is surrounded by cloisters and fine gateways. At the main entrance all visitors must remove shoes and socks and wash their feet in a tank; unworn socks are provided for non-Sikhs and yellow dusters to cover their heads if they have no turbans. They must carry no tobacco or alcohol. Then one walks round the marble pavements, very cold in winter but provided with long strips of coconut matting.

The temple stands in the middle of the lake, at the end of a causeway some two hundred feet long. Guards are posted at the silver gateway, armed with spears and swords, and yellow flags float above the gate bearing the Sikh emblems of ring and swords. The temple is three storeys high, the upper half gilded, and the roof of a gilded copper dome on lotuses, with cupolas in the corners.

The floors and passages are of black and white marble, and the walls of marble inlaid with representations of birds, bees and flowers. Pictures of Guru Nānak with Hindu and Muslim disciples adorn some of the walls. There are texts inscribed from the Granth, but no images.

In the lower inner sanctury a canopy covers the Granth and a rail round it keeps worshippers at a due distance. Blind musicians play drums and accordions and chant verses. Worshippers bow at the threshold, put their head or hand to the floor, throw money inside the rail and receive sweetmeats in return from the priest there. Then they circulate round the outside passage. In the upper storeys men sit chanting the Granth non-stop, being relieved at intervals. There is electric lighting and candles in reserve in case of a power failure.

The lake in which the Golden Temple stands is fed from a spring. It is surrounded on all four sides by black and white marble pavements, some five hundred feet long each side of the square. Old houses around the pavements have recently been demolished by voluntary labour to provide more hostels and arcades to beautify the temple precincts. At intervals along the pavements there are small shrines showing the sites of martyrs' deaths; one has a picture of a decapitated Sikh with his head in his hand fighting his way through to Amritsar. Sacred banyan trees decorate the paths, and steps down into the tank allow people to drink the sacred water or put it on their heads.

Outside the temple are open places where large congregational meetings are held on festivals of Sikh heroes. Here the Granth is placed under a canopy, with a speaker sitting behind it, and the audience in front sit on the ground, men on his right and women on the left with covered heads.

There are other temples in Amritsar; one of eight storeys is dedicated to the son of the sixth Guru and decorated with frescoes of his life story. At Tarn Taran, some fifteen miles away, is the temple of the fifth Guru, its outside walls decorated with scenes of saints, animals and birds. In many villages of the Punjab are small domed Sikh temples, marked by their spears and yellow flags. There are wayside shrines covered with yellow cloths at which passers-by place their gifts. In Lahore are famous Sikh temples which were closed after the expulsion of the Sikhs from Pakistan. Overseas temples may be more simple.

## Divisions and Revival

There have been many divisions among the Sikhs in the four centuries of their history, though the venerable scholar Teja Singh says that 'it is impossible for Sikhism to have any sects'. This is based on the principle that all ten Gurus were one in spirit and that after them the whole community became the Guru.

There were Hindu followers of Nānak, and others later who are Hindus rather than Sikhs. Others again have differed on matters of leadership (such as the Udasis); these hold the principles of Sikhism, and even recite the daily prayer invoking God and the Gurus, while disagreeing about the place of the Gurus. Others, 'gradual-adopters', believed in the Sikh faith but did not wish to distinguish themselves by dress or risk martyrdom during persecutions.

Modern movements of reform have sought to restore the worship of the Formless and Invisible God to its early purity; such are the Nirankāri, 'worshippers of the Formless', and the Nāmdhari, 'upholders of the Name'. Others again, the Singh Sabhā, have fostered Sikh education and revival, so that it may play a larger part in the modern world. A recent book by an educated Sikh that suggests the absorption of Sikhism in Hinduism, is regarded in Amritsar as merely seeking to please the rulers of the Indian Republic.

After partition in 1947, when the Punjab was divided between Pakistan and India, right across Sikh territory, great massacres took place. The Sikhs rose to seek independence and the Muslims retaliated. Finally nearly all the Sikhs who survived were expelled from the Pakistan Islamic State, and their temples were sacked or closed.

In India there is a secular state and freedom of religion. The Sikhs set about re-establishing themselves with great vigour. Amritsar is on the Indian side and its temples have been repaired and beautified, the free kitchens enlarged, and the faith is spread by education and literature. Worship is being revived and purified, and probably is performed with greater zeal and knowledge than for long past. The Sikhs claim about ten million adherents and say that their numbers are increasing as the faith is missionary. It is difficult to know how much success it has outside the Punjab, though there are Sikh temples in other parts of India, and even in Africa where there are communities of Sikh traders; but there is much ground to make up for the losses of recent years. In 1970 there were thirty-five Sikh temples in Britain.

### BIBLIOGRAPHY

Archer, J. C. *The Sikhs*, Princeton, 1946.

Archer, W. G. *Paintings of the Sikhs*, H.M.S.O., 1966.

Keay, F. E. *Kabīr and his Followers*, Calcutta, 1931.

McLeod, W. H. *Gurū Nānak and the Sikh Religion*, Oxford, 1968.

McLeod, W. H. *The Sikhs of the Punjab*, Oriel, 1968.

Singh, F., ed. *Sikhism*, Patiala, 1969.

Singh, J. *Sikh Ceremonies*, Bombay, 1941.

Singh, K. *The Sikhs*, Allen and Unwin, 1953.

Singh, T., ed. *Selections from the Sacred Writings of the Sikhs*, Allen and Unwin, 1960.

Singh, T. 'The Religion of the Sikh Gurus', in *The Cultural Heritage of India*, 2nd. ed., Calcutta, 1956.

## Chapter 5

# THE PARSIS

———

The origins and early history of Zoroastrianism have long been the subject of intense study in the West, and are still hotly debated. A religion which arose in Iran (Persia) from similar roots to Vedic Hinduism, but which thanks to a reforming prophet grew more and more akin to and indeed influenced Judaism, Christianity and Islam, yet whose modern followers are a tiny but highly educated minority in India, has many points of interest. Moreover the noble yet difficult scriptures present a great challenge to scholars. Here, however, we are not concerned to take sides with one or other of the opposing academic viewpoints on origins, dates and authenticity, but we shall try to give some picture of the faith and religious practices of the descendants of the ancient Zoroastrians in the Parsis of today.

ZARATHUSHTRA

Of the religion of Iran before Zarathushtra (whom the Greeks called Zoroaster and later Parsis Zartusht) nothing is known apart from his own teachings. The ancient gods (daēvas) were mostly turned into demons by his monotheistic reform. But a significant survivor was Mithra, a solar deity later to be supreme in the Mithraic religion, and who has persisted in Parsi religion down to this day. The sacred fire (ātar) which goes back to very ancient times in both Parsiism and Hinduism has become the best known symbol of the Parsis who are often wrongly called 'fire-worshippers'. Equally ancient is the sacred drink (*haoma*) used in the Parsi liturgy. All the other gods were rejected and the All-Wise Lord, Ahura Mazdā, exalted as the only God.

Zarathushtra (traditionally dated 660–583 B.C.) began from a vision in which the archangel of divine hypostasis Vohū Mana (Good Mind) took him to the heavenly court where the supreme Ahura Mazdā taught him the doctrines and duties of a reforming faith. So he opposed the gods and sacrifices of his day and taught the dualism of good and evil spirits. The spirit of good (Ahura Mazdā) is against the spirit of evil (Ahriman).

Some modern Parsis deny that there is a dualism, and insist on the monotheistic character of Parsiism and on the certainty of the final victory of good over evil. It was long debated whether Ahura Mazdā had created the evil spirit, or whether the two had co-existed from the beginning. One heresy postulated Zurvān, Infinite Time, as the original and superior principle to both. But all Parsis believe that the Good Spirit will ultimately triumph and the evil be hidden underground if not destroyed. Hence the religion is optimistic.[1]

This faith is affirmed at the initiation ceremony of every Parsi, and in daily repetitions: 'The Omniscient God is the greatest Lord. Ahriman is the evil spirit that keeps back the advancement of the world . . . May Ahura Mazdā be praised. May the Evil Spirit Ahriman be condemned.'[2]

The opposing powers of good and evil fight for possession of the human soul, and so each man has to decide for or against the right. This gave Zoroastrianism the highly moral character that it has always had. It may be remarked that because the dualism is not one of mind against matter (as in Indian and European beliefs), so the flesh has not been regarded as evil. Celibacy is abhorred, as among the Jews. Marriage is honoured; priests marry, and Zarathushtra himself is said to have had sons and daughters. There is more equality of men and women than in some other Eastern religions.

---

[1] R. Masani, *The Religion of the Good Life*, p. 102 f., and see R. C. Zaehner, *Zurvan, A Zoroastrian Dilemma,* and *The Teachings of the Magi.*

[2] J. J. Modi, *The Religious Ceremonies and Customs of the Parsees*, p. 183 f.

In course of time changes took place in the prophetic religion which are still visible. Zarathushtra became a godlike person, born of a virgin, and fighting demons from his cradle. Some of the divine hypostases became Immortal Holy Ones (Amesha Spenta). Mithra rose in importance. Increased powers were attributed to Angra Mainyu, who was assisted by many demons, and held responsible for all evils, disease and death. The moral struggle in man's heart turned to a fight against ceremonial impurity, in which powerful texts (*manthras*) were used as spells against demons.

The Magi, imagined in the West to be magicians, were missionaries of Zoroastrian teaching whose holy lives and simple rituals are acknowledged by some classical writers. When the Muslim Arabs overran the Persian Empire in the seventh century A.D. the Zoroastrians were respected at first as 'people of a book', like Christians and Jews. But about a century later many of them could no longer endure an alien rule and religion and they migrated from Persia, slowly travelling down the coastline until they reached India. A few thousands still live in Persia, called Gabars ('infidels') by the Muslims, tending the sacred fire, observing the old rites, and disposing of their dead in 'towers of silence'.

The Parsis (Persians) in India number about a hundred and twenty thousand today, most of them in Gujerat near where they first arrived, and particularly prominent in Bombay. But they are scattered about in many parts of India and East Africa. They have always been among the most educated and westernized Indians. The men, especially the older ones, are notable in their dark shiny rimless hats and tight white trousers; the women in saris over European dresses; and the priests with beards, turbans and white robes.

## Scriptures and Beliefs

The Zoroastrian scriptures are collectively known as the Avesta; formerly and inaccurately called Zend Avesta in the West which means really 'commentary on the Avesta'. The Avesta include the Yasnas (with the Gāthās), the Vīsperad, Yashts, Vendīdād, and other texts and prayers. They are of many dates, almost as diverse as the Bible, and written in the extinct Avestan which few Parsis now understand.

The oldest part of the Avesta are the Gāthās, which form seventeen poems of the Yasna, and have been regarded with special reverence as coming from Zarathushtra himself. They begin with an invocation of Ahura Mazdā, followed by the divine seeking for a prophet and the dedication of Zarathushtra. There are exhortations, insistence on choice, and teaching of the good kingdom and the Saviours (Saoshyants), Zoroaster and his sons.

The rest of the Yasna (a word which means 'worship') is composed of ritual and prayers. In Parsi ritual they are recited by a leading priest and an assistant joins in occasionally and meanwhile feeds the sacred fire with sandal wood and incense. In between some of the chapters sacred bread (darun) is eaten and the consecrated Haoma juice drunk.

The Vīsperad consists of unconnected pieces added to the Yasna which are always recited along with it. The Yashts ('worship by praise') is devoted to the angels and heroes of Iran; the god Mithra and the Fravashis figure largely here. The Vendīdād has been called 'the Leviticus of the Parsi canon', and consists of laws and purifications. One passage of the Vendīdād says that when Zarathushtra was tempted by Ahriman he conquered him by quoting a powerful Yasna text; this is still used daily by Parsis (the *Ahunavar*).

Parsis believe in a future life, and there are traces of this in the Gāthās where the righteous is to cross the Bridge of Judgement (Chinvat) and join the holy souls in the house of eternal light and song. Later works speak of the Future Saviours who will purify the world and destroy the works of Ahriman; even the souls of the wicked will be brought out of hell and purified.

Ormuzd (as Ahura Mazdā is now called) is creator of the spiritual and material worlds; he stands as self-existent at the head of all other orders of beings. Every day the Parsi invokes the name of God as his Lord and calls upon him in trouble.

There are seven Amesha Spentas ('Bountiful Immortals'), including Ormuzd himself, which are called archangels. Next come the Yazatas ('worshipful') which are regarded as angels; there are thirty of them which preside over natural objects and give their names to the days of the month. Zarathushtra is termed a Yazata, and properly is the only man so-called, since the rest are all spiritual beings. He stands at the head of mankind as the best of all.

Meher, the ancient Mithra, is a Yazata. He is judge of departed souls at whose tribunal every man has to appear. Since he is Yazata of light and justice, the temples of Parsiism are called after him. Dar-i-Meher, 'door of Mithra', is the true name of the so-called Fire-temples. His feast is in the autumn, at the time of one of the great ancient feasts of Mithra. The two middle days of the month bear his name.

The Fravashis are of great importance as guardian spirits. Everybody has one; gods, men, and natural objects. In one Yasht they are said to number 99,999, but properly speaking they are innumerable. Hymns of praise are sung to the Fravashis; first those of Ormuzd and the Amesha Spentas, then those of ancient Mazdā-worshippers, of Gayomard the first man, of Zarathushtra, and of all pious souls. The Fravashis of the dead are invoked in a special prayer.

When a man dies special ceremonies are performed for the departed soul on the third night and the mercy of God is implored for him. The soul then appears before Meher the judge who weighs its actions in scales; if the good outweighs the evil, even if only slightly, he may cross the bridge to paradise. The Fravashi of the dead one leaves him and goes to its place among all the Fravashis, but it remains as a link between living and dead.

So the Fravashis of the dead are invoked for help, and they on their part are supposed to take offerings made to them to God and to the departed souls. 'May these Fravashis come satisfied to this house . . . May they leave this house satisfied! May they carry back from here hymns and worship to the Maker, Ahura Mazdā, and the Amesha Spentas!' And it is said that those who 'treat the Fravashis of the faithful well' become happy and prosperous.[1]

## SACRED PLACES

Parsi temples are called Dar-i-Meher, 'door of Mithra'. In English they have been called fire-temples from the Indian name *agyari* (place of fire). They are, in effect, temples for the preservation of the sacred fire. Parsis insist that they do not worship the fire, but it is a symbol of God.

There are three grades of fire-temple, or rather of sacred fire. The Atash Dādgāh, the lowest grade, is consecrated fire in a house or very small temple. The Atash Adarān is the second-grade temple, which should be built where ten or more Parsi families are living. In the consecration fire is taken from the houses of the four classes of the community and consecrated with the words, 'Homage to thee, O Fire of wise Ahura Mazdā, the benefit-giving great Yazata'.[2] The Atash Behram is the most important and there are less than a dozen of them in existence. Their rare nature is due to the long, involved and costly methods required in obtaining, preparing and consecrating the sacred fire.

The sacred fire is spoken of as 'King'. The stone on which its urn stands is its 'throne'. In the domed roof of the temple above the fire is a bronze 'crown'. Swords and maces hang on the walls of the chamber. The fire is so placed that rays of the sun may never fall on it lest they appear to dim its light.

Only priests can enter the sanctuary where the fire is burning. Lay Parsis come barefoot to the threshold to offer sandal-wood and money, and the priest brings ashes from the fire in a ladle and applies them to the worshipper's brow. The priest cleans the room, arranges the cinders, and puts on fresh sandal-wood at least five times a day. As he does this his mouth is covered with a piece of cloth to prevent his breath defiling the fire. Alone among the religions of the world Parsiism refuses to allow anyone of another religion to enter any of its sacred buildings, and there is no missionary impulse.

[1]Modi, op. cit., p. 397 f.    [2]ibid., p. 228.

The Parsi temples are not architecturally distinguished buildings, and many of them are hardly different from the surrounding houses. In Bombay some of the larger temples are built of stone or concrete, in what is termed a neo-Persian style. The doors are often flanked by images of bearded men with bulls' bodies, on the dome of the roof may be a concrete flame painted red, and over the door a winged sun disc, a symbol of Ahura Mazdā in Persian monuments.

Quite a number of small Parsi communities have no temples, for according to tradition prayers may be said in the open air. Groups of Parsis may often be seen in the Back Bay of Bombay praying towards the setting sun over the sea; but they are not worshipping the sun for they pray there also in the early morning with their backs to the sun. There are several Parsi communities in East Africa, but the only temple is in Zanzibar.

The other notable Parsi buildings are the 'Towers of Silence', the English explanation of the Persian word Dakhma. These are the buildings where the dead are exposed to the vultures and so disposed of. To the Parsi the earth is sacred, and fire even more so, therefore he will not defile either with the commonest forms of disposal of corpses practised in India.

The Dakhma, usually situated on a hilltop, is a round stone or brick structure about forty feet high and some three hundred feet in circumference. Inside are three rings of stone slabs, for men, women and children, sloping down towards a central well. When a body is placed there, the bearers retire and waiting vultures swoop down and usually pick the bones clean in an hour or two. Some days later the corpse bearers come and throw the bones on to the charcoal and sand in the central well, the charcoal having the purpose of guarding the earth from pollution.

The Dakhmas and their surrounding gardens are now completely closed to non-Parsis, following upon some critical visiting journalism and public agitation in Bombay a few years ago. There have been moves by one or two reforming Parsis in Bombay to adopt burial, or even cremation, but this has been strongly overruled by the feeling of the community. In many small Parsi centres, however, there are no Dakhmas, partly because of the expense and also the shortage of vultures. There are no Dakhmas in East Africa, and Parsi dead are buried in coffins in special cemeteries.

### PRAYERS AND FESTIVALS

The commonest of all Parsi prayers is the Ahunavar. It is the very first prayer learnt by a child, is used daily in temple worship and home prayers, and is used at initiations and before all events of importance. The name comes from the second and third words of a Yasna text, *Ahuna vairya*, 'Lord supreme', which are said to have been used by Zarathushtra and even by Ahura Mazdā himself before creation.

The sincere recitation of the Ahunavar is worth the repetition of a hundred Gāthās. It is often said on a rosary, a bead being turned at each Ahunavar. It is not easy to translate, being so old and always in the extinct ritual Avestan language. Roughly it is said to mean: 'As Ahu is an independent ruler according to Order, so should a Ratu (temporal lord) rule according to fixed laws. The gift of the good mind is for the work of the world of Mazdā. He who gives himself as the nourisher of the poor gives kingdom to Mazdā.'[1]

The second most sacred formula is the Ashem Vohū, a prayer in praise of Asha or Order. It is learnt from childhood, recited on rising and going to bed, before meals, in temple worship and on countless other occasions. It may be translated: 'Piety is the best good and happiness. Happiness to him who is pious for the best piety.'

Every Parsi enters the religion as a child through an initiation (Naojote). This is essentially investing him or her with the sacred thread (*kūsti*) and shirt (*sudreh*). These should ever afterwards be worn, no matter what clothes are put on over them. The orthodox hold to this but some of the young are not so strict.

During the course of the initiation the child recites the Parsi confession of faith, from the twelfth chapter of the Yasna. 'O

[1]ibid., pp. 327, 328.

Almighty! come to my help. I am a worshipper of God. I am a Zoroastrian worshipper of God. I agree to praise the Zoroastrian religion, and to believe in that religion. I praise good thoughts, good words and good deeds. I praise the good Mazdayasnian religion which curtails discussions and quarrels, which brings about kinship of brotherhood, which is holy, and which, of all the religions that have yet flourished and are likely to flourish in the future, is the greatest, the best and most excellent, and which is the religion given by God by Zarathushtra. I believe that all good things proceed from God. May the Mazdayasnian religion be thus praised.'[1]

The confession of faith is recited daily and on many home occasions as well as in the temples. The sacred thread should be untied and retied on rising, answering calls of nature, bathing, praying, and before meals, and always facing the light.

Devout Parsis visit the temples daily, or at least on four sacred days in the month. Shoes are removed at the entrance, hands and feet washed, and a prayer of penitence uttered, condemning Ahriman and praising Ormuzd. Then the worshipper goes to the threshold of the sanctuary where the sacred fire is burning and receive ashes from the priest. He prays there standing, Avestan prayers such as Ahunavar and Ashem Vohū, and adds prayers in his own language for special needs. Then he retires backwards, takes his shoes and goes home.

Men and women can enter temples equally, and to the same places. Only the priests can enter the sanctuary where the fire burns. There are no images of any sort in the temples. Worship is not congregational and there is no sermon.

The temples have priests (Mobeds) and the office is strictly hereditary. Sons of priests need not take up the profession, however, and many do not because of greater opportunities and wealth elsewhere; but a layman of priestly descent may wear a white turban with ordinary dress. The high priests (Dasturs) wear beautiful shawls like stoles. Women of priestly family spin the sacred thread, and until this century they always married priests.

[1]ibid., p. 184 f.

## PRAYERS AND FESTIVALS

There are numerous Parsi festivals which can be observed more or less scrupulously. There are six Gahambārs, lasting five days each, which are seasonal feasts. The principal day is the last one; liturgical services come first, and solemn feasts of communal eating the offerings end the ceremonies. Important events are celebrated with Jashans ('praise'). Many of these are anniversaries, i.e.: of historical events of the Parsi faith or in honour of the dead.

The Farvardegān holidays are in honour of the departed, like All Souls' Day, when Parsis go with sandal-wood to the temples and flowers to the Dakhmas. Both the birth and death of Zarathushtra are celebrated with great veneration.

The New Year is of great importance. Its date has long been in dispute and resulted some two hundred years ago in lasting schism. The Kadīmīs ('ancient') observe the New Year in August, and the Shenshāhīs ('royal') keep it in September. The sects have separate priesthood and temples, but there is now easy intercourse between the two groups.

In modern times there have been reforming movements among the Parsis, protesting against innumerable repetitions in an unknown tongue and against superficiality and apathy. Efforts have been made to introduce sermons and religious instruction in the halls of the Anjuman, 'assembly'. Probably the Gāthās are better known now than for centuries past.

Some of these reforms have been resisted, and the Parsi community has suffered like others from the conservatism of the old and the carelessness of the young. Nevertheless the religion is living, and the practical outworking of the faith in deeds of charity and education is justly renowned.

## BIBLIOGRAPHY

Cumont, F. *The Mysteries of Mithra*, 2nd edn., Dover, 1956.
Dhalla, M. N. *The Nyaishes or Zoroastrian Litanies*, New York, 1965.
Duchesne-Guillemin, J. *Symbols and Values in Zoroastrianism*, Harper, 1966.

Frye, R. N. *The Heritage of Persia*, Weidenfeld, 1962.

Gershevitch, I. *The Avestan Hymn to Mithra*, Cambridge, 1959.

Hinnells, J. R. 'Iran' in *Man and his Gods*, Hamlyn, 1971.

Modi, J. J. *The Religious Ceremonies and Customs of the Parsees*, 2nd edn., Bombay, 1937.

Widengren, G. *Mani and Manichaeism*, E. T. Weidenfeld, 1965.

Zaehner, R. C. *The Dawn and Twilight of Zoroastrianism*, Weidenfeld, 1961.

## Chapter 6

# THERAVĀDA BUDDHISM

Theravāda, 'the doctrine of the elders', is the name properly given to that great branch of Buddhism which is found in Ceylon, Burma, Thailand, Cambodia and Laos. It is sometimes also called the Southern School of Buddhism. The term Hīnayāna, 'lesser vehicle', was better known for this school in the past, but it is a depreciatory title coined by the Mahāyāna, 'greater vehicle', school to show its own superiority. Southern Buddhists prefer the name Theravāda, and at the first conference of the World Fellowship of Buddhists, held in Ceylon in 1950, one of the resolutions adopted was that in all contexts the term Hīnayāna should be replaced by Theravāda.

It might seem that Buddhism, which was a later contemporary of Jainism, should have been discussed immediately after that religion. Or else, seeing that Buddhism is largely non-Indian today, it should come under a separate heading from the Indian religions. But the roots of Buddhism and the sacred shrines of its origin are in Indian soil, there is a revival of interest in Buddhism in India today, new Buddhist temples have been built in Delhi, Sarnath, and elsewhere, and the late Prime Minister Nehru spoke of the Buddha as 'the greatest of the sons of India'.

On the other hand, Buddhism is the link between India and adjacent countries, Ceylon and south-east Asia in particular. Buddhism is the transmitter of Indian culture to the rest of Asia, however much local colour the religion may pick up on its journey. So it is natural to turn to Theravāda Buddhism now and proceed thence to the Far Eastern religions by means of Mahāyāna Buddhism.

## The Person of the Buddha

European scholars have dated the death of Gautama the Buddha about 480 B.C. or even 370 B.C. Mahāyāna datings go back to 1000 B.C. or earlier. The dates now affirmed by Theravāda Buddhists are 624 B.C. for his birth and 544 B.C. for his death. It is declared that Gautama was born on the full moon day of the month of Kason (May), the first month of the Buddhist year, and that he attained both Enlightenment (*bodhi*) and entered final Nirvāṇa on the same day of the month. Therefore the Sixth Buddhist Council, the Buddha Jāyanti (victory), concluded in Rangoon on the 2,500th anniversary of Buddha's Parinirvāṇa, the full moon on the twenty-fourth of May 1956.

The popular Jātakas (birth stories) give accounts of many previous lives of Gautama and his final descent from the Tuśita heaven to be reborn and become a Buddha. His mother, Māyā Devi, had a dream in which a white elephant entered her side and this was interpreted by Brahmins to mean that she would bear a son who would become a Buddha. Other canonical works describe the birth of the child in the Lumbini Park, where he was received in a golden net by four gods who worshipped him, saying, 'Great Being, there is none like thee, much less superior anywhere.' The babe surveyed the ten quarters of the world, took seven steps, while Brahmā held a white parasol over him and other gods followed. In a lion-like voice the infant declared, 'I am the chief in the world, I am the best of the world, I am the first in the world. This is my last birth. There is now no existence again.' This is the general account as taught in Theravāda Buddhism.[1]

The scenes from the early princely life, the renunciation, temptations, and enlightenment of the Buddha have been depicted in innumerable sculptures and paintings in ancient and modern

[1]See *Buddhism for Students*, by C. Paññalaṅkāra, Ceylon.

buildings. After conquering Māra, the personification of death and symbol of attachment to the sensual world, Gautama abandoned asceticism and won enlightenment through meditation. Finally he attained the ending of desire, the stillness of Nirvāna, the knowledge of all things, and the cessation of rebirth.

At Benares he met five ascetics who had left him previously and who now became Arhats (or Arahats, 'worthy ones'), his disciples, and formed the first community of monks, the Saṅgha. Gautama told them that he was the Tathāgata, a title meaning perhaps 'he who has come and gone as former Buddhas'. In the deer park at Sarnath the Tathāgata preached his first sermon, setting in motion the Wheel of the Doctrine (Dharma). This taught the Four Noble Truths diagnosing the cause and cure of suffering, and the Middle Way between extremes in the Noble Eightfold Path.

This is not a history of the Buddha, but it is necessary to understand the importance of his person for Buddhists, and the care and imagination that have been lavished upon every incident in his life. The ideal is held out of 'the imitation of Buddha'. The places of his birth, enlightenment, preaching and death, at Lumbini, Buddh-Gaya, Sarnath and Kusinara, are the four most holy places of Buddhism to which pilgrims in India and from overseas go in ever increasing numbers today.

After his enlightenment Gautama is credited with 'the three-fold knowledge': he could remember his previous births as far back as he wished, he could see all beings passing away and being born, and with the destruction of lust and error he had attained to perpetual freedom and wisdom. The Tathāgata understood the ripening of karma, knew whither all paths lead, discerned the nature of the universe and the disposition of individuals. 'Anyone who should say of me, who thus know and perceive, that the ascetic Gotama does not possess superhuman qualities . . . he will find himself taken and thrown into hell.'[1]

Devotion came to consider the Buddha not merely in his earthly form but in his glorified body, 'the enjoyment body' as it was called, or 'the body which expresses the Buddha's own true

[1] E. J. Thomas, *Early Buddhist Scriptures*, p. 139 f.

nature'. From early time thirty-two 'marks of a superman' were ascribed to the Buddha's body. It could move about in the most tiny space, or in three huge steps, like Vishṇu, it bestrode earth and heaven.

The great size of many Buddha statues all over the Eastern world came from the belief that he was eighteen feet high. His body was a golden colour. 'Between the Lord's eyebrows there was a woolly curl (*urna*), soft like cotton, and similar to a jasmine flower, to the moon, to a conch-shell, to the filament of a lotus, to cow's milk, to a hoar-frost in blossom.'[1] This curl is represented as a tuft of hair, or a jewel, or a simple dot. It appears on sculptures of Jain saints also, and is related to the third eye of Śiva, and the eye of wisdom which yogis tried to produce by concentration.

Buddha statues, like many others of gods and saints, have long ears as a sign of holiness. Then there is the turban or cowl on the head, a kind of double crown of hair. There is also the halo which appears in the earliest statues. In later traditions it was said that, 'Around the body of the Buddha there is always a light, a fathom wide, on all sides, which shines constantly day and night, as brilliantly as a thousand suns, and resembling a mountain of jewels in movements.'[2] In Ceylonese Buddha figures the halo is a flame of fire, and in Java the flames are shaped like the sacred syllable OM, like an inverted question mark with a spiral tail. This aura or nimbus is of great antiquity. In the museum at Sarnath one ancient figure of Maitreya Buddha has flames behind its hair, which perhaps show its kinship to Mithra in his solar aspect.

The images of the Buddha have similarities of posture all over the Buddhist world. The commonest is the cross-legged seated figure, with an aureole behind the head. The position of the hands shows the different activities of the Buddha. The hands together on the lap indicate the Meditation posture; the right hand uplifted shows the Blessing posture; the right hand stretched down towards the ground is the Earth-touching mood, showing the strength that comes from the earth; the joined hands or

[1] E. Conze, *Buddhism*, p. 37.    [2] ibid., p. 38,

fingers in front of the breast are the Teaching mood. Some figures are standing, but usually the hands indicate the mood. The reclining Buddha, showing him passing into Pari-nirvāṇa (the state from which one is not reborn), is of great inspiration to his followers.

## THE BUDDHA AND THE GODS

Buddhists, like Jains, have been called atheistic, and with less reason.[1] To understand something of the attitude of the Buddha to the Hindu gods consideration must be given to the condition of the popular religion of his day. Even today Buddhist pilgrims to Sarnath have expressed distaste at the state of Benares, with its temples and images; while the sacrifices in the temples of Kālī in Calcutta fill them with horror. Things were certainly worse 2,500 years ago and human sacrifice was not unknown. The very multiplicity of deities, and the connexion of many ceremonials with fertility rites, would turn the ascetic mind elsewhere.

The early Buddhist stories do not deny the existence of the gods, indeed their existence is assumed. The Hindu gods figure frequently, but their significance is in relationship to the Buddha or his disciples. In the Dhammapada, the most famous text of the Theravāda canon, the gods are shown as admiring the Buddhist disciple: 'the gods emulate him whose senses are quiet as horses well-tamed by the charioteer'. And again, 'neither god nor demigod, neither Mara nor Brahma, can undo the victory of such a one who is self-controlled and always calm'.[2]

The gods, like men and animals, are part of the universe, but the Buddha is the greatest of them all. 'In the world with its gods, Māra, Brahmā, among beings with ascetics, Brahmins, gods, and men, the Tathāgata is the Master, the unmastered, the complete seer, the controller. Therefore he is called Tathāgata.'[3]

[1] H. Zimmer said that Jainism and Buddhism are not atheistic but transtheistic; the Hindu gods are common to both but are surpassed by the Jinas and Buddhas.

[2] W. D. C. Wagiswara, The Buddha's 'Way of Virtue', pp. 34, 36.

[3] Early Buddhist Scriptures, p. 138.

The gods most frequently mentioned in the Buddhist works are Indra (usually called Śakra) and Brahmā. Brahmā rules in a higher heaven than Indra, but he is not the supreme creator and omniscient ruler of the universe. Indeed, in one story Brahmā admits to a questioning monk that he does not know the answer and advises him to go and ask the Buddha. The idea of a personal creator hardly arises in Buddhism, and if Brahmā thinks that he occupies this post then he is suffering from pride.

Indra is much milder in Buddhism than in the early Vedas, and in the Jātaka tales he is frequently shown as a pious king who protects true religion. Indra and Vishṇu survive to this day in the Buddhism of Ceylon where their images are to be found in every temple. The legends of Rāma and Krishṇa both appear in the Jātakas in modified form.

It has been seen that in later Hinduism Vishṇu and Śiva are supreme, each being taken by his worshippers as very God, while Brahmā has practically disappeared. It might be said that a similar, though not identical, process has been at work in Buddhism. The Buddha himself is the central and all-powerful figure, the object of devotion and the subject of a million images. This applies especially in Theravāda Buddhism. In the Mahāyāna lands there are many other figures to be worshipped, and some of the Bodhisattvas are undoubtedly perpetuations of ancient deities, Mithra, Tārā, and the like.

Whatever the faith of Gautama himself, his later followers came to accord him supreme honours. The question sometimes raised, 'Is Buddhism a religion?', finds its answer in the temples and images, the reverence and devotion of all forms of Buddhism.

## THREE JEWELS

The Three Jewels (*triratna*) of Buddhism are the Buddha, the Dharma (doctrine) and the Saṅgha (order of monks). At every Buddhist shrine and meeting the Three Jewels are invoked thrice in the Refuge Formula: 'I go to the Buddha for refuge, I go to the Dharma for refuge, I go to the Saṅgha for refuge.'

It is believed that when the Buddha first enunciated the Dharma all heaven was shaken. 'The earth-dwelling gods raised a shout: "This supreme Wheel of the Doctrine has been set going by the Lord at Benares at Isipatana in the Deer Park, a Wheel which has not been set going by any ascetic, Brahmin, god, Māra, Brahmā, or by anyone in the world".'[1]

The first conference of the World Fellowship of Buddhists resolved that 'the Dharma-chakra (the Wheel of the Law) with eight spokes, representing the Noble Eightfold Path, be accepted as the International Buddhist symbol'. A similar wheel has been adopted into the flag of the Indian Republic.

The Dharma is the universal law discovered by the Buddha and summed up in the Four Noble Truths: the truth of suffering, of the cause of suffering which is desire, of the cessation of suffering by the elimination of desire, and the Noble Eightfold Path that provides the way out. The Noble Eightfold Path is a scheme of moral and mental self-development. But it is more than this; it is a model of religious progress, beginning with enlightenment, and proceeding through discipline to the final stage of ecstasy or contemplation of reality.

Nirvāṇa is release from the limitations of existence, the supreme goal of Buddhist endeavour. Nirvāṇa is variously described as cessation of striving, the extinction of desire, or an absolute bliss. The early texts speak of it as 'unborn, unoriginated, unformed', contrasting it with the created world. In Theravāda, Buddhism Nirvāṇa is often viewed as escape from life by renouncing its pleasures. In the Mahāyāna it is perhaps more positively the fruition of life, the unfolding of the Buddha-nature.

The significance of Nirvāṇa for religious striving is great in Buddhism, and some writers have suggested that the ideal it holds out and the place it takes in religious effort make it the Buddhist substitute for God. It may fairly be compared with the Christian seeking after the kingdom of heaven, or heaven itself, with the mystical conception of the latter as bliss coming close to the Theravāda teaching. In the Pāli scriptures (the Theravāda canon)

[1]ibid., p. 32.

it is said that 'the religious life is lived as plunged in Nirvāṇa, with Nirvāṇa as its aim, and Nirvāṇa as its end'.[1]

The monk is the norm of Buddhism, perhaps the only true Buddhist. It is said that a layman might gain Nirvāṇa, but only if he had been a monk in a previous existence. The attraction of the order (sangha) for a layman who seeks the perfect life is set out in a soliloquy in the Nikāya scripture: 'It is not easy for one who dwells in a house to practise a perfectly complete and pure religious life, polished as a pearl. What if I remove my hair and beard, put on yellow robes, and go forth from a house to a houseless life.'[2]

The yellow or saffron robe, consisting of three garments, and shaven head and beard, are the outward signs of the monk. The monk (bhikshu or bhikkhu) should only possess his robes, an alms-bowl, a razor, a needle, and a water-strainer. He should beg for his food. In Burma and other south-east Asian lands to this day monks are to be seen on their begging-round every morning, with their brown lacquer bowls held in both hands in front of them. The monk should only eat one meal a day, before noon.

The ordination ceremony to the Sangha takes place before at least ten senior monks. At a great ceremony in Rangoon in May 1956 2,500 youths donned the saffron robes, after listening to exhortations from heads of monasteries. But the monk is not bound to the monastery or monastic life for ever; he may leave the order at any time if he wishes to do so.

Moreover in some countries, Burma and its neighbours, all boys pass some time in the monastery as part of their religious education. Others may enter the monasteries for short periods of meditation, during the rainy season. So all males know the monastic life from the inside and the monks are much closer to the people than in some other religions. There are also convents frequented by smaller numbers of nuns.

Special meetings for the order are held weekly, at the new moon, the eighth day, the full moon, and the twenty-third day of the lunar month. These Uposatha, or 'sabbath', days are for special

[1]ibid., p. 102.   [2]ibid., p. 58 f.

meetings of the order. Disciplinary rules are recited which serve as a confession. Ten rules are laid down for monks, of which the first five are incumbent on the laity as well. The latter are: to refrain from taking life, refrain from what is not given, refrain from incontinence, refrain from falsehood, and refrain from strong drink which engenders sloth. These are called the Five Precepts (Pansil or Pancha Śila), and are the fundamental moral rules which every Buddhist should observe. Monks are further enjoined to refrain from untimely food, dancing and music, scent and garlands, a high or large bed, and gold and silver.

There are homilies on the duties of kings, and on social ethics for householders. They are warned against the evils of gambling, idleness, bad companions, roaming the streets at night, and drunkenness. The Dhammapada, the Way of Virtue, has always been a popular handbook of good living, with its warnings against anger, hatred, desire, vice, greed, and exhortations to the discipline of the mind, zeal, calmness and non-attachment. 'Play the man and stem the flood of passion . . . Cut the thongs of lust and hate, so wilt thou come to Nirvāna.'

Originally it seems that little provision was made for the religious devotion of the laity, many of whom probably continued to worship the Hindu deities while appreciating the Buddha's teaching. There was little ritual and ceremonial in which they could take part. Later, there was relic-worship in the stūpas and pagodas which provided them with a focus for worship.

## TEMPLES

In the third century B.C. the great emperor Aśoka did much to spread the Buddhist faith; it is said that he became a monk himself, and sent out missionaries to Ceylon, Syria and Egypt. A number of his pillar and rock-carved edicts remain, as the earliest monuments and texts of Buddhism. The best of all is at Sarnath where the magnificent capital of polished stone is topped with four lions of Persian style which once supported a stone wheel. The edict on the column includes the decree, 'Whoever, monk or nun, shall break up the order, shall be made to don white clothes and made to dwell in another dwelling . . . On every Uposatha day regularly shall each superintendent of the law come to the Uposatha service to be inspired with faith in this order . . . The laity should also come.'

The edicts tell us little else of the Buddhist doctrines, but it is said that Aśoka made a pious tour of the traditional sites of the life of the Buddha and erected commemorative pillars and stūpas. The stūpa was a 'mound' (from *chaitya*, a funeral pile), and so a small or large mound or building raised over relics of the dead, and embodying a relic-chamber. The great stūpa raised at Sarnath still remains, partially ruined. A famous and beautiful stūpa at Sanchi replaces a smaller one built by Aśoka. The famous caves at Ajanta, not far from Bombay contain many later statues and frescoes of Buddhist story, making, it is said, 'a harmonious fusion of old Indian naturalism with the infinite gentleness of Buddhist mysticism'. Modern art is not so successful, and a new shrine at Sarnath is decorated with slick and sensuous paintings by a Japanese artist.

Buddhism eventually disappeared from India, except for Nepal in the north, leaving only splendid monuments behind. But in the Theravāda countries there are countless splendid shrines.

In Ceylonese tradition it is written that the Buddha himself visited the island, flying through the air and leaving his footprint on Sumanakuta (Adam's Peak) which is a great place of pilgrimage. Aśoka's son Mahinda took the faith to the island again, on the orders of the god Indra. Soon there was a demand for relics: 'there is nothing here for us to worship . . . If we behold relics we behold the Conqueror'.[1] So the Buddha's collar-bone was brought and placed in a casket of gold, covered with a stūpa. Later a branch of the sacred Bo-tree was brought by Mahinda's sister and today this tree at Anuradhapura is said to be the oldest tree in the world and attracts pilgrims from all lands. The most famous of all relics was the sacred tooth of the Buddha, smuggled out of India in the hair of a princess, preserved despite the Portuguese claim to have

[1]W. Geiger, tr., *The Mahāvamsa*, p. 116.

destroyed it, and housed now in a miniature gold and jewelled pagoda in the Temple of the Tooth in Kandy.

Characteristic of Ceylonese Buddhism are the great bell-shaped Dāgobas, larger developments of the stūpas, and like them 'relic-cavities'. The largest dāgoba at the old monastic centre of Anuradhapura is some three hundred feet high, repaired and whitewashed in recent years. The dāgoba is completely solid and built of millions of bricks, except for a small closed relic chamber in its heart. A small shrine room is built on one side where are four Buddha images, three of past Buddhas and one of Metteya the Buddha to come. There are images of Vishṇu and Indra behind curtains, a huge and highly decorated Buddha's footprint, and frescoes of the three worlds and stages of life.

In Burma the pagoda is typical of the Buddhist life of the people and all over the country these graceful structures are built as acts of devotion. The word pagoda is said to be a deformation of the Singhalese dāgoba, and to mean a stūpa enclosing relics. The building is more conical than the dāgoba and tapers to a spire, often crowned with a delicate metal casket ever tinkling with brass pipal leaves.

The famous Shwe Dagon or Golden Pagoda in Rangoon is reputed to contain hairs of the Buddha, a sandal, and robes of previous Buddhas; these are kept in a barred underground basement. This pagoda stands a little higher than St. Paul's Cathedral, is said to be 2,500 years old, and to contain twenty-five tons of pure gold in statues and many precious jewels. Its golden spire is shrouded in scaffolding for applying the gold leaf brought by pilgrims, for the whole cone is covered with gold. Lit up at night with little electric lamps it looks in the distance not unlike the Eiffel Tower. There are four main entrances, with pinnacled gateways guarded by giant leogryphs. At the top of long flights of stairs from these entrances are four main chapels, in each of which a pure gold Buddha sits behind iron bars. The whole building is surrounded by large courtyards and small chapels containing countless sitting or reclining Buddhas. Many of these are the property of families which come to pay their devotions at their own shrine. Rooms surround the courtyards, for reading and meditation of the scriptures by monks and laity.

Of many other Burmese centres Pagān had the most extensive of all displays of pagodas, 5,000 of which can still be traced. In 1954 a great World Peace (Kaba Aye) pagoda was built in Rangoon for the Buddha Jāyanti Conference, and near by is a great artificial cave made to resemble the pattern of the cave in which the first Buddhist council was held.

In Thailand (Siam) the temples are called wats, groups of several edifices guarded by leogryphs. The stūpas (phras) are made of piles of stone discs of decreasing size, tapering away into metal spires. There are many Buddha images, and also Hindu motifs appear in decoration.

Similarly in Cambodia and Laos Theravāda Buddhism has its many monuments, and all youths have to spend some time in the monasteries. The great temples at Angkor Wat are renowned as relics of Hindu and Buddhist medieval art. Java also has its Buddhist memorials, notably at Borobudur, though the island is now Muslim. While in Vietnam the Mahāyāna Buddhist school prevails.

## WORSHIP

To the great temples, dāgobas, pagodas and wats endless streams of worshippers go with their needs and the gifts of their devotion.

In the dāgobas of Ceylon flowers, paper lamps and incense sticks abound. Cloth rosettes are popular as gifts. In some shrines coloured tiles are sold by the priests for twenty-five cents each and laid on the shrines. The offerers kneel in front of the priest while he utters sacred sentences.

The pagodas and wats of Burma and neighbouring countries are surrounded by stalls of sellers of paper umbrellas, lanterns, flowers, joss-sticks, images, candles, rosaries and flat bells. Great vases of flowers are put in front of the Buddha images. Boxes for gifts of money stand at the porch or in the shrine itself. Flat bells hanging from the roof are struck as gifts are made.

The worshippers join their hands in front of their faces, bow, kneel, and prostrate themselves. They call upon the name of the Buddha in the invocation that is recited in the canonical Pāli tongue throughout the Theravāda world: 'Homage to the Blessed One, the Venerable One, the All-Enlightened One. I go to the Buddha for Refuge, I go to the Dhamma for Refuge, I go to the Order for Refuge.' This is repeated thrice, and then other verses follow. Undoubtedly prayers for help and blessing are uttered. Men and women kneel with their hands clasped and their faces to the ground in the attitude of most humble deprecation and prayer.

'*Worship* (*pūjā*), the act that relates the devotee to the sacred symbols and to what the sacred symbols represent, is central to Buddhism as to other religions. It consists of offerings gifts and services to the Three Jewels—Buddha, Dharma and Sangha . . . The services consist of chanting the liturgy and Scriptures; performing ritual acts of reverence such as pressing the palms of the hands together in the attitude of worship, and offering incense . . . These are external acts of worship. Inner worship consists of contemplating a Buddha or Bodhisattva, focusing faith and devotion on him. Buddha-contemplation is rather like the Christian "prayer of contemplation".'[1]

Worship is individual, not communal, and congregational services are not normally held in the pagodas. They are not designed to take large audiences, and the many small shrines are for personal and family use. Worshippers come alone or in groups, go to their favourite shrine, and perform their devotions as they wish.

Great temples, however, may have their special public services. Every day there is communal worship (*pūjā*) at the Temple of the Sacred Tooth in Kandy, which is crowded for the ceremony. Drummers, bare to the waist, make a deafening noise with their instruments, and trumpeters ring out their call. Crowds of people throng in the ante-chambers and jostle up the steps leading to the shrine. There a priest takes their gifts of yellow and white flowers,

[1] R. H. Robinson, in *The Concise Encyclopaedia of Living Faiths*, p. 328.

bears them into the shrine and places them on a silver semi-circular altar before the caskets in which the tooth relic is ensconced. Rice is consecrated and distributed, as in many a Hindu temple. Pilgrims to the sacred mountain where the Buddha's footprint is to be seen begin and end their journey at this temple.

The monasteries, which are generally built around or near the pagodas, have their regular times of devotion. The Uposatha, or weekly sabbath days, are primarily meant for monks to gather and keep fast. Special meetings of the order are held then and the Pātimokkha confession recited, to cure infringements of monastic rules. There is often a lay audience which follows reverently while monks chant scripture passages, and the people bow to the floor at appropriate places. One of the monks will mount a preacher's dais where he sits cross-legged and reads from a palm-leaf manuscript. When this is over lay people remain there in meditation, or talking and drinking tea.

## PILGRIMAGES AND FESTIVALS

The dāgobas and pagodas are essentially shrines which enfold relics. The veneration paid to relics is one of the differences between Buddhism and Hinduism. In Hinduism temples may be erected over stones in which the footprint of a god appears to be impressed, e.g. especially to that of Vishṇu at Benares or Gaya, but reverence is not paid to fragments of human bone or hair as in Buddhism. No doubt this is because of the historical character of Buddhism, and the deep veneration in which the founder is held. Similar devotion to relics appears in other historical religions: Islam and Christianity.

The veneration of relics commended the faith to the laity and the early stūpas, and later great dāgobas and pagodas, were built not so much for monks, who had their monasteries, but for the populace. It is said that ten stūpas were erected over the ashes of the Buddha, and later on stūpas were also put up which contained the remains of various Buddhist arahats or saints.

Something has been said of the arrival of the Buddha's collar-bone, tooth and Bo-tree in Ceylon. In Burma it is believed that two traders received eight hairs from the Buddha's own hands which were enshrined in the Golden Pagodas at Rangoon and Pegu. Similar relics, footprints and hairs, are venerated in the other Theravāda lands. Most great shrines owe something of their renown to possession of a relic or image about which tradition has much to say.

New relics have been installed. In the nineteenth century the remains of two of the chief disciples of the Buddha, Sariputta and Moggallana, were found in the ruins of the great stūpas at Sanchi in India and taken away to the Victoria and Albert Museum in London. In 1947 they were formally returned to the people of Ceylon who had asked to be allowed to rehouse them for a time. They were received with great enthusiasm, brought in a golden casket and carried by elephants, to the accompaniment of salutes of guns, to the Colombo Museum. There they remained, the object of endless pious visits, till they were finally installed in a new shrine at Sanchi in 1953.

Even at ruined temples and monasteries, and before apparently insignificant stūpas, one may see little piles of fresh marigold flowers laid there by modern pilgrims doing the round of sacred spots. Such pilgrimages are of great importance in Buddhism.

Aśoka in his edicts decreed that religious processions with elephants, cars and illuminations should be arranged to please and teach the people about Buddhism. This undoubtedly has done much to attract the laity, for there may seem little difference to the uninstructed between the procession of a Hindu deity and the showing of a Buddhist relic or image.

At Kandy in Ceylon there is the celebrated Perahera festival in August, which is one of the most gorgeous spectacles of the East. The procession consists of five sections, in which are carried relics from the Temple of the Tooth (though it is said not the Tooth itself), as well as objects from shrines of Hindu gods near by. Hundreds of drummers and dancers and gaily caparisoned elephants take part in the processions, and there are flares and torches at night.

The chief Buddhist festival is that of Wesak (Kason), held in memory of the triple events of the birth, enlightenment and entry into Nirvāṇa of the Buddha. It is the full moon, usually of May, which marks the climax. Houses and streets are decorated, and gifts made to the poor and to monks.

The beginning of the rainy season, or 'Lent', from July onwards, is marked with special offerings to monks. It is said that this is the time when the Buddha sojourned in heaven and preached the Dharma to the assembled gods. No weddings or festivals are held during the time of this retreat. At the end of the rains there is a great festival at the full moon, marked by illumination of all pagodas and houses. The lamps signify the return of the Buddha to earth, when the gods illumined his path all the way down. Robes are given to the monks and alms to the poor.

At the new year, especially in Ceylon, is a water festival when water is splashed on friends and strangers, rather similarly to the Hindu Holi. There are parades of decorated cars and floats, Buddha images are ceremonially bathed, and monks entertained. In Laos and Cambodia processions of monks and young men pass through the streets and are splashed with water by the bystanders. At the pagodas they pay reverence to the Buddha and then engage in national dances. Despite the mingling of traditional customs with Buddhist celebrations the festivals of Theravāda Buddhism bring the faith into the life of the people and give scope to their religious fervour.

## LAY RELIGION

Wirz, in his study of popular religion in Ceylon, stresses the part played there by Hindu gods, ancient Ceylonese deities, demons and devil-charmers. The monks and Buddhist priests have nothing to do with the popular exorcists who they rightly regard as being in entire opposition to the doctrines of the Buddha. But the laity frequent them, and exorcists themselves use the name of Buddha as a source of power which sets evil forces to flight.

Other writers have said similar things about the attention paid to nature-spirits (Nats and Phis) in Burma, Thailand and elsewhere. So Wirz concludes, 'It is the same here as in other Buddhist countries; only very few comprehend the true Buddhist dogma in its real profoundness; the rest are Buddhists in name only.'[1]

The same might be said of the laity in many religions, and the truth is perhaps somewhere between the extremes of orthodoxy and superstition. Men are quite capable of holding contrasting and even contradictory beliefs at the same time, and popular religion is often syncretistic. At all events many Buddhists believe in gods and demons, as well as in the historical or mythical past Buddhas. It is a mixed religion.

In their homes the laity have pictures and images of the Buddha, to which candles and incense are burnt; but other spirits may be venerated as well. The threefold Refuge formula, 'I go to the Buddha as my refuge,' etc., rises many times daily from millions of lips. Prayers are also made to other beings. The name of the Buddha is met at every step, even in the magical *yantra* drawings which have come over from Hinduism.

The dāgobas and pagodas are used by the laity because of the relics and images there, the monasteries are also open to them for instruction. 'The laity should also come', declared Aśoka, and the Uposatha days are used for listening to expositions from the holy books. Lay people enter the Vihāra hall, bow to the image of the Buddha, offer silent devotions, and hear instruction. In our day, special halls have been built for congregational meetings, and 'Sunday' or Dharma schools are provided for teaching children, after the Western model.

The laity learn precepts drawn from various parts of the scriptures. A collection called the Mangala Sutta, which contains thirty-eight beatitudes, has been learnt by heart in the past by every Burmese child, and recently examinations in its teachings and similar ones have been widely instituted.

The rainy season has always been the traditional time for teaching and meditation in Buddhist lands. As it is not possible to work in the rice-fields then, many laymen retire to the monasteries for a

[1] P. Wirz, *Exorcism and the Art of Healing in Ceylon*, p. 236.

period, especially in Burma and Thailand, where they live abstemiously and meditate. Plays, in which the Burmese delight, are not allowed at this season. At the end of the rains, when gifts are brought to the monks, the pagodas are full of flowers and incense by day and of light at night.

Account must also be taken of modern influences, education, and the Buddhist revival. The great growth of education on the Western pattern is antagonistic to superstition and only an advanced religion can stand up to it. Buddhism has suffered in the past both from stagnation and persecution, the latter particularly in Ceylon from the Tamils and later on from European powers. Today there are Buddhist revivals in many lands in which laymen are taking a leading part. This has a marked effect on lay observance of religion. Buddhism is taught in schools and universities.

A recent writer, who has had long experience of Burma, says, 'It is impossible for an outsider to assess the total effect of this religious revival, but it can be asserted with confidence that the climate of opinion now regards religious observance as an essential duty . . . Neither the Deputy Commissioner nor his clerk would pass a pagoda in their town without stopping to make obeisance at the shrine.' And of the lay leaders of the country it is said that their 'driving-force is a Buddhism which permeates every thought and action'.[1]

## BIBLIOGRAPHY

Appleton, G. On the Eightfold Path, S.C.M., 1961.
Bunnag, J. Buddhist Monk, Buddhist Layman, Cambridge, 1973.
Conze, E. Buddhist Thought in India, Allen and Unwin, 1962.
Dutt, S. Buddhist Monks and Monasteries of India, Allen and Unwin, 1962.
Gombrich, R. F. Precept and Practice, Oxford, 1971.
Lévy, P. Buddhism: a 'Mystery Religion'? Athlone, 1957.
Ling, T. O. The Buddha, Temple Smith, 1973.
Morgan, K. ed., The Path of the Buddha, New York, 1956.
Pe Maung Tin, Buddhist Devotion and Meditation, S.P.C.K., 1964.
Spiro, M. E. Buddhism and Society, Allen and Unwin, 1971.

[1]H. Tinker, The Union of Burma.

# BIBLIOGRAPHY

Thomas, E. J. *The Life of Buddha*, 3rd edn., Routledge, 1949.
Wells, K. E. *Thai Buddhism, its Rites and Activities*, Bangkok, 1960.

# PART III

The Far East

## Chapter 7

# MAHĀYĀNA BUDDHISM

Buddhism, both Theravāda and Mahāyāna and kindred sects, reached heights of strength and propagation in the early centuries of our era. It entered China in the first century, and although it had a long struggle Chinese scholars got to work on translations of the Buddhist scriptures. These were of all schools, but eventually the Mahāyāna became the dominant Buddhist influence in China, Korea, Japan and Tibet that it is today.

The broader outlook of the Mahāyāna (or 'northern' school) allowed it to absorb new ways of thought and new objects of worship, thus affording scope for developed religious devotion. Armed with doctrines of Bodhisattvas and universal salvation Mahāyāna Buddhism spread across far eastern Asia with its Indian culture taking on local forms.

The introduction of the ideal of the Bodhisattva,' being of enlightenment', wrought a transformation in thought. The Theravāda ideal was that of the *arhat*, the 'worthy one', who followed the Noble Eightfold Path and finally attained Nirvāṇa. The Bodhisattva ideal meant that one could win salvation and become a Buddha, but also in the meantime, deferring one's own final bliss, work for the salvation of other men. So the *arhat* way was rejected as a Hīnayāna, 'lesser vehicle', whereas the Mahāyāna was the 'greater' or 'universal vehicle' of salvation for all. This was set out in the great Mahāyāna scripture, the Lotus of the Wonderful Law.

# MAHĀYĀNA BUDDHISM

The Lotus of the Wonderful Law (*Saddharmapuṇḍarīka*) or Lotus Sūtra has been called the 'Gospel of half Asia'. It was composed in Sanskrit about the second century A.D. It opens with the Buddha (Śākyamuni) living on a Vulture Peak with 1,200 arhats, 80,000 Bodhisattvas, and 20,000 gods, including Brahmā and Indra. While this assembly gazed at the Buddha he 'sent forth from the curl of white hair between his eyebrows a ray of light, which illuminated eighteen thousand worlds'. This was a sign that he was about to begin a discourse, which he declared to be a higher truth that only a Buddha knew and not the arhats. At this 5,000 arhats withdrew, as early monks may well have left a Mahāyānist meeting, rejecting its teaching of universal salvation by faith instead of works. 'The root of sin was deep in them, and their haughty spirit was so enlarged that they imagined they had already attained.'[1]

Then Śākyamuni declared, 'Never by a smaller Vehicle (Hīnayāna) (could a Buddha) save any creature. The Buddha himself is in the Great-Vehicle (Mahāyāna).' Those who pay the simplest act of homage to the Buddha will become Buddhas. 'Even children who, in play, gathered sand for a Buddha's stūpa; such men and beings as these, have all attained buddhahood.'[2] For these and for all Śākyamuni proclaims that he will cause them to attain to the same Way as himself. In a later chapter it is said that if one hear but a single word of the Lotus Sūtra and delight in it, his salvation is assured.

The last six chapters of the Lotus Sūtra deal with the Bodhisattvas, and contain the oldest reference to Avalokita, who in Chinese became Kwanyin. This Bodhisattva answers all prayers, and if crowds of people are in some great extremity the prayer of one alone will save them: 'If amongst them there be even a single person who calls the name of the Bodhisattva Regarder-of-the-cries-of-the-world, all those people will be delivered.'[3]

As the Mahāyāna doctrines developed many works set out the teachings for different types of audience. The Lalita-vistara gives

[1] W. E. Soothill, *The Lotus of the Wonderful Law*, p. 68.
[2] ibid., pp. 71, 76.   [3] ibid., p. 247.

a life of the Buddha with expanded Mahāyāna teaching. The Lankāvatāra Sūtra sets the Buddha in Ceylon uttering philosophical discourses. One of the best devotional works was written by Sānti-deva in India in the seventh century; his *Path of Light* has been called the 'Imitation' of the East. Here there is great devotion to the Bodhisattvas and expressions of compassion for others. 'With clasped hands I entreat the perfectly Enlightened Ones who stand in all regions that they kindle the lamp of the Law for them who in their blindness fall into sorrow . . . May I be a balm to the sick, their healer and servitor . . . May I be in the famine of the ages' end their meat and drink; may I become an unfailing store for the poor, and serve them with manifold things for their need. My own being and my pleasures, all my righteousness in the past, present, and future, I surrender indifferently that all creatures may win to their end.'[1]

Some centuries earlier a yet further development had been made in Mahāyāna doctrine which turned men's hopes to a Western Paradise into which the believer could enter immediately after this present life, before gaining ultimate Nirvāṇa. The ruler of this paradise is the Buddha Amitābha (or Amitāyus), the 'Buddha of Infinite Light'. Entry to paradise is through faith in Amitābha, who by his merits opened the way for all believers. Anyone who prayed devoutly to Amitābha would pass into paradise at death. Beginning in India, this doctrine received great development in Chinese and Japanese scriptures. A later but important work positively sets out the revolutionary teaching, for Buddhism, that salvation is by faith alone and not by works. 'Beings are not born in the Buddha country as a reward and result of good works performed in this present life. No, all men or women who hear and bear in mind for one, two, three, four, five, six or seven nights the name of Amitāyus, when they come to die, Amitāyus will stand before them in the hour of death, they will depart this life with quiet minds and after death they will be born in Paradise.'[2]

[1] L. D. Barnett, *The Path of Light*, p. 44 f.
[2] E. J. Thomas, *The History of Buddhist Thought*, p. 255.

Amitābha (Amitāyus) is one of the greatest objects of worship in Asia. He is O-Mi-T'o-Fu in China and Amida in Japan, where in the Pure Land sects faith in his name achieves rebirth into his paradise. The repetition of his name, Nembutsu (Namu Amida Butsu), is made countless times every day to ensure entry into paradise. In art his paradise is full of exuberant detail, in the midst of which he sits, a huge figure in a multi-coloured lotus to welcome those who enter his pure land.

Towards the end of the Lotus Sūtra the Hindu god Śiva comes with his wife Umā to ask for a prophecy, in which it is declared that they will both become Buddhas. Some of the other Buddhas and Bodhisattvas can be recognized as non-Buddhist deities, but many others seem to be imaginative developments. Avalokita, or Avalokiteśvara to use the full title, had Hindu features originally. His special function is to take his worshippers to the paradise of Buddha Amitābha, 'robed in pure white, flying with the speed of the wind they go, until all beings are released from all pains'.[1] The Dalai Lama of Tibet is believed to be his incarnation. His special text is the invocation Om Maṇi Padme Hūm, usually translated 'Hail to the Jewel in the Lotus', which is repeated millions of times every day in Tibet. In China he becomes Kwan-yin, usually represented as female, the name meaning 'The One who hears the cry' (not 'goddess of mercy' as misinterpreted by Europeans). Though really above sex this Bodhisattva appears in Japan as Kwannon in male form.

The Bodhisattva Mañjuśrī (Wen-shu in China) precedes Avalokita in the Lotus scripture. Both are unknown to the Theravāda Pali canon. Mañjuśrī's name means sweet or pleasant; he is the personification of transcendental wisdom, instructs Maitreya, and is depicted with a sword of knowledge and a book in a good many temples of the Pure Land school.

Maitreya (Mi-Lo-Fu in China) appears occasionally in the Pāli canon, but is very popular in the Mahāyāna. He is perhaps connected with the Vedic and Persian Mithra as a solar deity. He appears in Buddhist sculpture with a fiery halo, often of gigantic

[1] ibid., p. 191.

size, standing not sitting, and in paintings he is a golden colour. Maitreya is the 'Buddha to come', and in a Pāli sūtra we read of Gautama saying, 'there will arise an exalted one named Metteya . . . who will teach the Dhamma in its purity . . . whose followers will number thousands as mine number hundreds'.

There are many other Buddhas and Bodhisattvas, peculiar to Chinese, Japanese or Tibetan worship. Each has his shape and colour in imagery and painting, which are conventional representations of attributes. Vairochana, a Sanskrit solar title, is the chief Buddha (called Dainichi) of the Shingon sect of Japan. Kshitigarbha (Ti-Ts'ang in China and Jizo in Japan) is a Bodhisattva friend of children, helper of women in childbirth, and deliverer of souls.

## SCHOOLS AND TEMPLES

After its introduction to China in the first century of our era, Buddhism slowly won its way into Chinese life. The ideal of Nirvāṇa appealed to the Taoist intellectual, while to the common man prayer to Amitābha brought the language of devotion into religion, which no doubt could degenerate into vain repetition (it was called the 'short cut' school), but could also soar to heights of mysticism. Faith in Amitābha was not without works, for the Chinese householder had a deep concern with family and civic virtues.

Many of the scriptures were translated from Sanskrit and exist today only in Chinese. A most interesting transformation took place in art, where images of Buddhas and Bodhisattvas took on Chinese dress and characteristics while retaining their Buddhist serenity and grace. Monasteries and pagodas became typically Chinese.

Next to the Pure Land the Ch'an school was most important, said to have been brought from India by the monk Bodhidharma in the sixth century. The word Ch'an is from the Sanskrit *dhyāna*, 'meditation'; in Japan it becomes the well known Zen. This school taught the doctrine of sudden insight or intuition which came in the work of everyday life, and linked with Chinese Taoist teaching that one should abstain from striving and seek peace within. Another great school, the T'ien-t'ai, from the mountain where it originated, was all-embracing, recognizing all scriptures but claiming the Lotus Sūtra as the quintessence of the teaching of the Buddha.

Buddhism made a great contribution to the art of China. Its famous cave-temples in Shansi and Honan, hollowed out and adorned with colossal Buddha images, are among the greatest wonders of the east and still survive. In the Tun-huang grottoes in Sinkiang there are nearly five hundred caves with over two thousand statues, but even more marvellous are the mural paintings of Jātaka stories and scenes of paradise, all meant to instruct as well as to inspire devotion.

In India the stūpa had been the chief monument of early Buddhism; in China it was the pagoda. Its mast and tiers of symbolic parasols became distinctive and the greater the number of tiers the more important the temple to which it was attached. The oldest surviving pagoda in China today is said to be that on Sung Shan in Honan. It was built in 520 and has fifteen storeys, each of twelve angles.

The pagodas were not places of regular religious worship and were often situated away from monasteries, on sites dictated by the requirements of geomancy. Monasteries were usually outside towns and incorporated temples, while smaller shrines with priests were in the towns.

The temples were composed of halls, surrounded by·courtyards and monks' quarters. The halls contained shelves or alcoves for the images, and in front of them wooden tables with vases of flowers and incense sticks. There were many different images of deities and Buddhas. The first hall might contain the Four Lords of Heaven, gigantic and fierce images in bright colours. Then came Mi-Lo-Fu (Maitreya), a very popular figure, fat and laughing, with a bare stomach. Other images and figures of eighteen Lo Han (arhats) or disciples of the Buddha are very realistic. The most honourable places in the great hall would be occupied by images of the Buddhist triad, the 'three precious ones', Śākyamuni himself, O-Mi-T'o-Fu, and Wen-shu. Kwanyin would often be there too, but frequently with a special shrine of her own.

In the revolutions that have taken place in China during the present century there has been a great deal of iconoclasm, and even now it is hard to discover just how much temple worship is practised. Many temples have become disused or abandoned in recent years, and even turned into schools. Official pronouncements say that there is freedom of religion and protection of temples. In 1953 a Chinese Buddhist Association was founded, under governmental supervision, which declared that 'all Buddhist monasteries and temples are protected, and many well-known centres of worship have been renovated with money furnished by the people's government'.[1] It is said that Buddhism is recognized as a religion in which monks can perform their rites peacefully. There is certainly a desire to preserve buildings and sculptures that are of historic and artistic merit, as part of Chinese culture. But many other monasteries have been closed or taken over for public use and monks told to work; this continues a process that has been going on for the past fifty years.

It is not necessary to have a temple to perform one's devotions, and there are doubtless still many lay devotees who follow Buddhist precepts and practice as far as time affords. Though work is so pressing, and Communist lectures and meetings so numerous, that there is little leisure for long meditation. Buddhism in China has always played a large role in reciting 'masses' for the dead; death is always with us and funerals still tend to be elaborate. There has been a strong movement in Chinese Buddhism from monastic life to lay leadership, and the future may lie on this path.

In Japan Buddhism has both appealed to the masses by its splendid temples and images, its processions and priests, and it has also made a great impact on intellectuals. Whereas in China Buddhism too easily pandered to the superstitions of the masses, in Japan it held the élite as Theravāda Buddhism has done in Burma, Thailand and Ceylon.

[1] cp. *Buddhists in New China*, and *Statues and Pictures of Gautama Buddha*, by the Buddhist Association, Peking, 1956.

Japanese Buddhism succeeded in gaining a firm foothold from the sixth century, the century of its introduction to Japan, through the patronage of the regent Prince Shōtoku. Shōtoku came to be regarded as the incarnation of Kwannon, and he is still praised in these terms: 'The mighty Bodhisattva of Compassion, he who is the Saviour, was made manifest in this world as Shōtoku the Prince, who, like a father, hath not forsaken us, and like a mother is ever with us.'[1]

Buddhism took root in Japan by its syncretistic policy of declaring that the ancient national gods were incarnations of various Buddhas. When the colossal bronze Buddha, said to be the largest bronze in the world, was begun at Nara the emperor sent to the shrine of the ancient sun goddess Amaterasu at Isé to get her approval, with a Buddhist relic as a present. The next night the goddess appeared to him in a dream, identifying herself with the Buddha Dainichi (perhaps also originally a solar deity) and blessing his enterprise. Buddhist priests took charge of many of the Shintō temples, and Buddhist shrines adjoin many of them. The synthesis, Ryōbu Shintō (Dual Shintō), combining Shintō with Buddhism will be discussed later with the former religion.

In the nationalist revival of the nineteenth century Buddhism came under severe attack, but it was soon realized how deeply it had entered into Japanese life and it was restored to peaceful existence. Japanese Buddhism profited by new Western influences to engage in scholarly research, social activities, and propagation of scriptures and literature. After the Second World War there seemed again to be a decline from Buddhism, but now it appears to be gathering strength and taking once more the leading part in the study and spread of Buddhism that Japanese scholars have long done.

Japan developed some of the Chinese schools of thought and produced other new ones. The Tendai school was for centuries the chief centre of Buddhist learning in Japan and continues its harmonizing tendencies, embracing every way of gaining the supreme truth and thus able to agree with other sects, while stress-

[1] S. Yamabe and L. A. Beck, *Buddhist Psalms*, p. 83.

ing the primacy of Śākyamuni. Closely akin to it is the Shingon school which has developed into a pantheistic mysticism.

The Jōdo school is the Pure Land from China, founded in revolt against scholasticism and monastic corruption, and teaching simple faith in the all-compassionate Amida, Lord of the Western Paradise or Buddha Field. A distinctively Japanese form of Amidism was founded by Shinran in the Jōdo-shin or Shinshū school. Shinran wrote many hymns and praised Amida above Gautama himself. 'Take refuge in him who is Holiest of Holy. Sun and moon are lost in the ocean of his splendour. Therefore is he named that Infinite in whose radiance Sun and Moon are darkened. Before whose Divine Power even that Buddha made flesh in India himself faltereth in ascribing to the Majesty of his true glory.' And always there is the burden of universal salvation: 'He who is infinite never resteth, for together with the Bodhisattvas of Compassion and Pure Reason he laboureth, that the souls of them that duly receive him may have salvation, enlightening them with the light of his mercy.'[1]

The Jōdo-shin is also remarkable for the rejection of monastic life. Celibacy was regarded as a sign of lack of faith in Amida. Shinran himself was married and advocated the marriage of priests. This helped in the popularization of the school and its congregational worship.

More than half the Buddhists of Japan today belong to the Pure Land schools. But a protest against them arose in the reformer Nichiren who denounced the worship of the later Buddhas and Bodhisattvas, and declared that images of Amida and Kwannon should be cast into the fire. Nichiren claimed to restore Buddhism to its original form, which he believed was set out in the Lotus Sūtra with its glorified Śākyamuni. He said that in his own flesh was 'secretly enshrined the great mystery which the Lord Śākyamuni transmitted to me on the Vulture Peak'. So great stress is laid by this school on repeating the Lotus Sūtra, enlightenment coming by repeating, 'Hail to the scripture of the Lotus of the Wonderful Law'.

[1] Yamabe, op. cit., p. 21 f.

The Zen school is a development of the Chinese Ch'an. It is particularly interesting because of the appeal it has made to the West, and the spread of Zen literature in Europe and America. Zen is described as a special transmission of enlightenment outside the scriptures, with no dependence on words or letters, but looking into one's own nature to attain Buddhahood. It is no easy way to enlightenment, however, despite its attraction for a western world impatient of discipline. The monks undergo strict training in za-zen, somewhat similar to Indian yoga, and having taken up an appropriate posture a special problem (kōan) is adopted for solution by intuition. 'The seeker after Enlightenment allows a few moments for his thoughts to become calm, and then strives to put his mind into a condition to receive the intuitive knowledge which, it is believed, enters only when the mind is perfectly still and devoid of thoughts.'[1] In a Zendō, Meditation Hall, the monks sit facing the wall and a watchkeeper goes round with a warning staff to give a blow to any careless monk. The Zen monks are the only ones in Japan who continue the daily begging-round prescribed by the Buddha. Due to its discipline and suppression of self-interest, Zen was taken up by Bushido, the military code of the Samurai warriors; both wrestling (judo) and archery were taught as part of the technique of self-mastery. Of the subdivisions of Zen, however, by far the most numerous in Japan is Soto which is much simpler yet less publicized in the West than the Rinzai sect with its stress on kōans.

The first monasteries in Japan struggled with the position of the pagoda as they had done in China, but eventually the Buddha Hall or Golden Hall came to dominate the scene. The principal figures in it were what are called the Shaka Triad, that is Śākyamuni, Miroku (Maitreya) and Jizō (Kshitigarbha), with Kwannon the compassionate.

An important development over the centuries was the building of halls of worship. It seems that in early periods the laity could not enter the image hall, at least during services, and had to stand

[1] J. Blofeld, The Jewel in the Lotus, and see the many books of D. T. Suzuki on Zen.

or kneel in the courtyard with or without some kind of shelter during the rains. The development of lay congregations in some of the schools led to much larger floor areas being covered. The popular Amida sects came to have large and sumptuously orna-mented halls for their congregations. The early buildings were monasteries; the later are popular temples with but few priests, who are usually married. The pagodas have disappeared, except in the Nichiren temples, and so have cloisters and dormitories, while the priests' quarters are walled off like private houses. Thus the temples are popular places of lay resort; to them parents take their babies and listen to scriptures being read; weddings and funerals are held there. Tea ceremonies are performed accord-ing to the school. Some sects specialize in dancing and play-acting.

In the Zen sects, however, monasteries are important. There are image halls with figures of the Buddhas, especially Śākyamuni, but the meditation halls are more important. Laymen sit outside them, seeking the guidance of a true master, and support them financially.

Many of the Japanese Buddhist temples have as principal figure the founder of the sect, Shinran, Honen or Nichiren. The many other images may stand or sit, alone or in groups, with a great flame-like reredos behind. Kwannon appears sometimes with a dozen heads and a thousand arms, holding symbols of swastika, arrows and wheels, in Hindu fashion. In severe contrast are some of the great figures of Amida Buddha.

From Japan, Buddhism has spread to the Pacific Islands, especi-ally Hawaii, and the western seaboard of North America, where-ever there are Japanese colonies. International Buddhist Institutes seek to spread the faith today in many lands.

Buddhism entered Tibet even later than it did Japan, crossing the great Himalaya mountain ranges some time in the seventh century. The first missionary, Guru Rimpoché, 'precious teacher', is revered today in Tibet as a second Buddha. The aboriginal gods of the ancient Bön religion are said to have submitted to Bud-dhism on condition that they became protectors of the new faith.

They exist in great numbers as Srong Ma, 'guardians of the Buddhist doctrine'. Most of them have been worshipped by all Tibetan Buddhists, and the lesser ones take possession of mediums through whom they utter oracles. In art the Srong Ma generally appear as angry figures in lurid colours; the chief guardian goddess of the Gelugpa sect, Paldan Lhamo, brandishes weapons in the manner of the Hindu Kālī.

Tibetan Buddhism has been divided between two orders, the Gelugpa or 'Yellow Hat' order, a reformed school to which the spiritual and secular leaders of Lamaism have belonged; and the Nyingma-pa, 'old ones' or red hats. Among the latter most of the ancient Bön practices have survived, their monks are not held to celibacy, and they claim to possess secret scriptures and esoteric revelations, which have deluded certain Asian and European writers who speak in hushed tones of Occult Mahātmas somewhere in Tibet.[1]

Tibet has been noted for the unique development and organization of the Buddhist church. The title Lama, 'superior person', is applicable especially to the higher grades of monks and abbots. The Dalai Lama has been the temporal ruler, from the Potala palace in Lhasa, and the Tashi (Panchen) Lama the spiritual head. These lamas are called Rimpoché or 'incarnation' lamas. They are not 'living Buddhas', in the sense of incarnations of Gautama, as sometimes miscalled, but incarnations of various great figures. The Dalai Lama is believed to be the incarnation of the bodhisattva Avalokita (Chenresi) and the Tashi Lama the incarnation of Amitābha.

It is difficult to speak of the state of Tibet. As I write the Dalai Lama is in exile, many monasteries and temples have been sacked and monks butchered or forced to labour by the Chinese, and Communist indoctrination is proceeding. Probably some of the greater monuments will be spared, as in China, and the Tibetan people have been much more profoundly Buddhist than the Chinese as a whole so that the national faith will be likely to survive.

[1] J. E. Ellam, *The Religion of Tibet*, p. 36.

The Tibetan version of the pagoda or stūpa is the chörten (from the Sanskrit *chaitya*, funeral pile). The chörten is found everywhere, not only in monasteries but at roadsides and hilltops, and even over gateways. It may contain relics or be a memorial to a departed saint. On a plinth representing earth stands a solid bell-like mass representing water, crowned with a spire symbolizing fire, and topped by a trident or leaf-shaped object for the ether. Two eyes are often painted on the base and the spire may be gilded.

Prayer or praising wheels are everywhere. They range from small hand wheels, twirled as one walks, to huge wooden cylinders, six feet or so high, in the temples, which are turned by levers and ring bells as they turn. Paper prayer wheels, like lanterns, turn slowly over candle flames in the temple. Cowls on chimney pots, with sacred texts attached, revolve in the wind. The wheels have inscribed on them the formula uttered millions of times a day by Tibetans, *Om mani padme hūm* ('hail to the jewel in the lotus'). Prayer flags flutter from temples, houses and sticks in fields; they bear texts and designs of horses and dragons. On 'prayer walls' are depicted bodhisattvas, gods, sacred symbols, texts, and always *Om mani padme hūm*.

The so-called 'devil dances' of Tibet, which have been notorious, are ancient folk dances in which later the victory of good over evil was symbolized. Masked figures represented evil beings fighting with lamas, who used their magic arts to save the souls of the dead. Bodhisattvas fought with demons, first in mild form and then in terrifying aspects to ensure victory. Opponents of Buddhism were put to flight, and the performances were supposed to have moral and educational value. These are different from the prophetic trances into which oracle-priests went in order to be possessed by a spirit.

The great monasteries have had elaborate services for monks which have often been compared with those of Roman Catholicism for pageantry: 'candles, censers, bells, rosaries, mitres, copes, pastoral crooks, adoration of relics, confession, intercession of "the Mother of God", litanies, chants, holy water, the Trinity, organized priesthood, and so forth.'[1] It must be said, however, that many of these features have been found elsewhere in Mahā-yāna Buddhism.

## LAY WORSHIP AND PRAYER

'It is hard to say whether Chinese Buddhists "pray" without misleading the reader. Certainly many believers petition to Bodhi-sattvas Kuan-yin and Ti-tsang and the Buddhas Tao-shih and Amit'o for relief from personal troubles and for personal favours. The liturgies, such as "The Daily Offices of the Ch'an Sect", include wishes for the welfare of the nation and all living beings that are rather like intercessory prayer. But in fact the fulfilment of these wishes is to be achieved through transfer of the merit arising from recitation of the liturgy . . . True worship, how-ever, belongs properly to the great superhuman Bodhisattvas and Buddhas, whose merit, insight and power of good means are unlimited . . . There is a vast lore about the miraculous responses of Kuan-yin to the cries of people in trouble.'[2]

Every house in Tibet has had its image or picture, in front of which are placed seven bowls of water daily, with flowers and incense, and prayer is made there. Sacred books have been wor-shipped and read aloud, since there is a high degree of literacy, and the family would gather to listen three times a day.

In Japan Buddhist households have their *Butsudan*, Buddha shelf or altar. This is frequently an elaborate shrine with a central figure of Amida painted on silk, radiating rays of grace in all directions, and perhaps a small statue of Prince Shōtoku in front. There are elaborate decorations and utensils with flowers and lamp oil regularly renewed. In China some houses still have a shelf or altar of Śākyamuni or Amitābha.

In the Mahāyāna temples the monks and priests have performed

[1] Ellam, op. cit., p. 35.

[2] R. H. Robinson, in *The Concise Encyclopaedia of Living Faiths*, p. 328 f. Kuan-yin is the Lady Giver of children, especially prayed to by women; clay images of her, daubed in bright colours, are in many poor homes, while richer people have images of porcelain, or bronze, silver or gold.

their rituals several times a day, and the laity may assist. Generally they attend only a few of them, at festival time or when somebody in the family is ill or dying. They may come towards evening when work is done and light candles and joss-sticks. In Tibet and Nepal prayer-wheels are set going and the air is full of tinkling of bells as the wheels revolve. The people walk round the shrine clockwise, as demanded by Buddhist teaching, keeping the central image on their right, murmuring texts and prayers. To go round a holy image anti-clockwise is iniquitous and a practice of evil cults. The incense sticks glow in the dusk and light from the lamps throws strange shadows on the images and paintings of Buddhas and demonic figures. Gongs sound as people give their offerings. The worshippers bow and kneel before the images, and pour out their hearts to the serene dwellers in the Pure Land.

Rosaries are widely used in Buddhism; large ones by monks, smaller ones by the laity. The larger ones have a hundred and eight beads, with the two halves representing fifty-four stages of becoming a Bodhisattva. The large bead in the middle stands for the Buddha. The rosary is carried on the left wrist when walking, and encircles the two hands when placed together in prayer, thus it is said that Buddha's hand is embraced by the wearer.

The Amidist sects, especially in Japan, favour congregational worship. These buildings face east, so that worshippers turn to the west where sits Amida in paradise. The priests sit in a chancel, in brocaded vestments, while hanging lamps shine on the gold surfaces of the altar furnishings. The air is full of incense and the packed lay worshippers in dark clothing, except for girls and children in flowered kimonos, look on in wonderment at the glowing scene and hear the chanted responses. The chancel is often fully visible and the images not closed up in shrines.

These temples (often called Hongwan-ji) are made of black wood, and the principal edifice is a great hall with its roof supported on huge pillars. The only colour is in a few inscriptions in golden letters. In some of the Shin worship halls the drama is heightened by closing off the rear of the hall by a partition. This is shut while the congregation is assembling, and the priests begin the service with their chants within a railing at the end. At the climax of the service the screen is opened (as in the Eastern Orthodox churches), and the altar, images, hangings and lamps appear all shining and glittering with gold. The atmosphere can be made even more inspiring by using higher levels of floor for the priestly choir, and even higher for the altar which appears as on a royal dais.

The simplest prayers of the laity are the invocations, prefaced by the ejaculation Om, like *Om maṇi padme hūm* in Tibet. The most famous of all is 'Homage to the Buddha Amitābha': *Nan-mo, O-mi-t'o-fu* in Chinese, *Namu Amida Butsu* in Japanese. According to Amidist teaching a single act of devotion, a single thought of the Buddha, even for a single moment, can procure salvation. Since it is an article of faith that the Bodhisattvas have vowed to save all mankind, so they are believed to be able and willing to take the vilest sinner to paradise through their own abundant merit. Hence prayers are both thanksgiving and petition. In time of danger their cry to Amitābha or Kwanyin tends to be of pitiful beseeching.

The vow of the Bodhisattva is fourfold: 'However innumerable beings are, I vow to save them; however inexhaustible the passions are, I vow to extinguish them; however immeasurable the Dharmas are, I vow to master them; however incomparable the Buddha-truth is, I vow to attain it.' These vows are repeated after services in monasteries and temples of all schools.

Common prayers uttered on many occasions are invocations of the Buddhas: 'Adoration to the Buddhas in the ten quarters; adoration to the Dharma pervading the ten quarters; adoration to the Sangha in the ten quarters; adoration to Sakyamuni the Buddha who is our Master; adoration to Kwanzeon the Bodhisattva, who is the great compassionate and pitying one, ready to save beings from all afflictions.' Or again, 'We pray to all the Buddhas, all the Bodhisattvas-Mahasattvas in the ten quarters, of the past, present, and future, and to Mahaprajna-paramita, that by virtue of this merit universally prevailing, not only we but all beings shall equally attain Buddhahood.'[1]

[1] D. T. Suzuki, *Manual of Zen Buddhism*, pp. 16–18.

PILGRIMAGES AND FESTIVALS

Buddhism was recommended to China by the importation of images, scriptures and relics. In the early centuries Chinese travellers to India braved great hazards to bring back tangible remains of the Buddha or his associates. A single hair was received with great ceremony. One of the reputed teeth of the Buddha was enshrined in the Pagoda of One Thousand Painted Buddhas in the Western Hills near Peking. This pagoda was destroyed by foreign gunfire in 1900, but the tooth-relic was unearthed from the ruins by monks and is now housed in a golden lotus in a seven-jewel pagoda in Kwangchi monastery, Peking. In 1955 it was lent to Burma for a state visit which sought to bind together the political interests of Theravāda Burma and Mahāyāna China.

Every land sought to have its own relics, or at the very least copies of some of them. The design of the Buddha's footprints was sent from India to China, whence copies were fetched in due course by Japanese artists and some of them still preserve the Indian style of the first models. The belief was also held in Japan that the Buddhas and Bodhisattvas had visited Japan in the guise of the ancient gods and so left their footmarks in many places.

Sacred mountains have been associated with different members of the Buddhist pantheon. Four especially sacred mountains in China were the abodes of Bodhisattvas, and even where such places were the site of ancient cults yet Buddhism performed its rites there. In Japan, where so many peaks are sacred, there are many holy spots of Buddhism to which pilgrims go.

Holy days observed in Mahāyāna Buddhism include the birthdays recognized for Buddhas and Bodhisattvas, events of the life of Śākyamuni and those of founders of the schools. On the anniversary of the death of Nichiren in Japan pilgrims go to the spot where he died, carrying drums and long poles with lanterns decorated with designs and mottoes ascribed to Nichiren, and shouting as they march 'Glory be to the Gospel of the Lotus of Truth'.

At dedications of temples or images there are public processions, led by groups of small children in ceremonial robes and gold headdresses, followed by young men holding white ropes which pull the shrine containing the image, often of Śākyamuni. Then come priests, monks, and chanters with bells, and the regular choir.

Holy days are observed, where possible, at the full moon and two or three other days in the month. The birth, enlightenment and Parinirvāṇa of the Buddha are commemorated, usually in May. There are festivals at the new year, many of them combining with older traditional feasts.

Festivals of the dead were early taken into Buddhism, and their priests in Mahāyāna lands came to be regarded as experts in offering prayers for the departed, since they taught belief in the Western Paradise. The popular Chinese 'festival of hungry ghosts' (or 'seventh month, fifteenth day') has adapted some Buddhist rituals to ancestor worship. Offerings have been made for the lost and lighted candles placed in paper boats to guide their spirits. The observance is tending to diminish in the new China.

The Japanese Higan occurs twice in the year, for a week at the spring and autumn equinoxes, and most schools offer prayers and gifts for the dead at this time. The Shinshū assert that Amida has all the dead safe in his keeping and so they do not need to pray for them, and they are content to offer thanks on this occasion and listen to sermons at congregational meetings. In the seventh month there is the festival of lanterns, called Bon, when the spirits of the dead are supposed to revisit their homes and their relatives try to help them. The Shinshū call it the festival of joy and celebrate the happy lot of the departed in paradise.

Services (Hoji) are held in all Mahāyānist sects in memory of those who have passed away. In Japan they are held on the anniversary of death; the first after a week then weekly for seven weeks, then on the hundredth day, the first year, the third, seventh, thirteenth, seventeenth, twenty-fifth, thirty-third, fiftieth and hundredth years. These are services for private families but conducted by a Buddhist priest.

# TĀNTRA AND MYSTICISM

## TĀNTRA AND MYSTICISM

The Buddhist Tāntrists probably gained their inspiration from India, but developed in their own way. Magical practices are seen in the circles and maṇḍalas, like the Hindu and Jain maṇḍalas and yantras. These maṇḍalas are diagrams showing Buddhas and deities with the cosmic connexions. They are painted on cloth or paper, or portrayed on the ground with coloured rice or stones, or engraved on metal or wood. The maṇḍalas painted on Tibetan banners, representing the Wheel of Life, are famous.

Tāntric rituals in the Japanese Shingon temples necessitated large floor space and complete screening for private performances. Although magical in origins the maṇḍala is set forth as a basis for winning insight into the spiritual law. The Shingon school has elaborate exercises designed to develop supernatural powers such as clairvoyance, telepathy, and recalling former lives, and these can become a form of yoga.

There is a left-handed Tāntra, which may seem strange in ascetic Buddhism. But the transition was made with the introduction of the goddess Tārā in the early centuries and the personification of wisdom in Prajñā-pāramitā in female form. The Tāntric adept was supposed to cultivate sensual pleasures so as to pass beyond them. Ideally the left-hand path seeks to strip a man of his ego so that he becomes one with the divine principle.

The Zen and Bushido teaching sought similar suppression of self, or merging of it in the absolute. The swordsman's hall is called the Place of Enlightenment. After long and painful years of training the adept attains to 'the "artless art" which must be the goal of archery if it is to reach perfection . . . Indeed, he is the artless art itself and thus Master and No-Master in one. At this point archery, considered as the unmoved movement, the undanced dance, passes over into Zen.'[1]

In the Amidist cults one finds the development of *bhakti*, 'devotion', such as is widespread in India. The person of Śākyamuni, with the marks of a superman, is a focus for adoration.

[1] E. Herrigel, *Zen in the Art of Archery*, p. 89.

Just as much, or even more, are Amitābha in the Western Paradise, and the bodhisattva Kwanyin who 'hears men's cries'.

The Masses for the dead contain many expressions of adoration to Amitābha:

> *Thou perfect master, thy great compassion passes not by a single creature, thou art the Great Physician for a sick world.*

The Japanese Amidist, Shinran Shonin, expressed in his psalms his sense of unworthiness yet adoration to Amida in paradise:

> *Though I seek my refuge in the true faith of the Pure Land, yet hath not mine heart been truly sincere. Deceit and untruth are in my flesh . . . Yet the virtue of the Holy Name, the gift of him that is enlightened, is spread throughout the world . . . Unchanged may be our sinful body, but our heart is in Paradise for ever.*[1]

And another mystical poet Saichi sang of the immediate presence of the Buddha: 'I am in Amida-Buddha', 'this is my Pure Land', 'the whole world is my Namu-amidabutsu', 'O Saichi, if you wish to see Buddha, look within your own heart . . . the Namu is myself, Amida is myself too'.[2]

## BIBLIOGRAPHY

Ch'en, K. K. S. *Buddhism in China*, Oxford, 1965.

Conze, E. *Buddhist Scriptures*, Penguin, 1969.

De Bary, W. T., ed. *Sources of Chinese Tradition*, Columbia, 1960.

De Bary, W. T., ed. *Sources of Japanese Tradition*, Columbia, 1958.

Dumoulin, H. *A History of Zen Buddhism*, Faber, 1963.

Eliot, C. *Hinduism and Buddhism*, Routledge, 1921.

Eliot, C. *Japanese Buddhism*, Routledge, 1935.

Evans-Wentz, W. *Tibetan Yoga and Secret Doctrine*, 2nd edn., Oxford, 1958.

Herrigel, E. *Zen in the Art of Archery*, Routledge, 1953.

Herrigel, G. L. *Zen in the Art of Flower Arrangement*, Routledge, 1958.

Hoffmann, H. *The Religions of Tibet*, E. T. Allen and Unwin, 1961.

[1]Yamabe, op. cit., p. 86 f.

[2]D. T. Suzuki, *Mysticism, Christian and Buddhist*, pp. 151, 152, 189.

# BIBLIOGRAPHY

Luk, L. *The Secrets of Chinese Meditation*, Rider, 1964.

Morgan, K. W., ed. *The Path of the Buddha*, New York, 1956.

Paine, R. T. and Soper, A. *The Art and Architecture of Japan*, Penguin, 1955.

Seckel, D. *The Art of Buddhism*, Methuen, 1964.

Sickman, L. and Soper, A. *The Art and Architecture of China*, Penguin, 1971.

Snellgrove, D. L. *Buddhist Himālaya*, Cassirer, 1957.

Suzuki, D. T. *Mysticism Christian and Buddhist*, Allen and Unwin, 1971.

Suzuki, D. T. *Zen and Japanese Culture*, Routledge, 1959.

Watts, A. W. *The Way of Zen*, Penguin, 1970.

Wright, A. F. *Buddhism in Chinese History*, 2nd edn., Collier, 1968.

*Chapter 8*

# CHINESE CULTS AND TAOISM

## NATURE AND HERO WORSHIP

Long before Buddhism came to China from India there existed the indigenous Chinese religion of nature and hero worship that persisted down to the present century. Confucius and Lao Tzu were roughly contemporary with the Buddha, and the religious complexes that later came to be associated with these three names led, rather inaccurately, to the use of such phrases as 'the three religions of China'. More happily it was said that 'all three claim to teach Tao'. There never were three organized churches, and even Buddhism had no nation-wide organization until modern times.[1]

The Chinese masses sought the help of whatever deity seemed available. Buddhist or Taoist temples were visited, and their priests called in for ceremonies, but as part of a general syncretistic practice. Some writers distinguished between the religion of the enlightened and that of the masses. The enlightened might honour Heaven, the ancestors, and possibly Buddha, Lao-Tzu or Confucius, but few other spirits. The masses worshipped natural objects, thousands of deities, including Buddhist and Taoist divinities, and practised a great deal of magic as well. The fact is that the ancient religion was polytheism, and therefore no gods were barred that promised favour.

The popular gods have been under heavy attack since the early years of this century, intensified since 1935 and again after the

[1]For Buddhism in China see the previous chapter.

Communist revolution. In a movement comparable to the Reformation vast masses of old junk have been swept away. Fragments remain, but in any case the old faith is still in the background and may exercise unconscious influence.

In an agricultural society the oldest gods were those of the earth, and every village had its temple or at least a mound to serve in fertility and harvest rituals for the earth spirits. At Peking the great Altar of Land and Grain was made of earth of different colours, and down to the end of the empire at the beginning of the present century the emperor himself made offerings to the gods of earth and agriculture on behalf of the people. Human fertility was associated with the earth, and betrothals and marriages held at spring and autumn festivals.

The emperors worshipped heaven too, and were called 'sons of heaven'. At the winter solstice in Peking the emperor sacrificed to heaven on the beautiful white marble terraces of the Temple of Heaven. To the educated heaven was the power that decreed destiny, but was not regularly worshipped. Confucius believed in his divine destiny, 'Heaven has called me'. The people would be more concerned with the heavens and hells of Buddhism and Taoism.

The elements were of great importance: winds, thunder, clouds and rain, all had their presiding deities. The cult of the Dragon King was ubiquitous. Dragons were said to fly across the sky as omens of wind and rain, and at festivals of the Dragon King paper dragons lit with candles inside were carried through the streets to ask for rain on the crops. Other gods were credited with the power of driving away pests, like plagues of locusts. Then there were many gods of disease and medicine, protecting against plague, eye disease, and the like. In addition to reputable doctors, there were priests who carried the image of a god of disease to a sick man's door, read out the names of suitable medicines and applied the one that the spirit seemed to indicate.

Towns and cities had their tutelary deities, 'Wall and moat', whose temples were visited by officials for the purpose of reporting on activities in the town to the god. Public and private prayers were offered, for health and good fortune. In addition the city deity was supposed to summon dying men and judge them according to their deeds in life.

There were innumerable local deities and spirits giving help to individuals. Such were the household gods, and especially the Kitchen God whose picture was found at every hearth. Divination was a great occupation and much attention was devoted to geomancy, 'Wind and Water'.

Many of the gods were deified heroes, some of them historical characters of recent times. Such was Kuan Ti, the god of war, originally a general of many adventures. His fierce red face and great size was shown in many pictures and images in his innumerable temples, and he was worshipped also as patron of literature and riches. Such attitudes of veneration were encouraged by the empire on account of the value of the hero's example, and when finally his godhead was decreed it did but confirm his place in popular esteem.[1]

## THE ANCESTORS

The cult of the ancestors was called by some writers 'the real religion of China'. Other authorities, following the early Jesuits, claimed that only reverence and not worship was paid to the ancestors. But the ancestral cult was developed in China as hardly anywhere else. Even today, while much of the ritual is neglected yet great expense is often lavished on funerals and the dead may be thought nearer than the gods.

Confucius is said to have revived the ritual for the dead in his day, and to have enjoined that children should give three years to mourning for their deceased parents. Buddhism was attacked at first because of its celibacy and monastic orders which withdrew sons from tending their fathers' graves. But in time Buddhism became popular through its prayers for the dead which supplemented the ancient burial rituals.

When the funeral rites had been performed a tablet was set up

[1]See J. Shryock, *The Temples of Anking*, p. 66 f.

for the deceased in his own home. Traditionally this was done to the chanting of passages from the classics, while Buddhist and Taoist priests intoned prayers for the departed soul. The tablets of immediate ancestors were kept in a special room, with an altar in front of them and often Buddhist and Taoist images nearby. The attention paid to the tablets has varied very much with the piety of the family, especially in modern times, but formerly a pious Chinese would light incense sticks every evening, placing one in the crack of the front door lintel, another before the Kitchen God, and a third before the ancestral tablets.

As the tablets of new dead members of the family arrived the older ones were put in collective ancestral halls, which were usually in the country in spots surrounded by trees and shared by relatives who had the same surname. The halls were tended by poor members of the clan living on the spot; they lit candles on the altar and kept long cones of incense burning before the tablets. The tablets were arranged on shelves, with the family founder on the highest shelf. Other rooms adjoining the ancestral hall are used for schools and public meetings.

Ancestors were welcomed back from the halls to their homes at the end of the year, with offerings of food which would after-wards be recooked and eaten by the family. The chief officiant at the great sacrifice, held before dawn at the winter solstice, was the head of the clan, who stood outside the entrance to the hall in front of the altar and to whom clan members came and kow-towed. Food of several kinds was held up before the altar and placed before it, to the accompaniment of chants and flute-playing. In addition to sacrifices clan matters were discussed, for several days. Then the halls were not officially visited till the next festival. In modern times such rituals have been performed only by the old and in the country.

## CONFUCIUS AND CONFUCIANISM

Confucius was a teacher of moral and social doctrines and not of religion, despite what later ages tended to make of him. It was said that after his death (479 B.C.) his employer, the Duke of Lu, built a temple for him. At any rate from three centuries after and onwards emperors came and bowed before his grave. His tomb is still to be seen, a stone tablet with a stone altar in front of it, standing on a plant-covered mound. On the tablet is inscribed, 'Confucius, the Primal Sage'.

From the first century A.D. sacrifices were ordered for Confucius in every school in China and his cult became hero-worship. But there was constant oscillation between the hero and the deity. Both under the Manchus and the recent republic there were moves to make Confucius a state deity, but they met with considerable opposition. In the early centuries Confucius and his disciples were represented in temples by images, but these were later removed and replaced by carved and gilded tablets on the ancestral pattern.

Confucian temples were under the direction of scholars and town officials, and there was no priesthood. Divination was not practised in the temples as in Buddhist and Taoist buildings. It is true that the state cult of imperial times, which centred in the worship of Heaven, Earth and the gods by the emperor, was under the control of Confucian scholars, but that was because they dominated the state until the fall of the empire in 1911. Confucianism was called Ju-chiao, 'the doctrine of the learned'.

The Confucian temples were beautiful places, with courtyards and fine trees. The Great Hall contained the tablets of the Sage and his followers; there was often a library and a school. At least until after the Second World War there were annual sacrifices in Confucian temples on the Sage's birthday. These are still continued in Korea and Formosa. There were sacrifices, liturgical essays read, and speeches given. An American scholar so described the ceremony:

'It is in reality one of the most impressive rituals that has ever been devised. The silence of the dark hour, the magnificent sweep of the temple lines, with eaves curving upward toward the stars, the aged trees standing in the courtyard, and the deep note of the bell, make the scene unforgettable to one who has seen it even in its decay . . . The great drum boomed upon the night, the twisted torches of the attendants threw uncertain shadows across the lattice scrolls, and the silk embroideries on the robes of the officials gleamed from the darkness . . . The altar was ablaze with dancing lights, which were reflected from the gilded carving of the enormous canopy above. Figures moved slowly through the hall, the celebrant entered, and the vessels were presented towards the silent statue of the Sage, the "Teacher of Ten Thousand Generations".'[1]

This author adds his opinion that Confucius himself would have been surprised, if not shocked, by this ceremonial. In recent years there have been strong attacks both on Confucius and his cult. Yet a Chinese author gives his conviction that Confucius would not have been disappointed but pleased with the reversal of the fortunes of his cult, for the Chinese people have not really forsaken him but only certain aspects of Confucianism.[2]

## TAOISM

If Confucianism was not properly a religion, but an ancestral cult or at most state-worship, Taoism can claim to be the truly native and personal religion of China, its original contribution to the religious development of the world. Covered over with a mass of superstitions, often regarded as nothing but exorcism and magic by outsiders, Taoism has nevertheless been claimed as the flowering of personal religion, the way of mysticism.[3]

The nature religion of China was largely a collective affair. The rituals performed at the altars of soil and grain were for the village and the family, but did not satisfy the individual's religious cravings. Moreover, the feudal organization of society was reflected in the religion with its clan, city and imperial cults. The larger the state became the harder it was for the people to take part in rites performed on their behalf. Taoism came as China's own religion for the individual.

[1] J. Shryock, *Origin and Development of the State Cult of Confucius*, p. 69.
[2] Wing-tsit Chan, *Religious Trends in Modern China*, p. 19 f.
[3] H. Maspero, *Le Taoïsme*, p. 15 f.

The great classic of Taoism, the *Tao Tê Ching*, 'the Book of the Way and the Power', was attributed to Lao Tzu (said to have been born about 600 B.C.), though many modern scholars consider that he had little to do with it. The word Tao has been of great significance in Chinese thought, and may be interpreted variously as truth, guide, way, and finally 'the way of the universe'. It precedes all things, even deity: 'Tao gave birth to the One; the One gave birth successively to two things'.[1]

The teaching of early Taoism was that of a nature mysticism, which urges quietness and submission because by them all things can be gained. A favourite symbol is water, which always seeks the lowest level but can overcome everything. The negative, passive, female element leads to Tao, and the cultivation of stillness.

> *Push far enough towards the Void,*
> *Hold fast enough to Quietness,*
> *And of the ten thousand things none but can be worked on by you . . .*
> *To be kingly is to be of heaven;*
> *To be of heaven is to be in Tao.*
> *Tao is forever and he that possesses it,*
> *Though his body ceases, is not destroyed.*[2]

The *Tao Tê Ching* is of course opposed to militarism and proud displays. It teaches that submissiveness will gain kingdoms, and that the great must learn humility. To think weapons lovely is to delight in them which means 'to delight in the slaughter of men'.

Two centuries later the book of Chuang Tzu elaborated the doctrine of the Tao and its transformations. The Yang and Yin, male and female, light and dark, spring from the Tao, influence and destroy each other and are ever renewed. All things are changing and equal, so the wise man takes no heed of time but passes to the realm of the infinite and finds rest there. A mystical way was taught wherein was practised a kind of yoga, or 'sitting in forgetfulness'.

[1] Tao is pronounced as Dow.
[2] A. Waley, *The Way and its Power*, p. 162.

# TAOISM

In its development Taoism came to be absorbed in the search for immortality. By becoming one with Tao, or recognizing Tao within the heart, life and death no longer had meaning. Men left their homes to live ascetic lives, by vegetarianism and fasting, to attain deathless existence. They practised gymnastic exercises, controlled their breathing, 'put on the sun's rays', and recommended sexual techniques akin to Tantrism. So it was said that the complete Taoist could achieve immortality, the ascetic could thrive on dew. Hence arose a quest for magical potions which would confer immortality. The association of magic and alchemy with Taoism, which became so fatal, began no doubt as a primitive science seeking the key to all knowledge and mysteries.[1]

With the arrival of Buddhism it might be said that Taoism took the natural way in imitating its rival. It became an organized religion, with priests and exorcists, liturgy and ceremonial. Lao Tzu was deified under the title 'Emperor of Mysterious Origin', and formed a triad with two other gods. Many other immortals appeared in huge images in Taoist temples. Heavens and hells were added, with blessings in mysterious islands, or tortures by fiends. Taoist priests gave themselves to incantations, spells, amulets and charms, and many of them know only texts which are used for talismans, and ignore the classic scriptures.

Despite the ignorance and superstition of many, Taoism had a strong moral side. Many lay societies took inspiration from Taoism, and practised virtue, almsgiving and asceticism. On the other hand Taoist secret societies were potent forces of political opposition, especially in this century, from the Boxer Rising to the 'Pervading-Unity Tao' society in recent years. As soon as the Communists came to power they crushed such potential centres of revolt.

However, like the Chinese dragon which cannot be grasped by head or tail, Taoism may well prove the most resistant form of religion to Communism. A recent writer says, 'Taoism as a religion is by no means defunct. It is as much alive as ever . . . It was, is, and probably always will be an integral part of the

[1] J. Needham, *Science and Civilization in China*, ii, p. 83 f.

Chinese way of life. It makes a direct appeal to the innate love of the Chinese for the beauty of their landscape and the spirit of veneration which the reflection of this beauty calls forth in the Chinese soul.'[1]

## TEMPLES

'The peaceful life of the temples, the architecture of which was, with consummate artistry, fitted into the Chinese landscape, and the quiet struggle for purification and union with Nature by meditation will never lose their attraction for the true Chinese mind.'[2]

The most famous Chinese temples are the imperial temples and altars at Peking. They are comparatively modern, dating from the time when the Ming Emperors made Peking the national capital in the fifteenth century. They have been disused for cult purposes since the fall of the empire in 1911, despite an abortive attempt to revive the cult under the republic. Since the Communists came to power the imperial temples have been repaired and opened to the public as part of China's artistic heritage.

The Temple of Heaven, where once the emperors, 'the sons of heaven', offered sacrifices is now open to public view. The famous buildings are within a double red wall, with 5,000 cypress trees dotted about the approaches and in the enclosure. The main buildings in the inner space are the Hall of Prayer for Good Harvests, the Imperial Vault of Heaven, and the Circular Mound Altar. These are circular, designed according to the ancient belief that the heavens are round and the earth square.

Across the other side of the city is the ancient Altar of Land and Grain, where sacrifices were made to the spirits of earth and agriculture. To the north is the Hall of Worship, now the Sun Yat-sen Memorial Hall. The Gate of Heavenly Peace in Peking was formerly used for reading imperial decrees. It was renovated in 1952 and used by Mao Tse-Tung for viewing parades on May Day. A giant portrait of Mao was hung in the centre, flanked by

[1] W. Eichhorn, in *The Concise Encyclopaedia of Living Faiths*, p. 401.
[2] ibid.

inscriptions exalting the People's Republic (plus ça change, plus c'est la même chose?).

Confucian temples or halls (a different word was used from those describing Taoist and Buddhist temples) were found all over the country. Most are now in decay, or turned into schools and public halls. They generally consist of three courts, within red walls. The first court contains school buildings. Memorial arches with inscriptions praising the virtues of Confucius led to the two other courts, the second with buildings for musical instruments and sacrificial vessels, the third and main hall above a terrace, with roofs sweeping upwards and bells hanging from the eaves. The red tablet of Confucius, five feet high, with gold lettering, held the centre, flanked by tablets of the master's disciples.

There are some beautiful old Taoist temples, especially in the western hills, some carved from the rock and often in conjunction with Buddhist temples at the same spot. In the towns Taoist temples were smaller and filled with images and scenes of the tortures of the damned in the ten hells; many of these were destroyed after the 1911 revolution, some later restored to be destroyed again in further upheavals. In addition to their own special temples, Taoist priests have served the cults of the deified heroes and city gods.

## WORSHIP AND FESTIVALS

To the temples people have come with their needs, burning incense and candles and offering prayers and supplications. Beggars slept in the courtyards, as it was thought lucky to die in the presence of a god, and so poor people at the point of death had themselves carried to a temple. Then Taoist and Buddhist priests performed rites for the dead, praying for the rest of the soul and its deliverance from one of the many hells to one of the heavens. Spirit marriages were performed on behalf of those who died young, and exorcisms for those troubled by evil spirits. Divination was practised in the temples, and fortune-telling and gambling in the courtyards gave them a bad name. Today schools and military exercises are often held in the grassy courts, and the temple may be deserted till the time of a great festival. Then, however, according to reports, many temples of those that remain in China are crowded. The older practices still abound in non-communist Chinese communities, in Malaya and Hong Kong, Korea and Formosa.

The chief temple festival is the birthday of the god, and many also come at the New Year. On the god's birthday the temple traditionally is crowded with people day and night, the altars lit with candles and the air laden with incense. The crowd is noisy, with drums, gongs, and crackers, and men dress up as 'ghosts' in fantastic masks and robes, in order to obtain a favour of the god, such as recovery of a relative from sickness. Images of the god may be carried in procession round the town; shops and houses put out tables lit with candles and incense sticks to honour the god as he passes by in a sedan chair.

At the New Year temples and images are cleaned, and so are private houses, thus driving away and drowning dirt and evil spirits. All the gods are supposed to report to the Jade Emperor the highest of all gods in the heavens. In the home, the Kitchen god, who has not received much attention all the year, now has a feast of sweet cakes, fruit, rice and honey. A small image is placed on bamboo sticks like a chair with a paper horse and this, and a report form on the family, is fired to the murmur of prayers by the head of the house. Thus the god goes to heaven to report favourably on the deeds of the family during the year. Some of the bamboo sticks are taken into the house and put in the hearth as a new fire. New bright pictures of door gods and auspicious texts are stuck on the doors.

Doors are sealed with red paper on New Year's Eve, to prevent luck from leaving the house. New door scrolls and inscriptions are hung up, and 'cash papers' express the desire for prosperity. The gods of hearth, well and bed are welcomed back. Sacrifice should be made to the family gods and the ancestors, by the father of the house. This ceremony is repeated the following day with prayers for the year then beginning. All the ancestors are supposed to be present, either in the ancestral room or at the small shelf on which their tablets stand. In olden days children prostrated before their parents at midnight, the doors were opened to let in good luck, and the family would stay at home in quiet for a few days.

On the fifteenth day of the first month is the Festival of Lanterns, when giant paper or cloth dragons were borne lighted through the streets as prayer for rain on the spring crops. At the summer solstice the Dragon-boat Festival was especially popular with boat people who decorated their craft with green for the occasion and rivalled other boats in shows of mock battles over demons. At the Autumn Festival, women celebrated the moon, climbed pagodas to get a good view of it, feasted and formulated wishes in secret.

The Festival of Hungry Souls (to which reference has already been made under Chinese Buddhism) is held at the full moon of the seventh month. Incense is burnt outside shops and houses, at which prayers are said and paper clothing and money burnt for the use of the dead. Paper boats are taken in great processions to the temples or rivers, with images of gods on board. After ceremonies by priests and prayers the ships are burnt, or in river regions put in the water with lights in them and they drift away till they sink one after another. The belief is that the dead can use the boats to help in their travels to or in the other world. Tiny lanterns in lotus leaves also light the way for the ghost ships.

There are many sacred mountains to which people have gone on pilgrimage to obtain help in need; women especially sought the gift of children, prostrating themselves many times on the way. In the Western Hills facing Peking are remains of magnificent temples, many of them destroyed by the Japanese in recent times, and thither many pilgrims have gone. The pace of life today, however, with great public works and collective enterprises, does not leave leisure for pilgrimages. Party rallies and doctrinal meetings crowd out many old festivals, but are themselves gatherings for teaching new beliefs.

The Tao can remain the mainspring of spiritual life. Even under the most adverse circumstances the Taoists always taught that perfection was not found in opposing nature but giving one-self up to it. Fundamentally Taoism has been the worship of nature, both within man and beyond man, and an endeavour to bring about the harmony of both. So high moral standards were attained and the best qualities of Chinese character owe their development to the teaching of the Tao. This is the clue to personal religion in China.

## RELIGION TODAY

With the revolutions that have broken over China during this century, religion has suffered a series of declines. Much reform was long overdue and cleared away centuries of superstition. The folk religion has come under many attacks; thousands of images have been smashed, priests driven out of temples, and monks and nuns from monasteries. Temples have been taken over for secular use, or demolished and their contents confiscated. In many cities the old city god disappeared and no image replaced him. The gods of earth and grain may still have small mounds, but few large temples.

Strangely enough it is Confucianism which seems to have taken some of the hardest knocks. In revolt against the classical system Chinese professors and students cried, 'Destroy the old curiosity shop of Confucius', and they burnt Confucius in effigy. By the Communists Confucius is suspect as a supporter of feudalism and Mao Tse-Tung declared, 'I hated Confucius from the age of eight'. The young spend far more time studying the works of Marx, Lenin and Mao than the classics of Confucianism and Taoism, though recent reports say that there is a steady demand for the latter from the libraries. Yet there have been some tendencies to regard Confucius also as a son of the soil and defender of the poor. Sun Yat-sen said that 'both Confucius and Mencius were exponents of democracy'. It may well be that in time more will come round to this point of view, and it is hard to think that China's Primal Sage can suffer lasting eclipse.

The ancestral cults continue, though in decline and the young take less part than hitherto. Masses for the dead are fewer. It is the women, in particular, who burn incense at the family tablets. But death is ever with us and veneration for the departed will no doubt remain.

After early attacks the Communist government appears to be keeping religion in check by bringing it under official control. Chinese Buddhist and Islamic Associations were first founded, in 1953, and it is likely that Taoism was more suspect because of its link with secret societies. But in 1957 a China Taoist Association was founded after a conference of priests and nuns from all over the country; temples are being repaired and images protected.

The magical side of Taoism and its search for material benefits are being replaced by modern science and medicine. Its leaders have long ceased to be men of the calibre needed for a national revival. But as a personal religion and an individual philosophy of life Taoism is of great and abiding value. Its exaltation of nature mysticism and inward calm have been and are likely to remain an integral part of Chinese life and culture. As a Chinese writer says: 'Taoism will certainly continue to be a Chinese way of life for the educated and the uneducated alike . . . Similarly Taoism will persist as a guiding principle of Chinese art, as its doctrines of spontaneity, simplicity, and *ch'i* (rhythmic vitality or vitalizing spirit) have been the great source of power.'[1]

The place of Taoism in helping to provide personal religion and mysticism may grow if its best scriptures become better known through research and education. In popular festivals Taoism will continue to play its part in guiding the feelings of the people and giving them expression. The festivals of the seasons, the new year and the dead, will still need expression in symbol and ceremony. Together with Buddhism it will provide the needed outlet for religious feeling. 'Is there not a possibility that Taoism as a religion will cease to be a set of superstitions and will become a source of spiritual motherhood, as in effect Kuan-yin has been to the millions of Chinese? If the West has felt the need of the Virgin Mary, will the Chinese not need her counterpart?'[2]

[1] Wing-tsit Chan, *Religious Trends in Modern China*, p. 154.
[2] ibid., p. 156.

## BIBLIOGRAPHY

Ahern, E. M. *The Cult of the Dead in a Chinese Village*, Oxford, 1974.
Blofeld, J. *The Secret and Sublime*, Allen and Unwin, 1972.
Burkhardt, V. R. *Chinese Creeds and Customs*, Hong Kong, 1953.
Chan, Wing-tsit, *Religious Trends in Modern China*, New York, 1953.
Christie, A., *Chinese Mythology*, Hamlyn, 1968.
De Bary, W. T., ed. *Sources of Chinese Tradition*, Columbia, 1960.
Dobson, W. A. C. H. 'China' in *Man and his Gods*, Hamlyn, 1971.
Eberhard, W. *Chinese Festivals*, New York, 1952.
Hsu, F. L. K. *Under the Ancestors' Shadow*, Stanford, 1971.
Needham, J. *Science and Civilization in China*, Vol. ii. C.U.P., 1956.
Rawson, P. *Tao*, Thames and Hudson, 1973.
Shryock, J. *Origin and Development of the State Cult of Confucius*, New York, 1932.
Shryock, J. *The Temples of Anking*, Paris, 1931.
Sickman, L. and Soper, A. *The Art and Architecture of China*, Penguin, 1971.
Smith, D. H. *Chinese Religions*, Weidenfeld, 1968.
Smith, D. H. *Confucius*, Temple Smith, 1973.
Waley, A. *Three Ways of Thought in Ancient China*, Allen and Unwin, 1939.
Waley, A. *The Way and its Power*, Allen and Unwin, 1934.

## Chapter 9

# JAPANESE SHINTŌ

---

### The Way of the Gods

The ancient religion of Japan was distinguished from Buddhism, which had come from China, by the title 'the Way of the Gods', in the Chinese words Shen Tao, whence Shintō. The Japanese pronunciation of the same characters is Kami no Michi.

In the *Nihongi*, 'Chronicles of Japan', is a cosmological myth: 'Of old, Heaven and Earth were not yet separated, and the In and the Yo not yet divided. They formed a chaotic mass like an egg which was of obscurely defined limits and contained germs . . . Heaven was therefore formed first, and Earth was established subsequently. Thereafter Divine Beings were produced between them.'[1] The In and the Yo are equivalent to the Chinese Yin and Yang, female and male principles; from them many deities appeared.

Amaterasu Ōmi-kami, the sun-goddess, was the chief deity of early Japan and has remained so to this day. Called in myths the Great-Sky-Shiner, she is the sun who shines upon sky and earth in all six directions. The phenomena of day and night, summer and winter, are explained in stories similar to many of ancient Europe. Her brother Susa-no-wo, the storm-god, ill-treated Amaterasu and she hid in the Cave of Heaven, thus bringing darkness to the universe until she was enticed out with the aid of a mirror. The mirror became chief treasure of her ancient shrine

[1] W. G. Aston, tr., *Nihongi*, p. 1 f.

at Isé, on the south coast; and every other Shintō shrine also has a mirror as a solar symbol.

Susa-no-wo was banished by the gods to Izumo, on the north coast of Japan, with his son the earth-god, Oho-na-mochi. Amaterasu dispossessed the latter from ruling the earth and sent her grandson Ni-ni-gi to rule in his stead. Ni-ni-gi came down from heaven, married the goddess of Mount Fuji, and his great grandson was the first emperor of Japan, Jimmu Tenno.

Thus the emperors of Japan claimed descent from Amaterasu, the sun goddess. Whether she is supreme deity, or chief of a council of gods, has been disputed. But Japanese writers claim her supremacy: 'There is one supreme deity, Amaterasu Ōmi-kami, the "Heaven-Shining August Goddess", to whom the Imperial family and some other clans and families trace back their descent. To her all the other deities are subordinate and from these deities nearly all Japanese claim to be descended. So that the worship of these deities is, at one and the same time, a genuine nature worship and also the worship of the ancestors and heroes, centring in the sovereign deity.'[1]

Next in importance is Uke-Mochi, the 'Food-Possessor', spirit of food and sometimes of drink. Another form of the god is Inari, the rice-god, who has shrines in every village. His messenger is the fox, which is sometimes identified with the god himself; at the shrines of Inari there are many images of foxes. Inari is also god of fortune; his clients are traders, actors, and anyone seeking good luck, and many arches are set up at his shrines by successful dealers.

There are innumerable other gods (*kami*), of wind and rain, mountains and trees, sea and harbours, food and healing and fertility. Japan was called 'the land of the gods' and the number set at a million or so. Mount Fuji is the chief of mountains, called 'a wondrous deity . . . and a guardian of the land of Japan'. Many pilgrimages are made to its heights, as proof of physical endurance and spiritual fervour. Earthquakes are a constant menace in this land, and men give ardent worship to the protecting deity.

[1] M. Anesaki, *Religious Life of the Japanese People*, p. 36.

The word *kami* for god is also used for human superiors, and some of the gods are deified heroes, as in China. The war-god Hachiman, was an early emperor, and the god of learning, Temmangu, a scholar and ruler reminiscent of Confucius.

The crucial place of the emperor, as descendant of the sungoddess, will be mentioned again. Here it should be said that the common assertion that Shintō is emperor-worship needs correction. There are few shrines of past emperors, mostly of recent construction. The imperial ancestors are worshipped collectively and in private in the Hall of the Imperial Ancestors in the palace at Tokyo.

## SANCTUARY SHINTŌ

Two kinds of Shintō are distinguished today. The first is Jinja, 'Sanctuary Shintō', or Kokka, 'State Shintō', as expressed in what were till recently state sanctuaries. The second is Kyōha, 'Sectarian Shintō', which has appeared as a series of popular movements with their churches. Long arguments went on till recent years as to whether the former was a state cult, and therefore more patriotism than religion, or whether the loyalty it demanded was truly religious.

We saw in an earlier chapter that when Buddhism came to Japan it was soon declared that the Shintō gods were manifestations of original Buddhas and Bodhisattvas, starting with Amaterasu herself.[1] Buddhism almost absorbed Shintō in Ryōbu or Mixed Shintō, 'The Two-fold Way of the Gods'. Buddhist priests took charge of all except a few of the main Shintō temples, and introduced imagery and ceremonial of their own. But after nearly a thousand years of triumph on the part of Buddhism, Shintō thinkers and priests sought to free their religion from Buddhist influences. Finally after the fall of the Tokugawa Shōguns (dictators) and restoration of the emperor to a central position, in 1868, Ryobu Shintō was abolished and pure Shintō declared the religion of the Japanese state.

Buddhism recovered from the early attacks, for it had entered

[1]For Buddhism in Japan see Chapter 7 on Mahāyāna Buddhism.

too deeply into the affections of the people to be destroyed. But Sanctuary or State Shintō was given official status and its shrines nationalized. There were over a hundred thousand of these, not only great temples but innumerable tiny shrines of heroes and spirits, and rice and fox deities. Buddhists and Christians were ordered to attend the state shrines, as a mark of reverence to the imperial ancestors. The emperor played a leading part in what was a national cult, with worship of the gods and administration of government as aspects of the same thing. The identity of religion and nation, taught by Shintō theologians led to fanatical loyalty to the emperor as a state cult.

All this was changed with the defeat of Japan in 1946. The emperor broadcast a repudiation of his own divinity: 'The bonds between us and our countrymen have been tied together from the first to last by mutual trust and affection. They do not originate in mere myth and legend. They do not have their basis in the fictitious ideas that the emperor is manifest god.'[1]

The State Shintō shrines were disestablished; the priests lost their state subsidy and many were reduced to poverty. The fortunes of Shintō must depend on popular support. But the great shrines at Isé and Izumo retained their importance, and in 1959 there were moves towards restoring their state subsidies.

Many other services, of course, were held at the ordinary Shintō sanctuaries, in addition to state rites, and these have continued in many cases.

## SECTARIAN SHINTŌ

After 'pure Shintō' was recognized as a state religion it became clear that a distinction would have to be made between the state shrines, where traditional rituals were observed, and the more recent sectarian bodies. These had grown out of Shintō but were more akin to churches. They had particular doctrines and definite founders. Hence only the officially recognized number of Shintō shrines were allowed to call themselves *jinja*, 'sanctuary' or 'god-

[1] D. C. Holtom, *Modern Japan and Shinto Nationalism*, p. 220.

house', while the other bodies were called Kyōha Shintō, 'sectarian Shintō'. Their institutions were treated as kyōkai or churches, on the same footing as Buddhism and Christianity.

The Shintō sects claim the allegiance of a considerable part of the Japanese peoples, 17 million out of 85 million being given as adherents of the thirteen recognized sects. Since the war, and the decline of State Shintō, the sects are claiming to be the native religion of the non-Buddhist Japanese, although a number of the sects have been influenced by Buddhism.

Some of the sects originated in pilgrimages to sacred mountains. The two most prominent peaks in Japan, Fuji and Ontaké, have always attracted pilgrims, whose struggles as they climb serve as physical and spiritual training. But many other peaks are regarded as sacred and pilgrims clad in white and carrying rosaries may be seen going to wayside shrines and on to the summit. Mountaineer priests, 'those who sleep among the mountains', lead such expeditions and give messages from the mountain spirits. Some of them are Buddhists, not regular priests but men who spend part of their lives as laymen and part as leaders of pilgrims and diviners. Three sects are recognized as authorized churches, with more or less of organization and hereditary leadership. One, the 'Order of the Conic Peak', is noted for its austerity. Others tend to practices of divination, exorcism, and fire-walking.[1]

The most important sects are popular movements in which faith-healing plays a great part. Konkō-kyō, 'the Teaching of Golden Light', was founded by Kawade Bunjiro in the latter part of the nineteenth century. Bunjiro was converted to the worship of the metal-god, which he interpreted as beneficent Gold, and this gave the church its name. He claimed to be possessed by the god, revealed to him as the one sole God who is good. This monotheism is a missionary faith, and claims 3 million adherents, with offshoots in Malaya and western America. Bunjiro became a Shintō priest, but he repudiated the narrow patriotism of his day and superstitious practices. He taught the need for sincerity of heart rather than much ritual and the value of extempore prayer.

[1] Anesaki, op. cit., p. 28 f.

'The vain making of a big noise by the clapping of hands avails nothing, for even a little sound is heard by God. It is not necessary to speak in a loud voice or to practise intonations in prayer.'[1]

The Tenri-kyō sect, 'the Religion of Divine Wisdom', was also founded in the nineteenth century, by a woman named Miki. It claims over four million followers, though such figures are always vague since no religious statistics are kept in the East; but it seems to have the strongest appeal of the sects and has been called Japan's most powerful religious movement. Miki belonged to the Pure Land sect of Buddhism but her husband was a Shintōist. At the age of 40 she became 'possessed' by the Lord of Heaven, sold all her family property and gave the money to the poor. Her movement gives special stress to faith-healing and has been called the Christian Science of Japan. Miki heard in her revelations that evil and disease were dust upon the soul and need to be purified away by ritual. She wrote down divine verses and taught methods of worship by dancing and movements of the hands. In the meetings of the sect dancing, drumming and incantation of psalms are used to induce 'god-possession'.

The Tenri church founded by Miki is highly organized and has missionary aims. It centres in a mother church, 'the Auspicious Seat', near Nara, where an ideal 'Terrace of Nectar' is to be established. There is a huge temple to which crowds come and bow before a Memorial Mirror. All the other churches of Tenri-kyō are linked to this central place in linear organization, and branches have spread to China, Manchuria and Malaya. A great deal of social and educational work is also undertaken and propaganda is spread in various modern languages.

### SANCTUARIES AND SHRINES

The Shintō shrine (*jinja*) is often a tiny hut standing at the roadside, in the corner of a factory, or on top of a block of buildings. Then it is like a little house and looks portable, but it is not moved because the spot where it stands is sacred.

[1]Holtom, *The National Faith of Japan.*

158

# SANCTUARIES AND SHRINES

The larger sanctuaries are nearly always in the midst of trees, on a hill or near the sea. The shade of the cryptomeria trees, and the quiet of the place, give an impressive atmosphere and encourage that love of nature which is a noted Japanese characteristic. An avenue of trees leads from the entrance to the hall of worship. At the beginning of the avenue there may be a wooden fence, and there is always a simple three-piece wooden arch, called *torii*. There may be several *torii* down the avenue leading to the shrine, and at some very popular sanctuaries there is a veritable forest of *torii* arches, with Japanese characters on them recounting the praises of the god who has answered prayer. Stone or metal lanterns light the avenue and give an air of solemnity at night.

There are no great stone temples or cathedrals in Shintō. The shrines are always built of unpainted wood, small and simple, much on the style of a dwelling house. A few straight pillars rise from the ground, with roof beams on them carrying a roof of bark or tiles. The beam ends project out cross-wise and give a conventional effect.

The main shrine is the *honden*, the dwelling place of the god. This is above ground, reached by a staircase. It is a single room never large, in the middle of which stands the symbol of the god facing the entrance; this is generally a mirror, or occasionally an image. The only other objects in the room are a few green branches of the sakaki tree, white tablets, and earthen vessels for offerings. The latter are flesh or vegetable and are placed uncooked in the shrine with water or saké rice beer.

Only the priests can enter the *honden*. There is a larger worship hall (*haiden*) in front of it, open on all sides, which is used for ritual ceremonies and music. Other structures may be stages for dramatic performances which the laity may attend. There may be a number of smaller shrines, dedicated to various other deities connected with the main one, and also sacred trees, rocks and fountains.

Every temple has its *gohei*, a small wooden or bamboo pole, split so as to hold a small piece of cloth or paper hanging down each side and looking as if it were plaited. This is a symbol of sanctity and a substitute for an ancient offering of cloth.

JAPANESE SHINTŌ

Every sanctified object and piece of hallowed ground within the sanctuary precincts is marked off by a piece of rope of twisted rice-straw hung before it. This is the *shime-nawa*, or demarcation rope, which is meant to keep away evil influences. Pieces of paper hang from the *shime-nawa*, and it is one of the commonest sights in temples and home shrines.

The most famous of Shintō shrines has always been the grand imperial shrine at Isé, dedicated to Amaterasu the sun-goddess. It is the most sacred spot in Japan and every Japanese is supposed to make the pilgrimage to Isé at least once in his life-time. The shrine is a simple wooden building, rebuilt every twenty years, standing in a forest of trees. Inside are the treasures, the divine imperial regalia of mirror, sword and stone jewels; all veiled from common sight.

The daily worship in the Shintō shrine is all performed by the priests. The green branches are renewed, offerings made, and ritual performed to the accompaniment of brief clapping of hands. It is very quiet, the priests gliding in and out with gentle footsteps. Shintōists are proud of the quietness and solemnity of their rituals, which reflect both its ancient character and the relation of the official rites to solemn court ceremonies.

There are, however, more lively and public performances in dances and songs with musical accompaniments, which are held in separate buildings in the presence of lay worshippers. Here old myths and legends are represented, but without systematic explanation by the priests. The dances are graceful horizontal movements, hardly ever any jumps, and while torches are used for lighting there are no fireworks.

The sectarian temples are conspicuous for their neatness and for the crowds of worshippers that throng them at all times. The mother church of the Tenri-kyō at Tenri Shi is believed to be built on the spot which is the cradle of the human race, and encloses a sacred column (*kanrodai*) indicating the centre of the world, and bearing a sacred cup for heavenly nectar. Long corridors connect the sanctuary with the shrine dedicated to the founder. All Tenri-kyō temples have three altars, one of which is dedicated to Miki, and often a hexagonal tower in remembrance of the sacred column. New temples are frequently built, in town and country, by the free labour of the members.

## LAY PRAYERS

There is no congregational worship at the Shintō sanctuaries. Lay worshippers come on their own, according to their wishes and needs. The layman stands in front of the shrine, pulling a white cord that rings a ball-shaped bell to attract the attention of the god, throwing special money ('homage coins') into a box, clapping the hands in prayer, or clasping the hands in Buddhist fashion, or simply removing his hat and bowing. Shintō or Buddhist formulas may be murmured in prayer but nobody raises his voice. Some people bring special offerings which are raised to the forehead in reverence, and later removed by the priests for their own use.

As special acts of piety worshippers may go backwards and forwards many times down the avenue leading from the *torii* to the shrine, or bathe in the ice-cold fountains or waterfalls among the trees. This may be done for a special deity or as part of a long pilgrimage.

There are no prayers in the most ancient scriptures, and when they do appear later they are litanies which request public benefits, peace and prosperity, for harvest and state affairs. The common people offer informal prayers, at time of sowing and harvest, on beginning some undertaking, and at times of family crisis, birth, marriage, sickness and misfortune. They visit the shrines to obtain charms and talismans which are sold there, to drive away evil spirits, or to give children, good harvest and successful deals. The more mystical type of prayer often comes from Buddhist influence.

Religion comes into the home of the laity by the use of the *kami-dana*, or 'god-shelf'. Most homes and many workshops and offices have one of these. They are sold on stalls in the streets, especially before the new year when they should be renewed. The *kami-dana* is a sort of long box, with partitions and small shrines with door wings that contain simple symbols. It is usually installed on the upper wall side of a room, above the door or screen. Above it hangs the *shime-nawa*, the twisted rope with pieces of paper hanging from it, which marks off all sacred objects. Vases of green sakaki twigs, and bottles of water or saké beer stand on the shelf. Memorial tablets of paper or wood also stand there, inscribed with the name of an ancestor or patron deity. The little shrines contain a sacred mirror, strips of paper with texts, and charms obtained from the shrines.

Every day domestic rites should be performed at the god-shelf, which may be no more than clapping the hands to attract the attention of the spirits, murmuring a prayer, and renewing the leaves and water. But on special occasions of family life, or in time of need, candles are lit, prayers made, and saké offered by the family head, while members sit on the floor before the shrine with bowed heads in attentive silence.

Priests can be called into houses to perform special rites and marriage ceremonies, and some of them minister not only at public shrines but also in private houses, and even at some of the sectarian churches. Many Japanese homes also have a Buddha-shelf, *Butsu-dana*, usually in another room, which is more elaborate than the Shintō god-shelf, with an image of Amida or other figures. Buddhist priests also come, especially for the funeral rites in which they are expert, and say prayers for the dead.

The laity take a much greater part in the worship of the sectarian churches than at the traditional shrines. The temples are large and are meant to accommodate worshippers within the courtyards. On great occasions tens of thousands squat on the mats laid out on the floors in the central temples. Public prayers are made by the leading priests: 'Thou, O God the Parent, hast created man and the universe out of chaos and thou hast ever since taken care of our growth . . . May God graciously deign to accept our sincere childlike hearts . . . May God grant that this world become a prosperous one in which people's minds will be purified completely.'[1] Music is played and dances performed,

[1] H. van Straelen, *The Religion of Divine Wisdom*, p. 117 f.

some of them in public, some, like the mystic dance of masked men and women round the *kanrodai* column of Tenri-kyō, in secret. The central ceremony of all Tenri-kyō temples is a public dance of six people in front of the chief altar to words and music composed by Miki. Sermons and instruction are also given at these public services.

## FESTIVALS

At the new year there are special family observances which seek to cleanse the house from evil influences of the past, renew the god-shelf, and invite good luck for the future. Great preparations take place beforehand, houses are cleaned, bills are paid, special food is prepared so that there may be no cooking for the first three days of the New Year. Pounded rice is the special new-year dish, prepared with much care and ritual. Houses are decorated with special arrangements of pine trees, bamboo plants, and straw and white paper cut in particular ways to indicate purification. Inside the house flowers are disposed in ways for which Japanese art is famous, in the manner appropriate to the new year. Families and friends visit each other, and notable shrines are visited, especially Ise. Family groups go there in brilliant costumes, and the priests dress in white kimonos with blue, purple and scarlet sashes. Some six weeks after the new year has begun special rites are performed in Shintō and Buddhist shrines for exorcizing evil spirits, and other rites are held in private houses.

A great festival of the dead is held in the middle of the year, called Bon, and akin to the Chinese feast of hungry souls. The souls of the departed are believed to return to their homes, where they are entertained and fed by their families. When the feast is over there are farewell fires, especially in mountain districts, to light the souls on their return journey. On the sea coast tiny boats, with lanterns and food, are put on the waters and sent adrift, their little lights as they disappear into the darkness and sink looking like the souls going away to rest beyond the floods.

Seasonal and occupational festivals mark the religious life of the people. Agricultural rituals are concerned with planting and harvesting, and those of fishing with the times of abundance and danger. The most important are the autumn harvest festivals, 'new tasting', with their rejoicing and communal feasts. There are processions with the sacred cart of Inari, the rice spirit, in the midst; and plays and singing, dancing with swords, torches and fans. The ancient character of this festival is shown by references to it in the *Nihongi*, and according to tradition the new rice should not be eaten until the festival has been performed and the rice-spirit honoured. A great form of this ritual was the 'Great Tasting', which was performed by the emperor in the eleventh month of the first year of his reign. He offered rice and saké to the gods and then partook of it with his court.

Other ceremonies take place in sowing the rice seed, and in prayers for rain and growth of the crops. There are seasonal flower festivals, of peach and iris blossoms. Flowers, dolls and lanterns are carried about in celebration. The Tenri-kyō celebrate the Great Vernal Festival in January, and the Great Autumnal Festival in October. Offerings are made of fish, vegetables, fruit and saké, as at any Shintō temple.

The Shintō gods have their own special festivals, when flowers and other gifts are brought to the shrines. The sects celebrate the birthdays or deaths of their founders, in public services with tens of thousands attending. They also observe their own special commemorations of the dead.

Artisans of most kinds have their own patron deities and observe special days in their honour. The workshop has its god-shelf, before which prayer is made when beginning and ending some special piece of work. Swords have always been regarded as particularly sacred, and the workshop of a sword-maker is decorated with the rope *shime-nawa*, as well as having its god-shelf.

Shintō has adopted many of the festivals, imagery and thought of Buddhism. State Shintō was also influenced by Confucian ideals. Sectarian Shintō has reflected both ancient animistic beliefs and also perhaps some Christian beliefs. The religion has been syncretistic, while at times seeking to revert to an indigenous nationalism. Many Japanese will go freely to Shintō, Buddhist and even Christian temples, and some maintain that the many gods of Shintō are but manifestations of the one God.

The mystical feeling of Japan has found superb expression in the many arts to which great care and discipline have been given, to swordsmanship and archery, to flower arrangement and the tea ceremony, to the placing and surroundings of the temples and their avenues of trees. In verse some of the most attractive lines of devotion are found in the Mikagura Uta, the sacred dance of Tenri-kyō, composed by Miki at the height of her spiritual experience:

> If you want to know, come unto Me and I will explain to you the origin of all things.
> I, God the Parent, reveal Myself and I will explain to you everything in detail; then the whole world will rejoice.
> I hasten to save the whole world; therefore you people in the world exult.

And God is not only the creator and parent, but is near to his followers:

> Whatever people may say of you, God watches you, so be at ease . . .
> Those who are around me, watch how God works . . .
> For I always hasten to save you, come to Me with a cheerful heart.[1]

## BIBLIOGRAPHY

Anesaki, M. History of Japanese Religion, 2nd. edn., Routledge, 1963.
Anesaki, M. Religious Life of the Japanese People, Tokyo, 1938.
Bellah, R. N. Tokugawa Religion, Collier Macmillan, 1959.
Creemers, W. H. M. Shrine Shinto after World War II, Brill, 1968.
De Bary, W. T., ed. Sources of Japanese Religion, Columbia, 1958.
Hammer, R. Japan's Religious Ferment, S.C.M., 1961.
Herbert, J. Shintô, Allen and Unwin, 1967.
Hori, I. Folk Religion in Japan, Chicago, 1968.

[1]Van Straelen, op. cit., pp. 132, 134.

Kishimoto, Hideo, *Japanese Religion in the Meiji Era*, Tokyo, 1956.

Kitagawa, J. M. *Religion in Japanese History*, Columbia, 1966.

Offner, C. B. and Van Straelen, H. *Modern Japanese Religions*, Brill, 1963.

Ono, S. *Shinto, the Kami Way*, Prentice Hall, 1962.

Paine, R. T. and Soper, A. *The Art and Architecture of Japan*, Penguin, 1955.

Piggott, J. *Japanese Mythology*, Hamlyn, 1969.

# PART IV

---

*The Near East and the West*

*Chapter 10*

# JUDAISM

The Western religions are notable in the importance they attach to history and while each has its special sacred events yet the Old Testament has the first. The patriarchs were founders both of race and religion and they are remembered in the Jewish daily prayers and many others: 'Blessed art thou, O Lord our God and God of our fathers, God of Abraham, God of Isaac, and God of Jacob.'

With Moses and the Exodus from Egypt the religion of Israel became historical, the first historical religion of the world with a founder earlier than any other. Ever after down their long history, even in the blackest days, the Jews have looked back to the time when God led their fathers out of Egypt, 'with a mighty hand and with an outstretched arm'. There are other great deliverances too: from the exile in Babylon, to the brave Maccabees, and in our own time in the return to Israel, a fact of deep religious significance.

Moses was the great prophet and law-giver, 'there hath never yet arisen in Israel a prophet like unto Moses'. The Commandments and laws which are attributed to him have been studied minutely ever since. His mysterious passing away was taken to mean that he had not died (Deut. 34, 6); he 'knew God face to face'; he gave the law which is enshrined in the central place in every synagogue. The Talmud said that Moses spoke in the words of all other prophets, the Cabbalists of the Middle Ages saw him

169

'reincarnated in every age', the modern state of Israel has been called 'a reincarnation of Moses'.

The great prophets of Israel, from Elijah in the ninth century B.C., and the written prophecies from the eighth century onwards, were the preachers of that ethical monotheism which distinguished Hebrew prophecy from the wild ecstasies of other peoples. 'Let justice roll down like waters and righteousness as a mighty stream', cried Amos, and Isaiah urged his hearers to 'relieve the oppressed, judge the fatherless, plead for the widow.' In Hosea the love and forgiveness of God are expressed and in the Psalms his nearness, 'Whither shall I go from thy spirit, or whither shall I flee from thy presence?'

The sixth century B.C. is often called the century of the great flowering of religious teachers in the world religious. Zarathushtra, Mahāvīra and Buddha, Lao-Tzu and Confucius, Pythagoras and Heraclitus, all lived about this time. The peak of Hebrew prophecy came then, in Jeremiah and Second Isaiah, but they were the successors of two centuries of prophetic writers, so advanced was this tiny Jewish people in the sphere of religion.

Elijah came to symbolize the later prophets, for he like Moses had ascended into heaven and so would come again to establish God's kingdom. To this day when the Passover is celebrated in Jewish homes the door is opened at the end of the meal for the entry of Elijah, a cup of wine is filled, 'the cup of Elijah', and the whole company rises to bless him.

The priests and levites were in charge of the temple in Jerusalem, the great centre of Jewish religion in late biblical times, which was destroyed by the Romans in A.D. 70, and the Jews expelled from Palestine. All down the ages Jews have prayed every day, 'And to Jerusalem, thy city, return in mercy, and dwell therein as thou hast spoken; rebuild it soon in our days as an everlasting building, and speedily set up therein the throne of David.'

After the Jewish Dispersion the teachers (rabbis) preserved the scriptures and traditions of Judaism. The canon of the scriptures was fixed towards the end of the first century. By the fourth century was produced the Talmud, 'teaching' or 'doctrine', applied at first to discussions of tradition (Mishnah) and finally to the whole text and commentary. Further ethical and religious expositions (Midrashim) were made later. Talmud and Midrash have been the guides of the Jewish people down the ages, with all aspects of faith and morals, civil and criminal law included.

The word Torah, 'law', is applied to the canonical scriptures, especially to the first five books of the Bible which are attributed to Moses, and are held to be divinely inspired; 'Moses received the Torah on Sinai'. The study of the Torah has been regarded as the most precious occupation in life and where ten people formed a congregation to study it the glory of God abode among them. In the daily liturgy it is said, 'Blessed art thou, O Lord our God, King of the Universe, who hast chosen us from all nations, and given us thy Torah.'

Portions of the Torah are worn on the person or placed in the house. During the week-day morning services men put on the *tephillin* (phylacteries), which are two small leather cases with straps attached to fasten them round the head and arm. This is in literal fulfilment of the verse, 'Thou shalt bind them for a sign upon thine hand, and they shall be for frontlets between thine eyes' (Deut. 6, 8). The *tephillin* enclose texts of which one is the famous Shema, 'Hear, O Israel: the Lord our God, the Lord is One.'

Similarly Jewish homes have a doorpost symbol, Mezuzah, in further fulfilment of the verse, 'thou shalt write them upon the door posts of thy house, and upon thy gates.' The Mezuzah are metal or wooden boxes, fixed to the right-hand doorpost of the house, and containing some of the above verses. On the outside of the Mezuzah may be seen the first letter of the name of God, Shaddai. Pious Jews touch the Mezuzah and kiss their hand on entering and leaving a room or house.

## THE UNITY OF GOD

As earliest of three great monotheistic religions Judaism has always stressed the oneness of God; 'He is One, and there is no unity like unto his unity', says the morning service.

The thirteen articles of the Jewish creed were formulated by Moses Maimonides in the twelfth century A.D. These are belief in God's existence, his unity, incorporeality, timelessness, providence, justice, and approachability through prayer. Then come belief in prophecy, the superiority of Moses, the revelation of the Law, the immutability of the Law, the coming of the Messiah, the resurrection and immortality. This creed is incorporated in the Yigdal hymn in the Jewish liturgy.

The existence of God is regarded as axiomatic in Judaism and not requiring proof. His unity was defended strictly, both against the polytheism of the Gentile world and against the Christian doctrine of the Trinity. That God has not bodily form was maintained by the rabbis, despite the many anthropomorphic expressions of the Old Testament which speak of God's face, finger and foot. These were interpreted symbolically: 'We borrow terms from his creatures to apply to Him in order to assist the understanding.'[1]

Yet men must believe that the noblest human emotions have some place in the divine, even if they are transcended there. So God was said to weep over the failings of his children, to visit the sick and to bury the dead. The fatherhood of God followed naturally from this. God is constantly referred to as 'Father who is in heaven'. He is a father who pities his children, and gives the soul and spiritual faculties to the newborn babe.

The name of God was so holy that for some centuries, at least, before Christian times the Jews never uttered the supreme name. This was represented by four letters, the tetragrammation YHWH, whose vowels are now unknown because the name is never spoken. The Christian pronunciation Jehovah is certainly wrong. Jews substitute another name for God, such as Adonai or Shaddai. The most holy name YHWH was revealed to Moses under the phrase, 'I am that I am', or 'I am who am', the self-existent one or the inscrutable.

God is so great, and his name unspeakable, yet his presence is known among men in the Shekhinah. This is the 'dwelling' or

[1] A. Cohen, *Everyman's Talmud*, p. 6.

glory of God. It was manifest in the pillar of cloud and fire that led the Israelites in the desert, and in the cloud of glory that filled the temple. Where righteous men gather it is present still. In Cabbalistic writings the Shekhinah is involved in the tragedy of the world and the task of man is to bring about its reunion with the infinite God, En Sof. The Spirit of God (or Holy Spirit) was another rabbinic concept by which the nearness of God and his influence on man were expressed.

In the Bible and Talmud there are many references to angels (divine messengers) and celestial beings. A popular night prayer invoked the four archangels as guardians, after the manner of the Christian invocation of the four evangelists. Michael was the chief guardian angel of Israel, Gabriel the messenger of God, Raphael the angel of healing, and Uriel the light of God. Ministering angels accompanied men to the synagogue and on returning home.

The Messiah ('anointed one') would be sent by God for the golden age of the future. It is an article of faith to believe 'in the coming of the Messiah, and, though he tarry, I will wait daily for his coming'. The rabbis believed that the Messiah would be a human being, of the house of David, and would restore the kingdom to Israel as it has ever been prayed daily. As the persecutions of Jews increased so did the belief that these were the 'birthpangs of the Messiah' who 'hath borne our griefs and carried our sorrows'. After travail and bitter warfare the Messiah would set up his kingdom in a reign of peace and happiness; the Holy City of Jerusalem would be restored and a new temple built.

## TEMPLE AND SYNAGOGUES

In the early days in Palestine there were many sanctuaries for God outside Jerusalem, where Samuel, Solomon, Elijah and others sacrificed. King Josiah in the seventh century B.C. tried to centralize all worship in his reduced kingdom at Jerusalem, in an effort to put down idolatry. After the exile this law was strongly enforced and Jerusalem was the only place for sacrifice. The country sanctuaries were gradually replaced by synagogues ('houses of assembly') where non-sacrificial worship flourished and this survived the dispersion of the Jews. Wherever they went they gathered in synagogues and here the Torah was central.

The architecture of the synagogue varies with country and age. Sometimes it is round, at other times octagonal. The most sacred object in it is the scroll of the Law which is kept in a sacred ark behind a curtain-covered recess at the east end. The ark is in the direction of Jerusalem towards which everyone turns in prayer. When the scroll is taken out of the ark, all rise as it is carried to the reading-desk with prayers. It is held up before being returned to the ark: 'this is the Law which Moses set before the children of Israel . . . It is a tree of life to them that grasp it'.

The Torah is written by hand in black ink on a parchment scroll, in square Hebrew characters without vowel points. It is mounted on wooden rollers, which often have silver heads. Before a synagogue is consecrated the scroll of the Torah is carried round it seven times and then put in the ark.

In the centre of the synagogue is the Bema, or desk, for the reader of the service who faces the ark. Candles stand at this desk. Round three sides of the building are seats for the congregation, often with galleries above. According to tradition women should sit in a separate 'court', marked off by a partition, or in a gallery. Until recently this was covered with a grille. In reformed synagogues the women's gallery is open and men and women may sit together.

There are no images or pictures in the synagogue. Texts from scripture are inscribed on the walls. But on the ark there is often the figure of a lion or an eagle, a crown or a symbolic representation of the two tablets of the Ten Commandments. The six-pointed Star or Shield of David is a common decoration.

The chief functionary of the Jewish congregation is the rabbi. He is teacher and lawyer, but does not necessarily read or preach in the synagogue, though he often does. Descendants of the priests (*cohanim*) are honoured but have no official position. It is the reader (*hazzan*) who is the chief officiant at the service, reading the Torah and praying. Any adult male Jew may lead prayers, but in a large congregation there is at least one reader who is called the minister. He must have a good voice for chanting and reading Hebrew correctly and must know the prayer book well.

## SERVICES AND PRAYERS

In most of the eastern religions that we have studied so far congregational worship is not frequent and only occurs in great festivals and processions. The chief exceptions are the Pure Land schools of Mahāyāna Buddhism and the Shintō sects. In most Eastern temples the shrine is small and entered only by priests who perform their rituals there, while the laity use the temple courtyards and pray in the open air.

In the Western religions, Judaism, Islam and Christianity, congregational worship plays a great part. While most Eastern mosques have open courts, because of the hot and dry climate, Jewish synagogues and Christian churches hold their services within doors. This is especially true in the cold northern latitudes. The congregational services expect considerable co-operation from the laity and will therefore be considered in some detail, as showing what worship means to the laity.

There are three services every day in the Jewish synagogue: Evening Prayer (the day begins at sunset), Morning Prayer, and Afternoon Prayer. These three daily prayers date from biblical times, and the morning and afternoon prayers are of greater importance because they correspond to the approximate times of the daily sacrifice in the old temple. The morning prayer is often held as early as 6 a.m., to enable workers to pay their devotions before beginning daily work.

Public service can only be held in the synagogue if ten adult males are present. The worshippers bow on entering the synagogue and also during certain portions of the prayers, which are said standing or kneeling. Orthodox Jews wear a prayer shawl over the head during prayers. The traditional language of the prayers is Hebrew, but some are in Aramaic and some in modern languages according to the country. Instrumental music is not used, except by Liberal Jews, but a number of passages in the service are sung in unison and this practice is being extended.

At all services the prayer called Amidah ('standing') or Eighteen Blessings is recited, while the congregation stands. Each individual recites this in an undertone and then the reader says it aloud on behalf of all. The Amidah begins with confessions of faith in God, and ends with prayers for the restoration of Jerusalem and for peace. It is preceded by several benedictions, notably the Shema: 'Hear [Shema], O Israel: the Lord our God, the Lord is One. And thou shalt love the Lord thy God with all thine heart, and with all thy soul, and with all thy might.'

Readings from the Torah are made at morning services on Monday and Thursday, and on all Sabbaths and festivals. Many psalms and scripture portions are recited at all services. On Sabbath and festival mornings there are selections from the prophets.

Many Jews pray at home on week-days and attend the synagogue on the Sabbath and festivals. Home prayers follow the outline of public prayers, with small omissions. The Shema is repeated by devout Jews every morning and evening, it is the first prayer learnt as a child and the last repeated by the dying.

In home life the religious Jew is constantly blessing God; in the Amidah with its eighteen blessings, 'Blessed be thou, O Lord our God, King of the universe', and on many other occasions, on taking different kinds of food, on smelling sweet things, on seeing lightning or a rainbow or the sea, at the sight of wise men or kings, in fact for any fine object or person. It is a religion which blesses the material and is generally opposed to asceticism. Celibacy and barrenness are unnatural, the divine command to man is to 'be fruitful, and multiply, and replenish the earth'. So marriage is highly honoured and the home is a religious centre whose ritual both at weekly Sabbath and annual Passover, is as significant as that of the synagogue.

The Sabbath, the observance of the seventh day of the week as a day of rest and prayer, has always been regarded as a festival. In a beautiful hymn sung in the synagogue on the Friday evening, the

Sabbath is compared to a bride, the crown of her husband God who awaits her. This service is generally attended by the men of the family and on their return home they find the house prepared for the Sabbath observance.

The Sabbath candlesticks, polished by the eldest son, are set out at dusk on Friday and the mother of the house surrounded by her husband and children lights them with the blessing to God 'who hast sanctified us by thy commandments and commanded us to kindle the Sabbath light'. The table is spread with a clean cloth, and at the head where the father sits are two loaves in memory of the double portion of manna which was gathered on the sixth day by the Israelites in the desert over three thousand years ago. They are covered with a napkin and next to them stands an empty cup and a jug of wine.

The father then takes a cup of wine and recites over it the Kiddush or hallowing of the day, and the verses from Genesis referring to creation and rest on the sixth and seventh days.The cup is blessed with the invocation of God 'who createst the fruit of the vine', sipped by the father, and handed to his wife and she to the children and on to all the others. Then the hands are ritually washed and the bread blessed, then it is sliced or broken and passed to the family. Then come special hymns, prayers in Hebrew, the Sabbath meal, the blessing after the meal.

On the Sabbath morning there is usually no breakfast, since it is improper to eat before prayers. The synagogue morning prayers are much longer than the daily services, lasting about three hours. There are special prayers and readings. The central point of the service is bringing the scroll from the ark and reading the Torah. The Pentateuch (first five books of the Bible) is divided into sections for Sabbath use, so that the whole book is read through once a year; some of the sections are very long. Traditionally seven men should be called up from the congregation to read the Sabbath lesson but nowadays they simply stand by the reader while he reads the portion.

The noonday Sabbath meal at home is similar to that of the evening before, consisting of blessing of wine and bread, breaking and distribution, followed by a meal and blessing. A third meal may be held late in the afternoon to complete three Sabbath meals. A bottle of wine and a box of incense are put on the table, a light struck, and thanks given to God for these three things, and for separating the Sabbath from the week. This ritual is also recited in the synagogue for those who cannot observe it in their own homes.

## FESTIVALS AND FASTS

The Passover is the best known Jewish festival and the 'Passover-holidays' are times of family reunion, even to those who have neglected strict religious practice. The Passover commemorates the Exodus of the Hebrews from Egypt, and anchors the religion to the history of Moses. The offering of firstlings of the flock and the use of unleavened bread were traits from the pastoral and agricultural days of Israel.

The Passover lasts eight days, from the fourteenth day of the month Nisan (March–April). It is preceded by a thorough cleaning of the house and on the festival eve a formal search is made throughout the house with a lighted candle, looking for leaven. Any leaven in the house is put aside till next morning and then solemnly burnt, after which only unleavened cakes are eaten during the remainder of the festival.

The chief feature of the Passover is the home-festival (*seder*) on the first two nights of the feast. The whole family gathers and strangers may be invited. The table is set and gaily decorated. In front of the place taken by the head of the family or leader of the service are placed: three unleavened cakes (*matzot*), a dish with a roasted lamb bone and a roasted egg, another with horse-radish or lettuce, a dish of parsley or cress, a saucer of salt water, a dish of mixed apples, nuts and raisins, two unlighted candles, a large goblet for wine. There is also a wine glass for every person present.

The leader or father begins with the Kiddush, kindling the lights and filling the cups, and the large one which is 'Elijah's cup', then some parsley or cress is distributed. After setting aside the bone and egg, the seder-dish with unleavened bread is raised and all who are hungry invited to share the festival. Then the youngest child asks questions on the meaning of the ceremonies, and the reply goes over the narrative of the Exodus and the redemption by God. The family joins in with blessings to God and the Shema. The leader continues on the mercy of God to the Jews, and finally all join in the Hallel (Praise) Psalms 113–15. A piece of unleavened bread which had been hidden is found by a child and distributed to the participants; three cups of wine have been drunk at intervals. Then comes the evening meal, recital of various Psalms, the great Hallel (Ps. 136), a fourth and final cup of wine, and a benediction of song.

In the synagogue there are special services during the Passover, with lessons from the Torah and Prophets and singing of the Hallel. The Song of Songs is read, and often in the home too at this season, giving its words an allegorical interpretation of the betrothal of Israel to God.

The Feast of Weeks (Shabuoth) begins on the fiftieth day after the Passover (hence its name Pentecost, 'fiftieth' in Greek). This came from the early wheat harvest and the synagogue is decorated with plants and flowers and special lessons include the harvest story of Ruth. Tradition also connected the season with the law-giving on Mount Sinai, and Reform congregations administer 'confirmation' to boys and girls at this time.

The feast of Tabernacles (Sukkoth) in the autumn is a fruit harvest which celebrates the wandering of the Jews in the desert when they dwelt in tabernacles or booths. Pious Jews build a kind of tent or hut with open roof, or adapt a greenhouse leaving the skylight open. This is not slept in usually but meals are taken in the Sukkah during the festival week. The walls and roof are decorated with all manner of flowers and fruit, branches and coloured lights. Every meal is like a feast, with abundant dessert, and prolonged by ceremonies such as blessing the Sukkah, blessing the vine, and special grace after meals. The synagogue is also adorned with branches and fruit at this harvest festival, and there are processions with palm branches around the scroll of the Torah, commemorating the processions of the old temple days.

Hymns with the refrain 'Hosanna' are sung, with seven Hosanna-processions on the seventh day, ending with a messianic hymn and discarding of the branches.

The feast of Hanukkah (Dedication) or Lights celebrates the victory of Judas Maccabeus over the Syrians in 164 B.C. and the rededication of the temple after its pollution by the rekindling of the temple lights. In the home candles are set in the windows to publicize the miracle of God's deliverance, and it is a women's festival on which games replace work. The feast of Purim in the first half of March celebrates the deliverance of the Jews as told in the Book of Esther. It is a carnival in which Esther's rescue is enacted and Haman's effigy burnt.

The two most solemn occasions in the calendar are the New Year and the Day of Atonement. The New Year (Rosh Ha-Shanah) is marked by sounding a ram's horn at synagogue services during, and sometimes before, the fast whence it has been called the Feast of Trumpets. The horn is sounded before, during and after morning prayers, to call the people to penitence. The ten days from the first of the New Year are called the 'Ten days of Penitence', and are described as days of judgement when all things pass before God. Many people go to the synagogue on the first day, and the most pious every day. These are solemn days rather than fasts; new bread and wine are eaten with honey, with the expression of the wish, 'May it be thy will that this year shall be happy and sweet for us.'

The ninth day of the month is marked with a festive meal. Each individual recites a confession of sins, and money is given to charity. A lamp is then lit to last for twenty-four hours, the mother kindles the usual festival lights, and the family goes to the synagogue for the great Day of Atonement. This is a time of repentance of sin, asking forgiveness of any who may be wronged, and hence of giving good wishes to relatives and friends. Many who do not normally go to the synagogue attend it on this day.

The ceremonies of the Day of Atonement (Yom Kippur) are based on the ancient ritual set out in Leviticus 16, but with modifications for modern times. It begins with the evening service before dark, which opens with a formula of remission of all ceremonial vows, so that pardon will not have to be sought for unfulfilled vows. On the following day there are four services which go on continuously: Morning Prayer, Additional Prayer, Afternoon Prayer, and Closing Prayer. Each service contains confession of sins and prayers for forgiveness. The most important part is during the Additional Prayer, which includes a summary of Hebrew history from Adam to Aaron, and a description of the ancient temple service on the Day of Atonement.

In the ancient ritual of Leviticus the high priest sacrificed bullocks and goats and then, laying his hand on the head of a live goat, he confessed over it all the sins of Israel and drove the scapegoat away into the wilderness, bearing away the sins of the people. The high priest made confession of his own sins, those of the priesthood, then those of the people, and uttered the awful name of YHWH at which the congregation fell on their faces. The old ritual has gone, but the elders of the synagogue still prostrate themselves at the appropriate places in the ceremony.

The concluding service for the Day of Atonement ends with a long prayer, 'Our Father, our King'. Then comes the Shema, a blessing repeated three times, and 'The Lord, he is God' is repeated seven times. Then the ram's horn is sounded and the Day of Atonement is ended.

## MYSTICS AND REFORMERS

It is sometimes said that Judaism is unmystical because of its belief in the transcendent holiness of God. Yet there have been many Jewish writers and movements that are commonly called mystical. And it might be said that Islam is even more transcendentalist in its teaching about God but undoubtedly has harboured powerful mystical activities. If mysticism is an advanced stage of communion with God then Judaism has included it both in past and present, though with its own special emphases. Cabbalistic mystical ideas were popularized in the Hasidist movements from the eighteenth century onwards.

The Jewish Cabbalah had a long history and often included forms of Gnostic and magical belief, but its very name meant 'tradition' so that this doctrine of communion with the divine was regarded as traditional wisdom. We have seen the importance of history to Judaism, and the mystic sought to recapitulate the national history in his own inner experience; the Exodus must mean leaving an inner Egypt in which the soul is enslaved, the stages of creation should be reversed so as to lead man back to God the source of all life.

In the Zohar, the classic of medieval Jewish mysticism, there is a close approach to mystical union with God, and the use of love symbols such as are found in Muslim and Christian mysticism. The Torah calls men in love, like 'a beautiful and stately maiden who . . . has a lover of whose existence she alone knows'. And God, the Holy One, has a Palace of Love where every beloved soul enters, and God 'unites them with himself'. There is a long description of 'holy union' with God expressed in highly symbolical and paradoxical ways.

The Shekhinah, the glory of God, is seen in the Zohar as the daughter and bride of God. She is the Community of Israel, mother of every individual Jew, 'Rachel weeping for her children'. This symbol of eternal womanhood both stresses again the idea of union with God and brings into Judaism a feminine element that was lacking but became very important in mysticism.[1]

Yet the constant Jewish stress on the transcendence of God preserved it from pantheism. As against Hindu ideas of absorption into and identity with the divine, a modern Jewish mystic, Martin Buber, maintains the doctrine of relationship as fundamental to the understanding of God and man. 'God comprises, but is not, the universe. So, too, God comprises, but is not, my Self.' And again, 'God, the eternal Presence, does not permit Himself to be held. Woe to the man so possessed that he thinks he possesses God.'[2]

In the movements of Reform Judaism that have sprung up in

[1]G. G. Scholem, *Major Trends in Jewish Mysticism*, p. 230.
[2]M. Buber, *I and Thou*, pp. 95, 106.

the last century there has been revolt against much ceremonial and tradition. But the reformers sought not just to destroy but to 'return to the Bible', by which they meant not so much to the prescriptions of the Pentateuch as to the lofty teaching of the Prophets and the Psalmists. The ethical teaching of the Bible was stressed and serious studies made of the teaching of Jesus. This went along with the use of more prayers in modern languages and modification of synagogue customs. Much of this paralleled the general liberal movement in Europe and did not necessarily affect Jewish worship.

The rise of the Zionist cause, leading to the establishment of the State of Israel, is a vast subject beyond our scope. But in some ways it has served as a corrective to the extremes of liberalism; at a liberal *seder* a great thrill was felt when the leading minister announced that he had brought the roast lamb bone from the Holy Land only two days before. In Israel itself, along with much of a secular spirit, there is determination to put Jewish ways into practice. Hundreds of new synagogues have been built in the new towns, Hebrew culture and religion are promoted through college and university, and Jews of all schools of thought hope for the acceptance of the ideals for which Judaism has striven all down the ages.

## BIBLIOGRAPHY

Cohen, A. *Everyman's Talmud*, Dent, 1949.

Epstein, I. *Judaism*, Penguin, 1970.

Fishman, I. *Introduction to Judaism*, Mitchell, 1964.

Gaster, T. H. *Festivals of the Jewish Year*, New York, 1970.

Gould, J. and Esh, S., eds. *Jewish Life in Modern Britain*, Routledge, 1964.

Hertz, J. ed., *The Authorised Daily Prayer Book*, with commentary, Vallentine, 1949.

Jacobs, L. *Hasidic Prayer*, Routledge, 1972.

Lehrmann, S. M. *The Jewish Festivals*, Vallentine, 1948.

Munk, E. *The World of Prayer*, Feldheim, 1950.

Oesterley, W. O. E. and Box, G. H. *The Religion and Worship of the Synagogue*, Pitman, 1907.

# JUDAISM

Rabinowitz, J. *Worship and Wisdom*, Soncino, 1955.
Scholem, G. G. *Major Trends in Jewish Mysticism*, Thames and Hudson, 1955.
Simpson, W. W. *Jewish Prayer and Worship*, S.C.M., 1965.

## Chapter 11

# ISLAM

---

### The Prophet and the Prophets

Islam parallels numerous Jewish and Christian beliefs and traditions, since it was later in time, arising in the seventh century A.D., and it goes beyond these religions in its own way. The monotheism of Islam claims to be as absolute as that of Judaism.

The religion is called Islam, 'resignation' or surrender to the divine will. Its followers are called Muslims, from the same root. Muslims do not worship Muhammad and should not be called Muhammadans; but they believe that he was the last and seal of the prophets and the Apostle of God. There are many books available which sketch the life and career of Muhammad; here some attempt must be made to indicate his significance in religion today.

'I testify that there is no god but God. I testify that Muhammad is the Apostle of God.' This cry, repeated from every minaret and by every Muslim every day declares the unity of God and the supreme revelation brought by the Prophet.

In the orthodox Muslim teaching Muhammad was a man, born in the normal way, who declared 'I am no more than man.' But he is believed to be the greatest of all men, and his person is essential to Muslim faith. He is regarded as the Light of all the prophets that came before him, and his revelation completes all the rest. He is the greatest of men, and in one ancient poem is called 'second only to God'. In many mosques the name of Allah appears on the right-hand side of the wall towards which prayer is made and the name of Muhammad on the left.

Muslims believe that Muhammad is the Intercessor for mankind, and will be so at the Day of Judgement, pleading for sinful believers to come out of hell, and for the faithful that they may rise higher in paradise. Among the two hundred and one titles traditionally given to him are Intercessor, Mediator, Forgiver, Holy One, Holy Spirit. He has been called the Light of all light, the loveliest of men, a rose in a garden, a pearl in a shell, and through him all blessings flow.

Ancient mystics spoke of Muhammad's love as 'our nourishment' and 'the celebration of him life in our hearts.' Modern Muslim biographers call him Prophet and King, both sinless himself and Saviour of sinful humanity. Muslims have long dedicated their lives to Muhammad in the words, 'May my life be thy sacrifice, O Prophet of God.'[1]

So whenever the Muslim takes the name of the Prophet on his lips he says, 'Peace and blessings of God be upon him.' He never utters the mere name of Muhammad alone, but always adds the blessed evocation.

Six great prophets are said in Muslim teaching to have founded dispensations of religion, and they were all sinless and interceded for mankind. These were Adam, Noah, Abraham, Moses, Jesus and Muhammad; and some thirty biblical characters occur in the Qur'ān (Koran). Moses (Musa) was the great prophet to whom the Torah (Taurat) was revealed and who talked with God. He gave the Jews their religion, but they were held to have fallen away from the true worship and to have corrupted the Torah which was replaced by the Qur'ān.

The position of Jesus ('Īsā) in the Qur'ān and later teaching is important. He is called Son of Mary, Messiah, the Word, a Spirit, the Messenger, Servant and Prophet of God. His Virgin Birth is taught, and his miracles and raising the dead. The Crucifixion is denied, perhaps under the influence of Christian heretics who held that Jesus was an appearance and not a man, but the Ascension is

[1] M. Ali, *The Prophet Muhammad*, p. 25 f.; A. Ali, *The Spirit of Islam*, p. 121.

affirmed. The Trinity is denied, if it teaches that Mary and Jesus are two gods beside God: 'The Messiah, Jesus, son of Mary, is only an apostle of God, and his Word which he conveyed into Mary, and a Spirit proceeding from himself . . . God is only one God. Far be it from his glory that he should have a son.'[1]

The pious Muslim always adds to the name of Jesus the phrase, 'on whom be peace', and normally the same to the name of Mary as well. Jesus is said to have foretold the coming of Muhammad as the 'other Comforter' who would perfect his work. It is held that every Muslim will have Jesus as his witness in the resurrection; Jesus will come again first from heaven at the end of the world, to destroy evil and reign on earth and this will be followed by the Last Judgement. When the idea of a Mahdī, a 'directed one' or Guide who shall come, appeared later he was sometimes identified with Jesus. Mystics have referred to Jesus as the perfect type of man, and the great philosopher Al-Ghazālī said, 'take Jesus as your pattern'. Today Muslims will say that Christians have no monopoly of Jesus and there is no reason why a Muslim should not celebrate Christmas.

## THE UNITY OF GOD

The basic creed of Islam is called from the mosque and uttered by the Muslim daily: 'God is most great. There is no god but Allah. Muhammad is the Apostle of God.' (*Allāhu akbar. Lā ilāha illā 'llāhu. Muhammad rasūlu 'llāh*). The unity of God is expressed clearly in sura 112, which is often repeated after the first sura: 'Say: He is God alone: God the eternal. He begetteth not, and he is not begotten; and there is none like unto him.' On this sura the heavens and the earth are said to be founded.

The Qur'ān repeatedly refers to God as the One, Al-Wāhid. The unity of God was the great passion of Muhammad, against the idolatry and polytheism of the Arabs of his day. God is unborn and does not give birth. The miraculous birth of Jesus is explained

---

[1] *Qur'ān*, sura 4. See my *Jesus in the Qur'ān*.

in the words, 'God will create what he will; when he decreeth a thing, he only saith "Be", and it is.' (Sura 3.)

The gravest sin is *shirk*, that is 'association' of other beings with God, or 'attribution' to others of the worship and knowledge that belong to God alone. The positive opposite of this is *tawhīd*, the assertion of the unity of God in faith and life.

God is the creator and man the creature, God the king and man the slave. The common description of human status before God is that of servant or slave, *ʿabd,* a prefix in many names, e.g. ʿAbdu 'llāh. From man's dependent relationship comes the nature of religion as Islam, submission or surrender to the will of God. This is a recognition of the utter supremacy of God over the whole of life, and the absolute nature of his will and decrees.

Traditionally there are said to be ninety-nine names of God; these are the Beautiful Names. They are inscribed on monuments, e.g. the Taj Mahal tombs, and in mosques, and are found in the Muslim rosary in three arrangements of thirty-three beads. Devotional sects tell over these names, to the accompaniment of bodily movements helping to concentrate the mind on God.

The most important names of God are the twin titles, 'the Compassionate, the Merciful' (Al-Rahmān al-Rahīm). These are found in the great invocation, the Bismillāh ('in the name of God') which occurs at the beginning of every sura of the Qur'ān but one and runs, 'In the name of God, the Compassionate, the Merciful'.

The other names give attributes of God, or emanations of his essence: God as Creator, Provider, King, Reckoner, the Real, the True, the Light. 'God is the Light of the Heavens and of the Earth. His Light is like a niche in which is a lamp—the lamp is encased in glass—the glass as it were, a glistening star . . . It is light upon light. God guideth whom he will to his light, and God setteth forth parables to men, for God knoweth all things' (sura 24).

There are innumerable spiritual beings which are believed to people the universe, as in Jewish and Christian tradition, but they are all subordinate to God. Angels, headed by the four archangels, praise and serve God and intercede for men, asking 'forgiveness for the dwellers on earth' (sura 42). Guardian angels watch over man, take account of his deeds, and examine him in the faith when he dies. Demons, headed by Iblīs (from the Greek diabolos, devil), and jinns (genii) prowl about the earth and lower heavens. At the end of all things men will be weighed in the balances before God, and pass over a razor-sharp bridge from which the lost will fall into hell, and the blessed be admitted to paradise which is like the most glorious of gardens.

## QUR'ĀN AND SUNNA

The Qur'ān, the sacred Muslim scripture, is believed to be eternal, the uncreated Word of God in book form. This is somewhat akin to the Christian teaching of the Logos, the Word which became flesh, and it has been said that it is the Qur'ān and not Muhammad which occupies in Islam a place similar to that of Christ in Christianity. For this reason there has not been a critical approach to the Qur'ān among Muslims like that of Christians to the Bible. An ancient writer said, 'The Qur'ān is the speech of Allah, written in the copies, preserved in the memories, recited by the tongues, revealed to the Prophet.'

Faith in the revelation of God in the Qur'ān is essential to Islam, for it is the best and final revelation. The original of the Qur'ān, 'the mother of the Book', was kept in the seventh heaven in the presence of God, and it was sent down to the lowest heaven at the end of the sacred month of Ramadān and revealed in the Arabic tongue.

It is held that Muhammad was illiterate, and hence the words of the Qur'ān are not derived from other scriptures but are what he received from God. The angel Gabriel brought the divine word to Muhammad and told him to 'read' or 'recite' it. This was sura 98: 'Recite (read) in the name of thy Lord who created.' The word Qur'ān comes from a root meaning to read or recite what is written, and hence Qur'ān means 'recitation'. The whole or portions of the Qur'ān are learnt by every Muslim and recited by heart.

# ISLAM

The Qur'ān receives the highest veneration from all Muslims, to whatever sect they belong. No one must read it or touch it without washing himself ritually as for worship. When read it should be kept on a stand. Strictly it should not be translated, though there is relaxation of this rule nowadays for private reading. Even so the Arabic text should be printed beside the translation. When the Qur'ān is quoted in sermons it is in Arabic, with explanations in the vernacular. Its 114 suras or chapters were revealed to Muhammad over some twenty years, later written down, and variant copies destroyed. The Qur'ān is believed to be of universal application and for all time. Jews and Christians are still respected as 'people of a Book', but the Qur'ān is held to be far superior to other revelations which have been corrupted and which it outdates.

While the Qur'ān is the first authority for all Muslims, all sects also base their faith and practice on certain traditions. These are gathered together in 'six correct books', with variations in some sects. In addition to the written word in the Qur'ān there are also traditions (Hadith), sayings of and about the Prophet on religious and social matters. A Sunna ('path' or rule of acting) is derived from the Prophet's practice or directions.

The great majority of Muslims, over 80 per cent, are Sunnis, traditionists, followers of the path. Shī'a Muslims, 'followers' of 'Alī the cousin and son-in-law of the prophet in the later history, also have their traditions of the Prophet and other holy books. Pictures of 'Alī and other Saints are used in Shī'a lands.

The Shī'a believe in twelve Imāms, 'leaders', who succeeded Muhammad, and the final one is the Hidden Imām who will come again as the Mahdī, the 'guided one'. The Imāms, like the prophets, are said to have been sinless and infallible and to have interceded with God for their followers. Husain, 'Alī's son, in particular is the great intercessor who died for the sins of his people in the battle against the Sunni at Karbala in A.D. 680; his sufferings are relived annually in the Passion Play of Muharram. The chief strongholds of the Shī'a are in Persia, the Yemen, Iraq, Pakistan and India.

MOSQUES

Religious worship in Islam is both congregational and private. The great communal prayers on Fridays are akin to the Sabbath services of the Jews and the Sunday services of Christians. Islam is both eastern and western, but as the religion of a book of common prayer, study and exhortation form a large part of religious life.

The English word mosque is a corruption of the Arabic *masjid*, a 'place of prostration'. For prostration in prayer it is better to use the mosque, but the Muslim has his prayer mat which he can unroll anywhere, find the direction of Mecca, perform the ritual ablutions, and pray openly or in private.

The mosque is a rectangular building, with a large open court and a covered hall, usually full of pillars, which often support graceful cupolas. The building is orientated in the direction (*qibla*) of Mecca and of the sacred Ka'ba building in that city; this means that prayer is to the east from North Africa, but to the west for Muslims in China. The direction of prayer is indicated in the mosque by the *mihrāb*, a niche in the central wall, often decorated with mosaics, marbles or tiles. There is no sculpture or painting in the mosque, for representations of human or divine beings are except by Shī'a and some others forbidden, but the artistic instinct finds its outlet in lettering which adorns the walls, and the graceful architecture of many buildings.

The pulpit (*minbar*) stands in front of the end wall. It may be a small wooden stand, a brick desk, or a high narrow structure crowned with cupola, as in Egyptian mosques. The pulpit is for the sermon on Fridays. There may also be a wooden stand in one of the bays next to the *mihrāb* for reciters of the Qur'ān.

The minaret, which is usually the most conspicuous and graceful feature of the mosque is a lofty turret, perhaps derived originally from a watchtower for fire signals. Many of the larger mosques have a minaret at each corner. The addition of minarets to Saint Sophia in Constantinople in the fifteenth century gave the old cathedral an Islamic character.

From the minaret the people are called to prayer by the muezzin (*mu'azzin*), the caller of the summons to prayer. Perhaps as a substitute for the Christian clapper or bell, and the Jewish horn, the human voice is used and is very impressive and effective. Nowadays megaphones and electrical aids are used to give the call to prayer a wider scope. The prayer call has already been given in outline, and it is repeated several times.

There are no seats in the mosque, the floor being used for placing the mat, sitting and prostrating. In the centre of the courtyard of large mosques is usually a fountain or small tank. However in countries of heavy rainfall, like West Africa, the whole mosque may be roofed in and have no courtyard apart from narrow verandas. Near the doors there may be running taps for ritual washing, or bottles of water. There are often fine and high porches at the entrance to the courtyard. There is frequently a room near the *mihrāb* into which the dead are borne before burial.

Every day worshippers may assemble in the mosque at the hours of prayer to perform their devotions, and continue them there at other hours if they wish. There they find quiet, the true direction of Mecca, and conditions of ritual purity. Special groups or sects may say their litanies and set prayers on rosaries. Teachers give instruction in the mosque and it may serve as a meeting-place. Women may go to the mosque privately, but not to the Friday prayers.

The Friday prayer, in which all faithful males should take part, is held at the hour of the midday prayer. During this time all shops and market stalls should be closed, though there is no obligation to observe the whole day as a day of rest. General purification and donning of newly washed clothes are recommended for the occasion. The Friday prayer demands the presence of at least forty worshippers, hence only where the population is large enough are several mosques allowed to hold the prayer at the same time.

The public prayers are on the same model as the ritual of private prayer (to be described below), and the main special feature is the sermon preached by the Imām or prayer leader. The sermon is composed of praises, warnings and exhortations; it is often extemporary and very short, it may comment on social and political affairs but is not directed to outsiders since they may not normally attend Friday prayers. The Qur'ān is quoted in Arabic but sermons are in the language of the people.[1]

The Imām is not a priest, he is not set aside by any ordination, and while he holds the title he will have a secular occupation as well. Shī'a prayer leaders, in humility, stand in a small cavity below the level of the congregation.

## PRAYER AND DUTIES

Prayer is one of the five pillars or duties of Islam. Every Muslim is bound to recite the prayers five times a day although, as in other religions, there are always those who are content with less than the rule. Prayer involves more than words and so the word ṣalāt for prayer includes the actions of ritual devotion. The times of prayer are daybreak, just after midday, afternoon, evening and night. Prayer is made on a small mat or carpet (musallā).

First it is necessary to be in a state of legal purity. Generally this means a bath after sleep and washing at other times. The worshipper washes in this order: the face, hands, forearms to the elbow, the wet hand passed over the head, and lastly the feet. Then in clean clothes, or at least undefiled, he responds to the call of the muezzin from the minaret who has announced that the time for prayer has come. If he is out of earshot he judges the time for himself. If he cannot go to the mosque, and apart from Friday there is no obligation to do so, he lays down his mat facing Mecca.

Standing, with his head covered but barefoot, facing Mecca (i.e. the Ka'ba within it), he repeats the call to prayer and makes a muttered or silent intention to offer sincere worship. This intention (nīya) precedes every Muslim act of worship which is invalid without it. This states the intention: 'I perform at its proper time the prescribed Morning Worship to God'. Then raising his hands

[1]For an example and analysis of a typical sermon see K. Cragg, *Sandals at the Mosque*, p. 29 ff.

to his shoulders the worshipper utters the *takbīr*, the expression 'God is most great' (Allāhu akbar), the most characteristic word of Muslim devotion. Then with the left hand in the right he recites the first sura of the Qur'ān, the Fātiha ('opening'). First the Bismillāh, 'In the name of God, the Compassionate, the Merciful'. Then the sura:

> Praise be to God, Lord of the worlds,
> The compassionate, the merciful,
> King of the Day of Judgement.
> Thee only do we worship, and to thee do we cry for help.
> Guide thou us on the straight path.
> The path of those to whom thou hast been gracious,
> With whom thou art not angry, and who go not astray.

After this he may recite as many suras of the Qur'ān as he wishes, and usually says 112 (The Unity). He bows, placing his hands on his knees, and says *Allāhu akbar*. He stands upright and then proceeds to the prostration, which is the culminating point of the prayer. He kneels on the mat, stretches out his hands, and touches the ground between them with his brow; he sits up and prostrates again. Shī'a place their foreheads on tablets of Karbala clay.

The sequence of movements that make up a complete act of prayer is called a *rak'a*, and two, three or four of these may be needed to fulfil the required prayer (*salāt*) according to the time of the day. Each *rak'a* ends with the confession of faith: 'I testify that there is no god but God.' At the conclusion come formulas of blessing for Muhammad: 'O God, have mercy on Muhammad and on his descendants'. Then there is a final salutation to left and right, which some say is addressed to guardian angels: 'The peace and mercy of God be upon you.'

The same prayers, with only slight variations, are said by the Shī'a sects. So they are common to the whole Muslim world and are uttered daily by millions of lips.

The five pillars of Islam are Faith, Prayer, Alms, Fasting and Pilgrimage. Faith is summarized in the confession (*shahāda*) which has been quoted several times. The unity of God, that there is none like him, none associated with him, and that Muhammad is his greatest and final Prophet, are stated in this short creed.

Almsgiving (*zakāt*) was insisted on from the very first as a religious duty, and it shows the communal nature of the religion wherein a man owes a duty to his neighbours and the poor. There is no collection taken in the mosque but it is the duty of all Muslims to bring alms for use in the cause of God, to support the Muslim community and to spread the faith outwardly, and to help the poor and beggars. Almsgiving has been assessed at times as the tenth of one's goods and the amount one distributes legitimates the private property that one retains.

Fasting (*saum*) is obligatory on all Muslims during the twenty-eight days of the ninth month of the lunar year, Ramadān, the month in which the revelations of God are said to have come. During Ramadān all adult male and female Muslims must fast during the day-time, from the first light of dawn until complete darkness at night. Children, the sick, pregnant women, and travellers are excused fasting, though the latter are expected to make it up some other time. Muslims keep the fast rigorously and abstain from all food, drink, smoking and sexual intercourse; after dark large meals may be taken. Fasting is very trying in dry lands and in the northern summer, when Ramadān falls then, when the hours of daylight are long.

The pious may fast at other times, though not on festival days, and may spend the time of Ramadān in additional prayers in the mosque. It is a time of special devotion and some repeat the whole Qur'ān during this month. Special fasts are observed by the Shī'a during the time of Muharram (see later). Fasts and special exercises may precede special prayers for rain, so much needed in the dry lands where Islam is strongest.

Jihād (holy war) was first enjoined in defence of the faith against its persecutors, and later to propagate it against idolaters. The Jihād was not exalted into one of the five pillars of Islam and schools of law defined its scope carefully as defensive and only to be undertaken on refusal of conversion and where there was a

good chance of success. The mystics and numerous modern inter-
preters saw the great Jihād as war against sin in one's own heart.

The fifth duty, Pilgrimage, is so important that it will be described in a section of its own. But before that a brief account will
be given of some of the main festivals of Islam.

## FESTIVALS

The fast of Ramadān ends with the little feast, the 'Īd al Fitr (or
Little Bairām in Turkish). It is celebrated with great joy and
feasting as soon as the new moon appears, and is the most popular
feast since it comes after the exhausting month's fast of Ramadan.
After sunrise everybody dresses in new or clean clothes, and the
men go to the mosque for prayers and sermon. Friends visit each
other's houses and presents are exchanged, often cakes and sweets
and greeting cards. Many families visit the graves of their relatives,
say prayers there, and give food to the poor.

The Great Festival, 'Īd al-Kabīr (also called 'Īd al-qurbān, or
Baqar-'Īd; Bairām in Turkish) is obligatory on every Muslim who
has the means of buying a sacrificial animal. This is for the sacrifice
which corresponds to part of the ritual of pilgrimage (see below).
Hence it takes place in the twelfth month, the month of pilgrimage, even for those who have not gone to Mecca. It is connected
in tradition with Abraham's sacrifice of the sheep instead of his
son (Ishmael in popular Muslim tradition, as father of the Arabs).

A fast precedes the feast, and food is prepared over which
prayers are made in the names of the Prophet and those of deceased relatives. In many parts there are praying-grounds in the
open air and thither the people go on the morning of the feast.
Prayers are made, with a sermon, and then sheep sacrificed, or it
may be a cow or a camel. Each head of a household slays his own
family animal, though a butcher may do it for him. The animal is
placed with its head towards Mecca and killed with one blow by
a thrust in the throat with a knife, while Quranic verses are recited.
If there is no praying-ground the prayers are said in the mosque
and sacrifice made at home. The flesh of the animal is cooked and

eaten by the family, and after that neighbours and the poor should have a share. Rich families may kill a sheep for each member of the family. After the feasting is over the cemeteries are visited.

The Sunnis strictly only have the Greater and Lesser Feasts, though others are added in places for favourite saints. The Birthday of the Prophet (Maulid an-Nabī) has become popular in many lands, following the example of Christmas.

Muharram, the first month of the Islamic year, begins with a ten-day commemoration among the Shīʿa sects of the martyrdoms of ʿAlī and his sons Hasan and Husain. By Sunni Muslims the tenth day only is observed and that as a memorial of creation: Adam and Eve, heaven and hell, life and death, are said to have been created on this day.

To the Shīʿa, that is in Persia and the Yemen, much of Iraq, Pakistan and India, this is the great occasion for the performance of the Passion Play. Karbala, where Husain was killed, is the greatest Shīʿa shrine. It is a place of innumerable tombs, for many aged Shīʿa come to die here or ask for their bodies to be brought after death, since it is held that those who die by the sanctuary will be sure of entry into paradise. Husain is called 'the bond of reconciliation with God on the Day of Judgement'.

Some days before the festival, in all Shīʿa towns, black tents are erected in the streets, adorned with draperies, arms and candles. Shīʿa standards are set up showing Fātima's hand, or ʿAlī's hand, indicating by its five fingers the five members of the Prophet's family: Muhammad, Fātima, ʿAlī, Hasan and Husain.

In these 'ten-day houses' the people assemble on the first of Muharram, in mourning clothes and unshaven. From pulpits the story of Husain is narrated and chanted in great detail, while the audience sit on the ground, beat their breasts, cry 'Husain, Husain!' and weep. This goes on throughout the day, different preachers taking their turns. Groups of men go round the streets during the first nine days of Muharram with their half-naked bodies dyed black or red, beating themselves, pulling out their hair, dragging chains, cutting themselves with swords and performing wild dances. Fights often take place with Sunnis during

ISLAM

these processions, since the first three Caliphs after Muhammad (which the Shī'a reject) are abused.

The festival culminates in the Passion Play which re-enacts the sufferings and burial of Husain. On a stage some forty or fifty scenes portray prophets and angels foretelling the events of Husain's life, the happenings at the Battle of Karbala, the wicked Caliph Yazīd who ordered Husain's death, and the progress of the severed head of the martyr. These are witnessed with great excitement, and at times the audience has tried to lynch actors representing villains. The chief points are the exposition of the meaning of the sacrifice of Husain, and the value of his intercession, which are set out with great clarity. At the end Gabriel brings the key of intercession from God, and tells Muhammad to give it to Husain. Husain receives the key with the injunction, 'Go thou and deliver from the flames every one who has in his life-time shed but a single tear for thee, every one who has in any way helped thee, every one who has performed a pilgrimage to thy shrine, or mourned for thee, and every one who has written tragic verse for thee. Bear each and all with thee to Paradise.'[1]

## PILGRIMAGE

The pilgrimage (*hajj*) to Mecca is one of the five duties of Islam, obligatory on every adult Muslim at least once in his life, and to be performed at the due season, the twelfth month, so as to be part of a sequence of ceremonial actions. The Muslim who has performed the pilgrimage bears henceforth the honorific title of Hājjī, and in some places dyes his beard red.

The pilgrimage is the great bond of the Muslim world, a sacrament of unity. Nowadays about a million people go to Mecca every year. Special ships and aeroplanes bring pilgrims from afar, others walk great distances on foot. The city of Mecca, set in a dry waste, lives on the pilgrimage trade.

The pilgrimage to Mecca was pre-Islamic and people came

[1] S. Pelly, *The Miracle Play of Hasan and Husain*, quoted in G. E. von Grunebaum, *Muhammadan Festivals*, p. 94.

from many parts of Arabia to visit the shrine of the Ka'ba and kiss the Black Stone, an aerolite set in its wall. Muhammad incorporated this into Islam and said that the shrine had been built by Abraham and Ishmael. 'The first temple that was founded for mankind was that in Mecca; blessed, and a guide to human beings. In it are evident signs, even a standing-place of Abraham, and he who entereth it is safe. And the pilgrimage to the temple is a service due to God, from those who are able to journey thither.'[1]

The Ka'ba (a word meaning 'cube') is a cube-like stone building, about twelve yards long, ten yards wide, and ten yards high. In its south-east corner is the Black Stone, an oval of seven inches in diameter, of black and granitic appearance, and surrounded by a silver band. The Ka'ba is completely covered with a black cotton and silk cloth (*kiswa*) which comes from Cairo and is renewed every year. Verses of the Qur'ān are embroidered on it in ancient characters. The Ka'ba is only open for a few days in the year, or on special request by rich visitors, ordinary pilgrims do not enter it. The interior is unfurnished except for gold and silver lamps hanging from the ceiling. The building is surrounded by a sloping terrace, and then by an immense square courtyard, with colonnades on the four sides and porticoes, and with minarets at the corners and elsewhere.

A pavilion stands at some distance from the wall of the Ka'ba, enclosing a sacred stone bearing the footprints of Abraham, the reputed builder of the Ka'ba. Another building contains the graves of Hagar, Ishmael, and various prophets. A domed pavilion covers the well of Zamzam, an ancient sacred spring from which Muhammad drank and which pilgrims drink today. Farther on is a stone and marble pulpit where the Imām delivers the Friday sermon.

There are many other sacred buildings and tombs in Mecca but visits to them do not form part of the ritual of pilgrimage. Visits used to be made to the house of Khadīja, the Prophet's first wife, the house of Muhammad's birth, 'Ali's house and other dwellings of his companions. The Wahhābī sect which now controls Arabia

[1] Sura 3.

has destroyed some of the tombs, and forbidden practices that suggested worship of Muhammad and his family.

The whole district of Mecca is holy ground (*harām*). As the pilgrim enters it he utters a prayer of thanks and sanctification of God. He must come in pilgrim dress, which is two lengths of cloth which leave arms and right shoulder bare. Women wear the *burqa'*, the complete veil which covers them from head to feet. Pillars on the road to the town indicate where the pilgrim dress must be put on.

On entering Mecca the pilgrim goes to the great mosque, the Masjid al-Ḥarām, crossing the threshold with his right foot. He traverses the court to the Ka'ba and kisses the Black Stone (or gets as near as he can through the great crowds), then goes round it seven times anti-clockwise, keeping it on his left and trying to touch the stone each time round. Then he goes to pray behind Abraham's shrine. He leaves the mosque and goes to two near-by hills, Safā and Marwa, reciting verses of the Qur'ān.

The pilgrimage proper begins on the seventh day of the month (the month of pilgrimage, Dhū 'l-Ḥijjah) with a sermon in the mosque. On the following day processions go to a hill called 'Arafāt, on foot, or by camel, and motor car. The night is spent there by the thousands of pilgrims, and on the evening of the next day there is a great rush back to the sacred valley of Minā, near Mecca, where stones are cast on to a cairn and animals sacrificed with the ritual observed elsewhere at the same time in the Great Festival (Bairām). Then the pilgrim has his head shaved, washes and having circumambulated the Ka'ba again the pilgrimage is complete. Some return to Minā for several days and cast more stones. Pilgrims generally stay a few more days in Mecca, and take some Zamzam water home with them and pieces of old *kiswa* cloth.

Pilgrims usually go on to visit the tomb of the Prophet at Medina, some two hundred miles to the north of Mecca. Medina too is holy ground though visit to it is not part of the pilgrimage ritual. The Prophet's mosque is in the oldest part of the town, it arose round his tomb and is a vast rambling structure. There are marks where the Prophet's pulpit stood, the pillars against which he leaned and many other memorials. A wooden screen surrounds the tomb and this the pilgrim kisses and utters invocations. Other graves of early heroes may also be visited.

Some pilgrims who can afford time and money may go on to Jerusalem. The Holy City is sacred for Islam, as well as for Judaism and Christianity, and is mentioned in the Qur'ān, hence the importance attached to keeping it within the Arab world. Here the centre of interest is the great mosque, the Dome of the Rock, 'Omar's mosque', on the site of the old Jewish temple, where according to ancient tradition Muhammad left his footprint.

## RELICS AND SAINTS

In a historical religion the veneration tends to be accorded to relics of saints, that elsewhere is given to symbols of gods. The mystical virtue of the saint, his blessing or supernatural power (*baraka*) is believed in the Muslim world to be available to those who follow him or touch some object associated with him. The holy person may be alive or if he is dead then his tomb becomes the centre of his *baraka*.

The saints may have been great mystics, emperors, tribal chiefs, founders of religious brotherhoods, or wild dervishes. The shrine may be simply of local interest, or a sanctuary that is the centre of pilgrimage. For example, at Ajmer in India is the tomb of Chishti, one of a family of saints which has other graves in towns nearby. To Ajmer the great emperor Akbar used to come on an annual visit. The tomb is inside a mosque courtyard, in a white building with a silver door. The tomb itself is square and silver-plated, guarded by a family which takes payment from visitors. Pilgrims come with offerings of flowers and coconuts and pray kneeling at the tomb. Women come to pray for children, while the room in which the tomb stands is hung with horse shoes from dealers who have given them in thanks for successful deals.

At many shrines relics of the Prophet or his companions are treasured, and there is a tradition that whenever he trod on a rock his foot left its mark in the stone. In Delhi, for example, the

Mughal emperors gathered together a reliquary which contained the reputed shroud of the Prophet, one of his sandals, a red hair from his beard, part of ʿAlī's Qurʾān, and two Qurʾāns of Husain, and these are still shown to visitors. Other great mosques have their own collections of relics.

Many of the tombs of the saints are on the site of old pagan shrines, replacing those that stood at springs, wells, trees, stones and hilltops, 'on every high hill and under every green tree'. As in Catholic Europe old shrines and customs were baptized into the new religion. The shrine is connected with some holy man, a shaikh whose life story may be forgotten or legendary but whose *baraka* lives on. His protecting influence extends over the locality or tribe which reveres him. His shrine is a holy place which extends its sanctity to all that is done there.

Festivals are held on the saint's birthday, with prayers in the mosque and processions, and in many places these are very popular events. The saint is called 'friend of God' and the divine blessing is invoked upon him. As in other religions there are many popular practices which the more orthodox or educated would not take much part in.

In the Qurʾān it is stated that Noah prayed for forgiveness for himself and for his parents, and that Abraham promised to do the same for his father. In the traditions Muhammad visited his mother's grave and wept there. It has been a common practice down the ages to visit graves and pray for relatives. At both Great and Little Festivals the cemeteries are visited and broken palm branches are laid on graves. Prayers are said there and sometimes the whole Qurʾān is recited by professionals. Women may spend the whole day in the cemetery, especially if the family has a house there.

## MYSTICAL DEVOTION

The way of love or devotion to God, which was marked out by the Ṣūfī mystics, was already expressed in the traditional saying attributed to Muhammad: 'O Lord, grant to me the love of thee; grant that I love those that love thee; grant that I may do the deeds that win thy love; make thy love dearer to me than self, family and wealth.'

The name Ṣūfī for the mystic is most likely to be derived from ṣūf, wool, from the simple woollen clothes that the mystics wore, like the Christian ascetics. It is no accident that the movement flourished in Persia, a land which had been Zoroastrian, had Hindu and Christian influences, and finally became Muslim of the Shī'a school. From there the Ṣūfīs not only spread a movement of deep devotion throughout Islam, but also influenced both the Sikhs and the *bhakti* cults in India.

Many Ṣūfīs were men and women of great sanctity and wide sympathy. Others gave more prominence to ecstasy and the dances of dervishes. In more pedestrian manner today many repeat litanies on the divine name (*dhikr*) and seek to advance by slow stages through devout prayers and performance of duties.

The unity of God and his complete transcendence are central to Islam, and the great sin of *shirk* is the notion that anyone could share God's glory. But the Ṣūfīs taught the sinking of the self through love of God. Rābi'a of Basra said that the love of God had so possessed her that no room remained even for hating Satan. 'Love has come from Eternity and passes into Eternity and none has been found in seventy thousand worlds who drinks one drop of it until at last he is absorbed in God.'[1]

The doctrine of utter transcendence and of predestination through omnipotent divine will could lead, strangely enough, to near-pantheism. For the infinite distance between God and man can be annihilated by God, and if God is all there is nothing beside him, the distinction of subject and object seems to disappear. So the Ṣūfīs taught of *fanā*, the passing away of consciousness in mystical union, and this could lead to identity of God and man. So Ibnu 'l-Fārid, an Arabian mystic of the thirteenth century, said that between God and himself 'the pronoun of the second person has gone out of use', and again 'Both of us are a single worshipper . . . None prayed to me but myself.'[2]

[1] M. Smith, *Rābi'a the Mystic*, p. 100.
[2] R. A. Nicholson, *The Idea of Personality in Ṣūfism*, p. 19 f.

It may well be understood how the orthodox reacted against one of the most famous mystics, Hallāj, saying 'I am the Real'. Yet while insisting on the mystical union with God, and abolition of self-will, Hallāj maintained the transcendence of God and his otherness from the creature. But he also set his personal experience against the claims of church and state and was crucified, yet even in death prayed for his persecutors.

One of the greatest of Ṣūfīs was Jalālu'l Dīn Rūmī who died in 1273. His popular Mathnawī, 'spiritual couplets', has been called the Qur'ān of Persia. He founded mystical dances, said to represent the revolution of the planets round the sun, which were perhaps the beginnings of the Dancing Dervishes. Rūmī ranges over the whole expanse of doctrine and religion, finding God even in Pharaoh's hard heart, and in the disobedience of Iblīs, as well as in the different ways of Christian and Muslim, Jew, Hindu and Zoroastrian. Love is the secret of them all, for the lamps are different but the Light is the same; 'the lovers of God have no religion but God alone.'[1]

The Ṣūfīs often aroused opposition but they served as a tonic to formalism and rigidity. They came eventually to be accepted by the orthodox largely due to the efforts of the great Persian philosopher, Al-Ghazālī, himself a follower of the mystic way, who died in A.D. 1111. It became recognized that revelations given to saints can supplement those of prophets, yet sainthood derives from prophecy and appeal was constantly made to the supreme authority of Muhammad.

The Ṣūfī movement developed among the Sunni away from the sole personal approach to God into associations of brotherhoods, 'seekers', who traced their descent through the saints back to the Prophet. The dervish fraternities are today numerous among the masses of the people, and many laymen follow them in a way that has been compared with that of the Franciscan tertiaries. The laity do not live in monasteries, but go there occasionally and take part in processions on great days. They take vows to follow daily or weekly religious rituals.

[1]R. A. Nicholson, *Rūmī*, p. 171 f.

# MYSTICAL DEVOTION

The Ṣūfī orders have been attacked in modern times for the superstition into which many of them degenerated and their reactionary influence in face of new social and political situations. But their influence is widespread and there have been revivals in countries, like Turkey, which sought to suppress them. Many holy men, Shaikhs or Marabouts, exercise great influence and are looked to for spiritual guidance and help. Nowadays there are mosques in Western countries, and in Britain, the first was built at Woking in 1889.

## BIBLIOGRAPHY

Calverley, E. E. *Worship in Islam*, 2nd ed., Luzac, 1957.
Cragg, K. *The Call of the Minaret*, Oxford, 1965.
Cragg, K. *The Dome and the Rock*, S.P.C.K., 1964.
Cragg, K. *Sandals at the Mosque*, S.C.M., 1959.
Gaudefroy-Demombynes, M. *Muslim Institutions*, Allen and Unwin, 1950.
Gilsenan, M. *Saint and Sufi in Modern Egypt*, Oxford, 1973.
Grube, E. *The World of Islam*, Hamlyn, 1966.
Grunebaum, G. E. von. *Muhammadan Festivals*, Schumann, 1958.
Guillaume, A. *The Life of the Muhammad*, Oxford, 1955.
Kamal, A. *The Sacred Journey*, Allen and Unwin, 1964.
Lings, M. *A Moslem Saint of the Twentieth Century*, Allen and Unwin, 1961.
Nicholson, R. A. *The Mystics of Islam*, 2nd. edn., Routledge, 1966.
Nicholson, R. A., *Rūmī, Poet and Mystic*, Allen and Unwin, 1950.
Padwick, C. E. *Muslim Devotions*, S.P.C.K., 1960.
Parrinder, E. G. *Jesus in the Qur'ān*, Faber, 1965.
Rahman, F., *Islam*, Weidenfeld, 1966.
Smith, W. C. *Islam in Modern History*, Oxford, 1957.
Trimingham, J. S. *The Sufi Orders in Islam*, Oxford, 1971.
Watt, W. M. *Muhammad, Prophet and Statesman*, Oxford, 1961.

*Chapter 12*

# CHRISTIANITY

I n discussing one's own religion several difficulties appear. There is so much known material, from a lifetime's acquaintance with one or more forms of the religion, that it is hardy to attempt a complete and balanced picture of the worship of the whole. Yet while the believer tries to maintain detachment and impartiality there is one sense in which the religious outsider may have better viewpoints, distinguishing the wood from the trees, and all the insider can do is to make rough estimates and judgements. Nevertheless the attempt must be made, in a survey of all religions, and since everyone is brought up in some religious environment each has some bias. We shall try to be objective, but pardon is craved for admitted inadequacy.

## CHRIST AND THE TRINITY

Christianity has always accepted and cherished the title 'Christian' for its members, who were 'first called Christians at Antioch' in Syria in the first century. The very name of the religion implies an attitude to its founder that Islam, for example, has not consciously adopted towards Muhammad. By its devotion to and worship of its founder, Christianity has expressed a faith that is only paralleled in Mahāyāna Buddhism. At the same time, Christianity, like Judaism and Islam, insists on a monotheistic belief in God and solves its dilemma by the doctrine of the Trinity.

That Jesus the carpenter-prophet of Nazareth was the Messiah or Christ, the 'anointed One', expected by the Jews as sent by God to deliver his people, was the faith which Jesus inspired in his disciples. He was not just an ethical teacher, indeed moral teachings were only incidental to his main message, which was the Kingdom of God which he was to inaugurate. At the crucifixion the faith of the disciples received a cruel shock, but it was re-established and reinforced by the resurrection experiences. Henceforth their faith was in a risen and glorified Christ: 'God hath made him both Lord and Christ, this Jesus whom ye crucified' (Acts 2, 36). Faith in Christ and the resurrection were cardinal points from which the Christian creed began and on which it has ever depended. The 'scandal' of the Cross showed the true humanity and vicarious suffering of the Christ and revealed the deep wisdom of God in reconciling mankind to himself.

Adoration of Christ is expressed early in the New Testament. Peter fell on his knees before the Messiah and said, 'Depart from me, for I am a sinful man, O Lord'. Stephen in his martyr's agonies saw Jesus standing to help him at the right hand of God and commended to him his soul, 'Lord Jesus, receive my spirit.' While Thomas is reported to have said to the risen Christ, 'My Lord and my God.' The effect of these acts of faith in Christ, and many other suggestive statements in the epistles, gradually worked up to the doctrine of the Trinity.

Paul was not a distorter of a simple ethical message, as some nineteenth century critics thought, but the great liberator of Christianity from Pharisaic legalism by taking the Gospel to non-Jews. In doctrine this ex-Pharisee stressed the majesty of Christ, and there is no evidence that any other Christians disagreed with this emphasis. He taught the incarnation, the coming of Christ as a man: 'Christ Jesus, being in the form of God, counted it not a prize to be on an equality with God, but emptied himself, taking the form of a servant, being made in the likeness of men' (Phil. 2). So he came to a cosmic conception of Christ, as agent of creation, 'Who is the image of the invisible God, the firstborn of all creation; for in him were all things created . . . he is before all things, and in him all things consist' (Col. 1, 15 f.).

Similar teaching is given by other writers, and notably in the prologue to the Fourth Gospel, where Christ is shown as existing from eternity and agent of creation: 'In the beginning was the Logos, the Logos was with God, the Logos was divine . . . all things were made through him.'

There has never been any doubt in Christian faith about the supremacy of Christ. He is first the historical and suffering Son of Man, but then also he is the pre-existent Christ, the Word become flesh, crucified, risen and alive for evermore. As long as the New Testament retains its place as the chief scripture of the Church, the doctrine of the divinity of Christ can never be widely rejected among Christians. But this raised serious problems on the nature of the godhead.

That God was Father was already taught in Judaism and emphasized by Jesus. The relationship of Christ to God was described as that of 'son', Son of God and Son of Man. The term 'son', which later in crude expositions gave offence to Muhammad, was not meant to be more than symbolical. There was never any suggestion of a divine family polytheism, father, mother and son. The Holy Spirit was the third person, and the Virgin Mary had not attained in the early centuries to that prominence for devotion that she was later to occupy. The relationship of Christ to the Father was expressed in such halting phrases as 'begotten, not made', so as to distinguish Christ from creation, like the divine Wisdom in Proverbs 8. The Logos was 'in the beginning with God'.

The word Trinity that came to express the orthodox doctrine was first used by Tertullian at the end of the second century, but there are trinitarian formulas in the New Testament (Matt. 28, 29; 2 Cor. 13, 14). The controversies that arose in the fourth century ranged round the question was Christ *homos*, of the 'same' substance with the Father, or was he *homoios*, simply 'like' the Father? The difference of the letter 'i' to the creed (which Carlyle ridiculed) was vital to the whole matter, and eventually the Church decided for the former and incorporated in the Nicene Creed the faith in Christ as 'Very God of very God'. This creed is recited in the Mass and Communion services of most churches today.

Certain reservations should be noted. Christ is Son, he is not God the Father but is subordinate to the Father. The medieval phrase 'God became man' is open to the objection that it might seem to imply the whole Godhead, whereas it is the Son of God who becomes man. Thus the use of the word Son ensures the recognition of the infinite nature of the Father and the incarnation of the Christ.

In Christian worship the place of Christ is assured, praises especially are addressed to him. But it is noteworthy that the great majority of liturgical prayers are made to God the Father 'through Jesus Christ our Lord'. In the Book of Common Prayer, which contains many ancient catholic prayers, only few and modern prayers are addressed direct to Christ.

The Holy Spirit, the third person of the Trinity, is the presence of God and his power as revealed on the day of Pentecost. He is also the one 'who spake by the prophets', thus linking the inspiration of the Old Testament with the New, and providing a means of connecting other manifestations of religion also with the New Covenant in Christ. The Church has been slow to recognize what a valuable doctrine is here, and it could be helpful today in bringing understanding of other religions.

## THE SAINTS AND THE VIRGIN

Christianity has shared with Judaism and Islam beliefs in angelic appearances, of which there are many accounts in the Bible. Guardian angels watch over churches and men, and especially protect children: 'In heaven their angels do always behold the face of my Father' (Matt. 18, 10). Doctrines of angels and demons have receded in modern Protestantism, though not in Orthodox and Catholic belief. Even so there are many Protestants who learnt as children the rhyme calling on apostles and angels to watch round the bed.

In the early Church, members of the family who had 'fallen asleep' were remembered in prayer, and soon requests came to be made for the help of the departed on behalf of the survivors: 'in

thy prayers ask for us, because we know thou art in Christ'.[1]
Prayers for the dead became part of the public and private devotions in the Greek and Roman communions. Suppressed because of abuses at the Reformation, they were permitted in modified form in the Revised Anglican Prayer Book of 1928. Many individual Protestants have prayed for their dear departed, and a Presbyterian writer says, 'No one, for instance, can logically object to such intercession who believes in future probation, or who thinks that the souls of the blessed gradually develop in holiness after they have departed this life.'[2]

The martyrs who gave their blood for Christ in the persecutions of Christians in the first three centuries came to be highly honoured, their bones enshrined, and their prayers asked for. To their number were added many popular names, of ascetics, saints, and other figures 'baptized' into Christianity. Originally prayers were made *for* the saints, but these were replaced by prayers *to* them, or at least requesting their intercession with God. At the Reformation the English Church rejected many festivals of saints, and retained those of apostles, evangelists, the Virgin, Stephen, the Innocents, and St. Michael and All Angels.

It was natural that the mother of Jesus, saluted in the Gospel as 'blessed among women', should be honoured among the greatest saints. However she was not a martyr and her cult arose slowly, until stimulated by controversy. Nestorius, patriarch of Constantinople, spoke in 428 against the title 'Mother of God' (theotokos, God-bearer) for the Virgin, and said the proper title was 'Mother of Christ'. His opponents supported the former phrase, as necessary to the doctrine of the divinity of Christ, and popular devotion to the Virgin upheld it. Festivals of the Virgin increased; the phrase 'Mother of God, and ever-virgin' were put into liturgies in East and West. The salutation 'Hail Mary' (Ave Maria) which ends 'Holy Mary, mother of God, pray for us sinners, now and at the hour of our death', is recited daily by millions in Orthodox and Catholic lands.

[1] H. P. V. Nunn, *Christian Inscriptions*, p. 57.
[2] J. H. Leckie, *The World to Come and Final Destiny*, p. 100.

The belief in the Immaculate Conception of the Virgin was made a dogma in the Roman Church in 1854, and her bodily ascension (assumption) to heaven was accepted in 1950. Rejected by Protestants, these doctrines have been claimed by the psychologist C. G. Jung as recognition of the feminine side of the deity, similar to Kwanyin in Buddhism.

Many devotions to the Virgin have been instituted in the West. Votive offices are said to her every Saturday and during the whole of May, 'Mary's month'. There are special Sundays celebrating her Most Holy Name, Seven Sorrows, Sacred Heart, Rosary, Motherhood, Purity and Patronage. Theologians have distinguished the invocation or homage (dulia) due to saints, the special homage (hyperdulia) to Mary and the worship (latria) offered to God alone.

## RELICS, SYMBOLS AND PILGRIMAGES

Since other religions have relics of founders and saints it is not surprising that there should have been many in Christianity, especially after the ages of martyrdom. In the Middle Ages pilgrims from the Holy Land brought back souvenirs, many of which were claimed as portions of the True Cross, and every great church had its quota as well as local relics of its own.

The importance of relics for church altars has remained in the Roman Catholic Church, where every altar must contain the relic of at least one saint and no priest may say Mass without the presence of a relic. But in the catechism children are taught, 'we do not pray to relics or images, for they can neither see nor hear nor help us'.

At first there was a distrust of pictures and imagery, inherited from Judaism, but in the Roman catacombs frescoes remain to this day dating from the second and third centuries and depicting Biblical scenes. Later the great growth of the use of images led to Iconoclastic controversies, and efforts were made to ensure that veneration but not worship was accorded to icons.

In the Eastern churches today icons, but not statues, are

everywhere. The icon is a picture of Christ, the Virgin, a saint, or a group of holy figures. It is often framed in a metal cover which leaves only the face and hands of the picture visible. Icons are found in all churches, and in many public buildings, shops and houses. They are carried about by travellers and used in prayers and processions. Only the Nestorians have no icons but a plain cross, to which they pay great reverence.

When the great Gothic cathedrals were built in the West they were adorned with masses of statuary unsurpassed anywhere except in India. In Roman Catholic churches today there are many images, and before them candles burn and the faithful kneel to pray to Christ, the Virgin or the saint represented. No difference is made between a picture or a statue.

In Lutheran churches pictures have been retained, though not prayers before them. In the English cathedrals the authorities generally managed to preserve much of the glass at the Reformation. Some of the Anglo-Catholic churches have introduced images but this is not general in the Anglican Church. The cross has been restored, but more rarely the crucifix representing the crucified body of Christ.

The bareness of many Reformed and Nonconformist churches is notorious, but today many of them have stained-glass windows and the cross appears with increasing frequency; flowers are used for decoration and a certain amount of wood carving is found and occasional paintings.

Christian art has been particularly rich in painting, and splendid triptychs have decorated many altars. Many medieval painters did not hesitate to depict all the celestial world and even God the Father; William Blake did the same in England. In modern times many churches call on painters and sculptors for decoration, e.g. Jacob Epstein and Henry Moore, Stanley Spencer and Graham Sutherland.

As in other religions, pilgrimages have occupied a large place in different periods of Christianity. These have been to famous cathedrals and shrines connected with saints and martyrs, and especially to the Holy Land. Both in East and West many devout people have hoped one day to go to Palestine and see for themselves the site of the sacred story and the great shrines which the churches have erected there.

In the West some of the most popular modern pilgrimages have been to Lourdes in southern France, where Bernadette Soubirous had visions of the Virgin Mary in 1858. Thither innumerable sick people have travelled and the grottoes are hung with the crutches of those who have been healed. Other popular modern pilgrimage centres are at Fatima and Lisieux.

## EASTERN ORTHODOX CHURCHES AND SERVICES

The Orthodox churches claim to be the oldest in Christendom and use the title of Holy and Catholic, Orthodox and Apostolic. Although the national churches are separately organized, they are one body through their common faith, government and worship. All are in communion with the Ecumenical Patriarch of Constantinople and with each other.

The worship of the Orthodox churches is a great uniting factor. There is no common ritual language, each nation having its own liturgical tongue which, however, is often not the vernacular. But the shape of the church and the order of the liturgy are substantially the same throughout Orthodoxy.

The central plan of the Orthodox Church, despite additional chapels and baptisteries, is that of a square Greek cross of which the central part is covered by a dome. Walls and roof are decorated with paintings and mosaics. High up in the dome is the picture of Christ, surrounded by rainbows, cherubim and seraphim.

Normally there have been no seats in Orthodox churches, since the congregation stands at worship; but nowadays many churches provide seats along the walls or back-rests with small seats. The choir stands in one transept, often out of sight. The singing is of great beauty and is unaccompanied by any instrument.

The east end of the church is completely closed off by the Iconostas, the great screen that hides the altar. It may be of wood, brick or stone, and is pierced by three doors of which double ones, the Royal Doors in the centre, reveal the altar when open. The Iconostas is covered with icons. The chief scene is above the doors where Christ sits in glory, with the Virgin and the Baptist to right and left and angels and apostles on either side. In other parts are the evangelists, the patron saint of the church, the Annunciation and the Last Supper. There are also pictures of Old Testament prophets and patriarchs, thus completing the Old and New Covenants with the angelic hosts in attendance.

The great act of corporate worship is the Liturgy, the Orthodox name for the Mass or Holy Communion, which may be said in any language. On entering the church the worshipper kisses a central icon picture, bows before it, crosses himself, says a prayer, and perhaps lights a candle. He stands, kneels or crosses himself during the service as devotion moves him. There are no congregational hymns, but there are responses, and he may join in the Lord's Prayer and the Creed.

The laity arrive on Sundays at the Liturgy of the Catechumens, which is preceded by a priestly preparation of the elements. Litanies, anthems and psalms lead up to the chief feature of this part of the service, which is the reading of Epistle and Gospel. The Epistle is chanted while the deacon censes sanctuary and congregation. Then comes what is called the Little Entrance, in which the Gospel book is brought out through the Royal Doors, chanted to the people, and then carried back to the altar.

The Liturgy of the Faithful follows on this directly; the catechumens used to depart here but now they stay on. It begins with a short prayer. Then comes the Great Entrance. The clergy, led by lighted candles, come out of the north door of the screen; the deacon carries the veiled paten (plate) on his head and the censer on his shoulder, the priest follows with the chalice. The people cross themselves, kneel or bow, while the procession enters the Royal Doors which are shut. Then comes a litany, with commemoration of the Mother of God and all the saints. The veil of the sanctuary is drawn back (or the doors opened in the Greek church). The Nicene Creed is chanted, followed by 'lift up your hearts' and the Trisagion ('Holy, holy, holy'). Then comes the Consecration, with a further litany, the Lord's Prayer, and the general Communion.

The priest comes out through the Royal Doors, holding the chalice in which consecrated bread has been put. Lay communicants receive the Communion standing, administered with a spoon. Children communicate first, receiving bread and wine; adults also receive both kinds, and sip wine and water at a side table. The people are signed with the cross, the chalice returned to the sanctuary, and the people dismissed with blessing. The priest brings out the cross from the sanctuary. Many people do not communicate every Sunday, but all now advance to kiss the cross, eat small pieces of blessed bread that remain, kiss the priest, and the service ends as a family gathering.

The Orthodox rite is long, there is usually a sermon, and what has been described above so briefly is the liturgy as seen by the layman, omitting the ritual performed by the priest behind the screen. Only one celebration of the eucharist is permitted in one day, so all the faithful try to gather at the one hour.

There are also daily offices, matins, vespers, and the like, which are chanted at various hours, often grouped together, and fully observed chiefly in monasteries. The services all include a good deal of biblical matter, Psalms and other lessons, and traditional religious poetry, with invocations of the saints and prayers for the dead.

There are variations in different parts of the East. For example in the Coptic Church in Ethiopia the sanctuary contains a sacred Tabor or Ark of the Covenant, which is regarded as equivalent to an altar stone. Drums and rattles are used in worship. Most worshippers stand outside the church, where the service is hardly audible, pursue their own devotions, and bow when the elements enter from 'Bethlehem', a shed where the bread is baked, and at the consecration which is announced by a bell ringing. Few people communicate but great crowds attend the churches.

## ROMAN CATHOLIC CHURCHES AND SERVICES

Roman Catholicism is reckoned to be the largest of all Christian churches, with about six hundred million members. The great cathedrals and churches are innumerable, many in the New World as well as in the Old. They are open for public and private devotion, and every Catholic[1] is under an obligation to attend Mass every Sunday. Thus congregational worship by the laity is essential.

Mass must be said every day by every priest, and hence in nearly every church. To the Catholic it is a great joy to know that at every hour, somewhere in the world, Mass is being said. It is said a number of times a day in churches where there are several priests, and three times by every priest on Christmas and All Souls' days. With several masses to choose from the faithful may fit their devotions to their free time, though the sung High Mass is the best.

High Mass is the full rite, and is sung by the priest and his assistants. With the Roman tendency to centralization the rite is similar everywhere, with only a few local deviations, and a number of old uses have disappeared. The language was formerly always Latin, but the laity used missals (prayer books) which have Latin and the vernacular in parallel columns, so as to be able to follow. Other services, such as Benediction in the evening, use vernacular hymns, and there may be sermons at Mass and other times. In many Catholic churches the people stand during the service and kneel at the appropriate places, and are not provided with seats; but portable chairs are in frequent use.

As the layman enters church he crosses himself with holy water from a stoup at the door and genuflects towards the altar. He then goes to his place and prays privately. He stands when the priest (celebrant) enters with his ministers to go to the altar; then the congregation kneel and cross themselves while the choir, with or without musical accompaniment, begins the introit. After invoking the Trinity and saying Psalm 42, the confession of sins is

[1]Others beside Roman Catholics claim the title 'catholic', but I have used it for convenience for Roman Catholics alone when the context is clear.

said and absolution given. Then at the altar the old Greek phrase Kyrie eleison (Lord have mercy) is sung and the Gloria in Excelsis (Glory be to God on high). Then follow Collect, Epistle and Gospel of the day, and the Nicene Creed, all chanted. Then the offertory and preparation of the paten and chalice is made and they are censed. Then comes the Sursum Corda (lift up your hearts), the preface and the Sanctus (thrice Holy).

The canon of the Mass, the central part, begins with the offering of the elements, the commemoration of the Virgin, Apostles, and Martyrs, and the consecration. As the host (bread or wafer) and the wine are consecrated they are elevated, a bell rings thrice each time, and the people kneel down in silence. The host is broken over the chalice and a particle dropped in; the Agnus Dei (Lamb of God) is chanted, and the kiss of peace given at a solemn Mass. The celebrant then receives the host himself. If there is a Communion, which was not usual at High Mass, a cloth is spread in front of the Communion rail, the deacon used to repeat the confession, the priest brings in the consecrated host (one kind only, the wafer) and administers it to the people at the rail. The priest then cleanses and veils the vessels and pronounces the benediction. The service ended with the first part of the first chapter of the Gospel according to St. John.

This very sketchy summary, for the benefit of those who have no acquaintance with the service, is far from being the whole rite, but gives the main parts that may be seen by the layman. Priest and servers have secret prayers, salutations and ablutions. Moreover the laity know both less and more than this outline. It was usually the custom in the Roman Church for the priest to say most of the rite either silently or almost inaudibly. The congregation, if it is instructed, knows what is happening but only joins in at certain points. Some may be occupied with their own prayers, and only bow and kneel at prescribed points, notably the elevation. On the other hand the externals of the ritual, the colourful vestments, the candles, crucifix, incense, bells, the general movement, create a drama that is both a spectacle and a means of devotion.

In recent years great changes have been made in the form of the Mass, under the influence of a liturgical revival and authorized by the second Vatican Ecumenical Council 1962–5. The service has been simplified, it is in the language of the people, and there is more lay participation, often with revival of an old practice of celebration behind the altar facing the people. An international committee on English in the liturgy produced an Ordinary of the Mass in 1969, stressing its shorter and 'more attractive' form. Confessions and prayers are modernized, God is addressed as 'you' instead of 'thou', except in the Gloria and Lord's Prayer, and names of many saints may be omitted. But the doctrine remains that 'the Mass is essentially the sacrifice of the Body and Blood of Christ offered to God for the living and the dead'.

There are other Masses, according to the season and circumstance. It is obligatory on the faithful to hear Mass every Sunday and on some other holidays of obligation, with local festivals in various countries. If he is in a state of grace, and fasting, the devout person may receive Communion on any of these occasions. First Communion, confirmation, nuptial mass at weddings, and Masses for the dead, are the occasions that come most personally into the lives of many of the laity.

Acts of devotions that are private rather than public, such as the Angelus, rosary, and fastings will be considered later. Special offices throughout the day from matins onwards, and devotions and litanies of the Blessed Virgin, the saints, the Holy Ghost, and the Way of the Cross, may also be said privately.

## PROTESTANT CHURCHES AND SERVICES

### (a) Lutheran

The Protestant Reformation of the sixteenth century was a less extreme reaction against Catholic ways among the Lutheran than in the Reformed or generally Calvinistic churches. Luther forbade images and relics but allowed the crucifix, and the Lutheran churches of Germany and Scandinavia are still often rich in carving and painting. Fine old cathedrals remain and many exciting new churches have been built in this century in Holland and Germany, Scandinavia and America.

Luther's eucharistic teaching laid stress on the mystery of worship, as against the rationalism of Zwingli but also against the Roman doctrine of transubstantiation. There was strong emphasis on the communion of the people, and this was taught by Calvin as well. Communion should be held on Sunday only, but it should be every Sunday, given in both kinds of bread and wine, to all confirmed Christians.

The canon of the Mass was pruned of what seemed to be accretions, put into the vernacular and hymns introduced. In time, however, the attempt at a full weekly Communion broke down and only a fragment of the original rite remained. The intention of the Lutheran rite was best worked out in Sweden, where Olaus Petri designed a Swedish communion Mass which for a time was celebrated alongside the Roman rite.

The Swedish liturgy begins with general confession and absolution, after an opening hymn, and this must precede every celebration of the eucharist. The eucharist proper (Högmässa, high Mass) begins with the Sanctus and confession, Lord have mercy and the Gloria. Then come the Collect, Epistle and Gospel. The Apostle's Creed is normally used, but the Nicene Creed at festivals. Then may follow a sermon and prayers. While the elements of bread and wine are prepared the priest sings the Sursum Corda and reads the words of the institution of the Lord's Supper from the Gospel. The Sanctus is sung, and then the communicants come forward while the people sing, O Lamb of God (Agnus Dei). The service ends with collects, blessing and hymn.

The Swedish liturgy is akin to the Anglican, and the Swedish bishops have kept the apostolic succession, so this Church is in communion with the Church of England. But the Swedish eucharist is only an occasional service, normally coming after the preaching service. Some other Lutherans have weekly eucharist.

In most Lutheran churches the emphasis of regular worship has shifted from the altar to the pulpit. The Reformation gave great prominence to the Ministry of the Word. The Bible was newly translated into Luther's sonorous version and the sermon became the centre of attention. The singing of Psalms in the vernacular, and later the composition of hymns by the Pietists, did a great deal to make non-eucharistic worship both normal and popular.

The stress laid on the Bible and preaching gave the pulpit pre-eminence, and the black gown and white bands of the preacher took the place of the more colourful eucharistic vestments. This affected the very architecture of the churches, since acoustics were vital. The pulpit took the dominant place. Spacious aisles once used for processions seemed ideal for building galleries for listening congregations. There arose thus a tension between altar and pulpit which is not yet resolved. If the congregation understood more, it was in danger of adoring less. This tendency went even further in the Reformed churches. At the same time the public exposition and private study of the Bible, and the use of strongly biblical hymns, made the worship fervent and evangelical.

## (b) Anglican

The Anglican Church claims to be both Protestant Reformed and Catholic, and in its reforms it retained the ancient cathedral and parish churches, together with the three-fold order of bishops, priests and deacons. The struggle of altar and pulpit has been pronounced, with the pulpit dominating in Puritan times and the altar regaining its place since the last century.

The title 'Mass' was dropped after the first prayer book of Edward VI, and the double title remains for the eucharist, 'The Lord's Supper or Holy Communion'. The proper vestments to be worn by the priest have long been in dispute and vary from church to church. The priest stood at the north end of the altar throughout the service, only in modern times standing in front of it or now sometimes behind the altar and facing the people. The liturgy must be in English (or the local vernacular), and it must be audible to everyone; this helps lay participation.

The priest begins the Prayer Book rite with the Lord's Prayer, said audibly but by himself alone, a collect and the Ten Commandments (two in the revised 1928 book). Then come a prayer for the king, and the Collect, Epistle and Gospel for the day. There follow the Nicene Creed, a sermon if desired, offertory and presentation of the bread and wine. A long prayer for the church comes next, then an exhortation (now usually omitted), confession of sins, absolution, and comfortable words. Next we have the Sursum Corda, preface, Sanctus, and prayer of humble access. The prayer of consecration contains the manual taking, but not generally elevation, of chalice and paten, fraction of the bread or wafer and consecration. The communion follows immediately, by the priest and people kneeling. Afterwards the conclusion is with Lord's Prayer all together, thanksgiving, Gloria in Excelsis, and benediction.

All this service may be simply spoken but today hymns are usually interspersed, and the Creed, Sanctus, and Gloria are often chanted. The 1928 book allows for introducing the Kyrie Eleison and Benedictus, a longer consecration prayer with invocation of the Holy Spirit (epiclesis) and remembrance of the resurrection and ascension. Shorter alternative services have been authorized since 1965, called Series One, Two and Three.

The rubric requires that there shall be no celebration unless a convenient number be present to communicate with the priest, in other words that non-communicating eucharist is forbidden. This helps to explain the prominence taken by the service of Matins or Morning Prayer in the Anglican Church. The Prayer Book begins with the services of Morning and Evening Prayer, to be said daily. These are based on old monastic offices of Matins and the like, and did not originally include a sermon. In the course of time Matins came to be the most popular Anglican Sunday service, with sermon, while Communion became occasional or at best an early service for the devout.

Since the Anglo-Catholic revival of the last century there is a great deal of variety, often confusing to the uninstructed, in Anglican services. The extreme 'high church' wing celebrates Mass in Roman style. The 'low church' has matins as principal service. Most churches have matins with sermon, but also weekly or daily Communion, and often sung eucharist with sermon. The double stress on Word and Sacrament is typical of the English Church and great efforts have been made to restore the Communion of the people. But the frequent practice of singing or intoning the Epistle and Gospel might well mean, if the eucharist became the main service, that most of the laity never heard the scriptures read and in course of time the chanting could make them unintelligible.

All churches have improved in modern times in decoration: the cross, but less often the crucifix, is re-established, candles are common, incense is less frequent. To the layman the church is more beautiful than in the past and there is more stress on his participation in the service. Fine new cathedrals have been built in modern times at Truro, Liverpool, Guildford, and Sheffield, and striking restorations at Coventry and Llandaff, as well as countless modern churches, and splendid buildings in America and elsewhere.

## (c) Reformed, Presbyterian and Nonconformist

The Reformed and Calvinistic churches on the continent of Europe rapidly slipped away from the ancient liturgy and eucharistic worship. Where they retained the old buildings they were stripped of all that suggested the old ways. New buildings made the pulpit central, with great stress on the Word of God and preaching.

The celebration of Holy Communion was occasional, though often observed with great devotion and large numbers when it occurred three or four times a year. The traditional liturgy was almost completely abandoned. In French and Swiss churches a long printed or extempore exhortation is followed by a confession said by the minister only in the name of the congregation, there being no written form for the latter to repeat. At most only the Lord's Prayer is recited together and there is no Creed. The words of institution of the Lord's Supper are read, the elements distributed by the deacons to the sitting people, and the service ends with a prayer and blessing.

In the Scottish Presbyterian churches there was more conservatism and struggles are again being made today to restore more of the liturgy. The Book of Common Order gives a service for the Lord's Supper or Holy Communion that is roughly similar to the Anglican Order, with the addition of an Old Testament lesson, extra prayers, Benedictus and Agnus Dei. Here there is stress on the place of the Bible and sermon, in the vernacular, within the framework of the eucharist. But this Communion is only celebrated once a quarter, and the weekly public service is based on psalms, hymns, lessons and sermon.

The English Puritans or Independents (later called Nonconformists) celebrated the Lord's Supper with decreasing frequency as the Reformation proceeded; some weekly at first, later monthly or quarterly. In many places the minister and deacons, with as many of the people as possible, sat round the communion table, in an endeavour to recapture the simplicity of the first Lord's Supper given by Christ in the Upper Room in Jerusalem. Five loaves or more were laid upon the table, broken first by the minister and handed to deacons and people each of whom broke off a piece. The cup or cups were circulated in similar manner. Later the people stayed in their pews while deacons carried the elements to them. The same practice obtains among the Baptists, who differ from some other Nonconformists chiefly in the administration of baptism solely to adults.

In the Nonconformist churches creeds are often no longer recited, and the Lord's Prayer remains the sole prayer, common to all Christians. The preaching service is the main act of public worship, the general order being roughly: hymn, prayer, Lord's Prayer, hymn, lesson, hymn, lesson (or children's address), long prayer, notices and collection, hymn, sermon, hymn, benediction. Despite its attempts at freedom from fixed forms this tends to settle into what one writer has called 'the rigid liturgy of Nonconformity', and another less kindly 'the hymn sandwich'. In the olden days sermons were much longer than now and the sandwich effect less noticeable.

The Nonconformists have always given great importance to the reading of the Bible and its exposition in preaching. Special occasions were often simply called 'Sermons', and these rallies and conventions had a great appeal. But the appeal was to the ear and intellect, and not to the eye, and only in this century have Christian arts begun again to flourish in this environment. With the shaking of biblical authority in the last century topical sermons tended to replace exposition; but today there are movements for more dogmatic interpretation of the Bible and stress on authority.

It is chiefly in Methodism that reaction towards sacramental worship can be seen among the Free Churches. Methodism was not a Reforming or Nonconformist movement. It was a child of the Industrial Revolution, arising from the desire to evangelize the unchurched masses of the new towns and mining areas. It taught no new doctrines, following the catholic faith and seeking to bring it to life. There arose again an attempt at frequent congregational communion. John Wesley celebrated Communion every Sunday and daily at certain periods of the year. He published books on 'the Christian Sacrament and Sacrifice' and spoke of the altar. His brother Charles wrote hymns on the 'real presence' and the epiclesis. Still in the Methodist hymn book is the verse:

> Come, Holy Ghost, thine influence shed,
>   And realize the sign;
> Thy life infuse into the bread,
>   Thy power into the wine.

But it was ultimately of small effect. Barred from many parish churches, the shortage of ordained ministers soon led to infrequent communion. But the Anglican rite for Communion is still retained in Methodism almost unchanged, especially in the churches of the Wesleyan tradition; a shorter order is also common. Communion is held monthly and tends to be a truncated service after the close of the evening preaching service. Methodism also laid great stress on preaching and the Bible and this brought its regular Sunday services into line with those of the other Free Churches, except for a few Methodist churches which use an abridgement of Anglican matins.

The Salvation Army was an offshoot of Methodism and continued its revivalist preaching. In a sense revivalism is a form of drama, with stirring hymns, fervent prayers, impassioned sermons and appeals for conversion. It provided religious drama, music and poetry for the emotionally starved multitudes of the eighteenth and nineteenth centuries. The Salvation Army with its banners, uniforms, bands and processions was an attempt at providing an appeal to the eye as well as to the ear. But the Army abandoned the traditional liturgy and has no Holy Communion or baptism; the sermon, Bible and hymns are the chief elements of public worship.

There are many Protestant sects, some orthodox in doctrine, some more or less extreme and heretical. The revivalist preachers are normally literal in their exposition of the Bible but follow the main doctrines of the church. Seventh Day Adventists, and even more Jehovah's Witnesses, have their own peculiar doctrines. Most of these sects stress preaching rather than the eucharist. A few, like the Plymouth Brethren, practise 'breaking of bread' every Lord's Day.

A complete sweep of the traditional liturgy was made in the Society of Friends (Quakers). Here the meeting-house replaces the church, and it is quite unadorned except perhaps for a text on the wall and some flowers. There are no hymns, bible-reading or sermon. There is no Communion or baptism. The people sit in silence for half an hour or so, until the Spirit moves one or more to speak. This is one of the principal places in Christendom, outside monasteries and mystical communities, where forms of meditation are practised that many in eastern religions would understand.

## CHRISTIAN FESTIVALS

The Christian Year begins at Advent, in the Western Church, four Sundays before Christmas. This celebrates the coming (advent) of Christ in his Incarnation and looks forward to his Second Advent in glory. The Advent climax is on Christmas Day.

Christmas is more popular today than for some centuries past. The old catholic name, Christ-mass, has been retained in English and was partly responsible for neglect of this feast under Puritanism. John Wesley revived the observance of Christmas, and for this was called a Papist; his brother wrote fine hymns for the occasion. In Scotland an effort to avoid superstition led to the other extreme of observing the secular New Year, but Christmas is now popular also.

Christmas is the favourite of all Christian feasts. It is the time of family reunions and of giving presents, even among those who never go to church. The many customs of Christmas trees, Santa Claus (St. Nicholas), yule logs, mistletoe, holly, turkey, plum puddings, mince pies and crackers are all secular and some pagan, but they are hallowed by association with the Babe of Bethlehem. Numerous churches have cribs with images of angels, wise men, shepherds, Joseph, and the Madonna and Child. Many other churches hold nativity plays and special services. Midnight services are held on Christmas Eve, in Roman Catholic and most Anglican churches, and increasingly elsewhere.

Lent, forty days before Easter, begins with Shrove Tuesday and Ash Wednesday, little observed by Protestants outside the Anglican Church. On Palm Sunday (the Sunday before Easter) palm branches are carried in Catholic churches. On Maundy Thursday the command (maundy) of Christ to wash one another's feet is observed by the Pope with his cardinals. In the Eastern churches the bishop washes the feet of his fellows, while they act in protest as did Peter in the Gospel. The English sovereign distributes Royal Maundy money.

Good Friday, the day of the crucifixion of Jesus, is the most solemn day in the whole year for all Christians. In many Catholic churches on the previous day the candles are extinguished one by one and the altar stripped. There is no consecration of the sacred elements on Good Friday. Many churches are draped in black and hold three-hour services, with prayers and long scripture readings. On Holy Saturday, in the Roman Church fire is struck from a flint, before the candles are lit and the altar reclothed.

Easter Day, the day of the resurrection of Christ, is celebrated with special fervour in the Eastern churches, where it is the greatest festival of the year. The Great Service takes place at midnight on the Saturday, and is preceded by a procession outside the church representing a search for the body of Jesus in the tomb. This is done in Jerusalem every year and has spread to other places, even to West Africa. A great liturgy and public rejoicing follow, and even in the teeth of Communist opposition vast processions have marched through Russian cities crying, 'Christ is risen'.

In Protestantism, where the Christian Year has often been poorly observed, Easter is yet a great occasion. Wesley's famous hymn, with twenty hallelujahs, gives the service the air of joy that characterizes it elsewhere. Popular Easter eggs, presents and cards, and public holidays over the long week-end preserve the general appeal of the season.

Whit-Sunday (Pentecost), from the white robes worn at christenings on this day dedicated to the Holy Spirit, is less popular. But it is important in the liturgical year. The remaining Sundays of the year are counted from here, in East and West. In England they are counted from the next Sunday, Trinity.

Popular religious festivals in Roman Catholic lands are Corpus Christi (the Thursday after Trinity) when the sacrament is carried in procession, the Assumption of the Virgin on 15 August, and All Saints and All Souls on 1 and 2 November. On the latter day all the dead are prayed for and cemeteries visited.

In Protestant countries favourite occasions are harvest festivals and Sunday School anniversaries. Even in industrial and urban areas harvests are greatly loved; there is no conscious memory of ancient pagan rites, but perhaps the modern love of nature finds expression here. The Sunday School anniversary expresses the devotion to children that marks our time: G. K. Chesterton said it was a substitute for the cult of the Virgin and the feminine element in religion.

Different lands and churches have their particular festivals. Dedication anniversaries of churches, feasts of one's own patron saint, and events in the church life of the believer, such as baptism, confirmation and first communion, all have their importance for the individual Christian.

In recent centuries new congregations and societies have appeared in the Roman Catholic world with special devotions and work. The society of the Sacred Heart of Jesus was founded as a devotion to Christ and an enterprise for educational work. Other congregations such as the Sacred Heart of Mary, and the Perpetual Adoration of the Blessed Sacrament, gave themselves to prayer and missionary work. The devotions to the Sacred Heart of Jesus have become very popular, and may link up with medieval devotion to the Five Wounds of Our Lord.

The Way of the Cross, with prayers and meditations at each of the fourteen stations set up on the walls of the church, is a widespread devotion and is promised special indulgences. The Blessed Sacrament is reserved in all Roman Catholic and some Anglican churches and is the focus of much adoration. People go to church during the week to pray privately here, or at the chapel of Our Lady, the altar of Holy Souls, or the image of a saint.

The rosary is a means of devotion to the Incarnation of Christ and to the Virgin. The full rosary consists of fifteen decades or sets of ten beads each, separated by fifteen larger beads, and with a crucifix at the end. The lesser rosary has five decades and five larger beads. In recitation the Creed is said on the crucifix, Our Father (Paternoster) on the large beads, Hail Mary (Ave Maria) on each of the small beads, and Glory be to the Father on the chain. Each group of five mysteries is known as a chaplet, and the mysteries meditated on are sequences in the life of Christ and his Mother: Five Joyful Mysteries of the Incarnation, Five Sorrowful Mysteries of the Cross, and Five Glorious Mysteries of the Resurrection and Assumption.

The Angelus bell is rung at morning, noon and evening, to remind the faithful of the Incarnation, and prayers are said privately wherever one may be. In the evening the laity observe this devotion especially, and say a Hail Mary. From Easter to Trinity is recited instead the Regina Coeli, 'Rejoice O Queen of Heaven'.

# POPULAR DEVOTION AND PRAYER

Before prayer the Catholic makes the sign of the Cross, says the Lord's Prayer, Hail Mary, the Creed, a confession of sins, and makes an act of faith. Prayers of dedication are said in the morning, and of committal at night, with invocation of the Virgin, saints and guardian angel.

The pattern of lay devotion in the Eastern churches is very similar. The sign of the Cross is from right to left, instead of the Roman left to right. Hail Mary is said in the liturgical or vernacular language. Prayer is said before icons at which candles burn. A simple and popular technique is the constant inward repetition of the Jesus-prayer: 'Lord Jesus Christ, Son of God, have mercy upon me'. It is said that this prayer can, if needed, replace all other prayers and liturgies for the power of God is in the Name of Jesus; 'the light of the Name of Jesus pours through the heart and irradiates the universe'.

Protestant devotion is less easy to describe because it has no fixed form. The centrality of the Bible has made it the mainstay of prayer and meditation. Large portions used to be read privately and in family prayer by the head of the family, or by a child, and then extempore prayer was offered. This practice has declined in modern times. But there are many popular books of devotion current and a number of systems of Bible reading are in vogue.

The Anglican has been fortunate in having well-known collects of morning and evening prayer to use, and canticles which most know by heart. The fixed form has provided a support when inspiration failed, but it may also suffer from rigidity. Most people have their own personal forms of prayer which, however, may become almost inflexible.

The use of the sign of the Cross is reviving among Protestants. Many people have a religious picture in the room where they pray, or in their Bible, but rarely an image. Readings from the great mystics have a wide sale.

Hymns have become very popular and are often used for private devotion as well as for public singing. The hymns of Wesley have been a mainstay of Methodist devotion, and have kept it both fervent and orthodox. Some of the hymns to Christ and the cross are as ardent as many Roman Catholic expressions of devotion. Not only such well-known lines as 'Jesu, lover of my soul', but many even more fervent words are commonly used in Methodist circles and some of them approach closely to the devotions to the Blessed Sacrament and the Sacred Heart.

## MYSTICISM

The tradition of mysticism in the Christian Church goes back to the Bible and has continued ever since. It provides an approach to *bhakti* and some of the devotional movements of other faiths. Paul prayed 'to apprehend with all the saints what is the breadth and length and height and depth', and wrote of union with Christ so that 'no longer I, but Christ liveth in me'. John wrote, 'Abide in me, and I in you'. And from them there has been a constant succession of Christian mystics.

The saints of Spain and Italy, France and Germany, Greece and the East are well known. But it is sometimes thought that the English are cold and unmystical, yet this is completely untrue. When the Mystical Theology of the Pseudo-Dionysius reached this country it is said that it ran across England like a deer. In the thirteenth and fourteenth centuries Mother Julian of Norwich, Richard Rolle, Walter Hilton, the author of the *Cloud of Unknowing*, and many others put England in the forefront of mystical writing. The metaphysical poets of the seventeenth century, the Wesleys of the eighteenth, the Romantic poets whom Dean Inge shows as true mystics,[1] the leaders of the Oxford Movement and a number of poets in the nineteenth century, and many devotional writers of the present, all witness to the strength of the mystical spirit in this country.

Among the many mystical teachers of Christianity there has been considerable agreement on the pattern of the mystical way. All of them agree on the necessity of purgation from sin and self as the condition of entry upon the way. St. John of the Cross, the Spanish writer who gave outstanding guidance, lays great

[1]W. R. Inge, *Christian Mysticism*, Chs. 7–8.

stress on the 'dark night of the soul', which may last several years, wherein the soul is purged of pride, avarice, sensuality, anger, gluttony, envy and sloth, the seven deadly sins, spiritual as well as sensual. After passing through the Purgative Way the soul advances to the Illuminative Way, where knowledge of God becomes clearer, though troubles, temptation and imperfections may still dog the aspirant. The final goal is the Unitive Way wherein 'the soul is oned with God'. This comes through contemplation and love where, independently of knowledge, the soul is united with God and centred on him.

There have been of course mystics of various opinions and a few of them have spoken of identification with God in terms little different from those of Hindu monists. Meister Eckhart is quoted with wearisome frequency to this purpose by synthesizers of religion. But their monotheistic tradition has kept the general run of Christian mystics from blurring all distinction of human and divine, and its doctrine of the Trinity has enabled Christianity to secure personal religion without a mystical dissipation of its Object. Like most Muslim Ṣūfīs it believes in union but not identity with God.

Through its mystics Christianity is speaking effectively to other faiths. If they are to understand each other as spiritual ways, and not just sets of rigid dogmas, then there must be dialogue at the deepest spiritual level. If they have anything to give, and to receive from each other, it is at this level that the faiths of the world must meet. If Christianity claims to be 'a light to lighten the Gentiles' it must show that it has important spiritual teaching and experience which fulfil men's deepest hopes. 'Here, and nowhere else, can it enter into a dialogue with Indian religion in terms that the latter can understand.'[1]

[1]R. C. Zaehner, *At Sundry Times*, p. 173.

# CHRISTIANITY

## BRIEF BIBLIOGRAPHY

Atiya, A. S. *A History of Eastern Christianity*, Methuen, 1968.

Brightman, F. *The Eastern and Western Liturgies*, Oxford, 1956.

Brilioth, Y. *Eucharistic Faith and Practice, Catholic and Evangelical*, S.P.C.K., 1930.

Brinton, H. *Christian Faith and Practice in the Experience of the Society of Friends*, Friends House, 1960.

Cross, F. L. *The Oxford Dictionary of the Christian Church*, 2nd ed., Oxford, 1973.

Davies, J. G. ed. *A Dictionary of Liturgy and Worship*, S.C.M., 1972.

Davies, J. G. *The Early Christian Church*, Weidenfeld, 1965.

Davies, H. *Worship and Theology in England*, 1900–1965, Princeton, 1966.

Davies, H. *The Worship of the English Puritans*, Black and Shepherd, 1948.

Dix, G. *The Shape of the Liturgy*, Dacre Press, 1945.

Dunlop, C. *Anglican Public Worship*, S.C.M., 1961.

Every, G. *Christian Mythology*, Hamlyn, 1970.

Frost, B. *The Art of Mental Prayer*, 5th ed., S.P.C.K., 1940.

Gieselmann, B. *Contemporary Church Architecture*, Thames and Hudson, 1973.

McArthur, A. A. *The Evolution of the Christian Year*, S.C.M., 1953.

Routley, E. *Hymns and Human Life*, Murray, 1952.

Underhill, E. *Worship*, Fontana, 1963.

Vipont, E. *Some Christian Festivals*, Joseph, 1963.

Wand, J. W. C. *Anglicanism in History and Today*, Weidenfeld, 1961.

Zaehner, R. C. *Mysticism Sacred and Profane*, Oxford, 1957.

Zernov, N. *Eastern Christendom*, Weidenfeld, 1961.

# INDEX

233

# INDEX

# INDEX

# INDEX

# INDEX

# INDEX